ESKIMO ARCHITECTURE

DWELLING AND STRUCTURE IN THE EARLY HISTORIC PERIOD

Molly Lee and Gregory A. Reinhardt

Foreword by Andrew Tooyak, Jr.

UNIVERSITY OF ALASKA PRESS *and* UNIVERSITY OF ALASKA MUSEUM ~ *Fairbanks*

International Standard Book Number: 1-889963-22-4

Library of Congress Cataloging-in-Publication Data

    Lee, Molly.
    Eskimo architecture : dwelling and structure in the early historic period /
    Molly Lee and Gregory A. Reinhardt ; foreword by Andrew Tooyak, Jr.
      p. cm.
    Includes bibliographical references and index.
    ISBN 1-889963-22-4 (cloth : alk. paper)
    1. Eskimo architecture. 2. Eskimos--Dwellings. 3. Vernacular
    architecture--Arctic regions. 4. Architecture, Domestic--Arctic
    regions. I. Reinhardt, Gregory A. II. Title.

    E99.E7 L4174 2002
    728'.089'971--dc21
        2002012706

This publication was printed on acid-free paper that meets the minimum
requirements for American National Standards for Information Sciences—
Permanence of Paper for Printed Library Materials, ANSI z39.48-1984.

*Publication of this book was supported in part by a fund established to honor
Tom English, in gratitude and respect for his scientific acumen, instructional
skills, and capacity to inspire research and researchers, by students who stud-
ied under his direction.*

Book and cover design by Dixon J. Jones, UAF Rasmuson Library Graphics.
Endsheet drawings of Eskimo oil lamps by Stoney Harby.

Printed in Canada

To Nelson Graburn, friend and teacher
—ML

To Karen, Allison, and Eric, with love
—GAR

To James W. VanStone—Jim—with fond remembrance
—ML AND GAR

CONTENTS

FOREWORD, IX

PREFACE, XI

INTRODUCTION, 1

Igloos and Accuracy ~ Scope and Definitions ~ Physiography, Prehistory, and Seasonality

1 GREENLAND, 9

WINTER HOUSES, 9

East and West Greenland Stone Communal Houses ~ Polar Eskimo Stone Houses ~ Alternative Winter Dwellings ~ Aspects of Winter House Life

TRANSITIONAL DWELLINGS, 22

SUMMER DWELLINGS, 22

East and West Greenland Large Single-Arch Tents ~ West Greenland Double-Arch Tents ~ Northwest Greenland Tents ~ Aspects of Summer Tent Life

SPECIAL USE STRUCTURES, 28

ASSOCIATED RITUALS AND BELIEFS, 30

NOTES, 32

2 CENTRAL ARCTIC, 35

WINTER HOUSES, 36

Labrador Eskimo Stone Communal Houses ~ Canadian Eskimo Snow Houses ~ Sallirmiut Stone Houses ~ Alternative Winter Dwellings ~ Aspects of Snow House Life

TRANSITIONAL DWELLINGS, 52

Central Arctic Stone/Bone/Turf Autumn House ~ Iglulik and Netsilik Ice Autumn House

SUMMER DWELLINGS, 55

Ridge Tents ~ Conical Tents ~ Sallirmiut Double-Arch Tents ~ Alternative Summer Dwellings ~ Aspects of Central Eskimo Tent Life

SPECIAL-USE STRUCTURES, 66

Lesser Structures ~ Birth, Menstrual, and Death Huts ~ Ceremonial Houses

ASSOCIATED RITUALS AND BELIEFS, 69

NOTES, 71

3 NORTHWEST ARCTIC AND BERING STRAIT, 73

WINTER HOUSES, 73

Mackenzie Delta Wooden Houses ~ North Alaska Coast Wooden
Houses ~ Pole-and-Turf Houses ~ Kotzebue Sound Wooden
Houses ~ Seward Peninsula Wooden Houses ~ Bering Strait Islands
Stone Pit-Houses ~ Alternative Winter Dwellings

TRANSITIONAL DWELLINGS, 93

SUMMER DWELLINGS, 94

Short-Pole Conical Tents ~ North Alaska Interior Dome Tents ~
Kobuk River Bark Houses ~ Bering Strait Island Stilt Houses ~
Alternative Summer Dwellings

SPECIAL-USE STRUCTURES, 104

Lesser Structures ~ Birth, Menstrual, and Death Huts ~
Burial Structures ~ Ceremonial Houses

ASSOCIATED RITUALS AND BELIEFS, 113

NOTES, 116

4 SOUTHWEST ALASKA, BERING SEA,
SIBERIA, AND GULF OF ALASKA, 119

WINTER HOUSES, 119

Mainland and Insular Alaska Men's and Women's Houses ~
Siberian Yupik Houses ~ Alutiiq Houses ~ Alternative Winter Dwellings

TRANSITIONAL DWELLINGS, 144

SUMMER DWELLINGS, 145

Norton Sound Wooden Houses ~ Norton Sound Dome Tents ~
Yukon River Wooden Houses ~ Siberian Eskimo Double-Arch Tents ~
Alutiiq Grass Huts ~ Prince William Sound Plank Huts ~
Alternative Summer Dwellings

SPECIAL-USE STRUCTURES, 152

Lesser Structures ~ Birth, Menstrual, and Mourning Huts ~
Burial Structures ~ Southwest Alaska and Alutiiq Ceremonial Houses

ASSOCIATED RITUALS AND BELIEFS, 154

NOTES, 156

5 SUMMARY AND CONCLUSIONS, 159

CONTRIBUTIONS TO THE STUDY OF ESKIMO ARCHITECTURE, 159

Similarities Shared by Dwellings Across the Arctic ~ Primary Summer and
Winter Dwelling Types

POSSIBILITIES FOR FURTHER RESEARCH, 162

FUTURE INQUIRIES, 164

Classification of Types ~ Gender Studies ~ Spatial Analyses ~
Meaning and Symbolism ~ Subsistence, Settlement, and Mobility ~
Energy Requirements ~ Ethnographic Details

CULTURAL DIMENSIONS, 168

NOTES, 170

APPENDIX, 171

REFERENCES, 183

NAMES INDEX, 203

SUBJECT INDEX, 206

FOREWORD

WHEN I WAS A BOY, I USED TO RUN FROM ONE HOUSE TO THE NEXT IN THE cold North wind, on my way to school. All the houses that I knew at the time were the wooden-framed houses built above ground. I do recall going to Nannie's house, though, when my mother visited the little old lady. It was a sod house on the western side of the village. A long, dark entrance hall led to a small, well lit, one-roomed home.

The house has collapsed on itself now, but the whalebone roof supports are visible, where the hallway still stands. The supports are made of jawbone and scapula, each pair representing one bowhead whale. I was asked once, "What is the significance of those whalebone standing over in the distance?" My answer was "clothesline," because, I thought, that is what whalebone was used for. Now I know a little better, thanks to the research represented by this book.

When I think of all the bone that washed out to sea during the fall storms from "Igloogroaks" (the place where we have our meat cellars), I can now appreciate the amount of work that went into building a shelter like the one that Nannie lived in. I have since learned that there may have been as many as 4,000 pieces of bone washed out from shore.

Outside the village in places such as Jabbertown, Singigraok, Kuukpuk, Itivlaagruk, and Kuunnuuk, the houses are made with driftwood and sod, the more abundant material. I have seen the house where my father was born, as have I seen the house where I was born. The difference between the two homes may represent just a millennia. I have lived amongst structures—ingeniously made—by the Inuit: the real people.

ANDREW TOOYAK, JR.

SUMMER DWELLING

When cold gives place to summer's glow,
And sun dissolves the ice and snow;
When verdure lies upon the ground,
And mosses, plants, and flow'rs, are found;
The Tribe forsake their winter haunt,
No more distress'd by pinching want.
Upon the plain, they bend their way,
While sledge, and dogs, their goods convey:
Onward they trudge, in merry mood,
At every step secure of food;
And when at night, fatiqued and spent,
They shelter all beneath the tent.
This is composed of walrus' skin,
Supported by a pole within;
Of broken spears, of bone and horn,
Or iv'ry, from the Unicorn;
While stones outside are scattered round,
The tent to fasten to the ground.

—Anonymous 1825

PREFACE

MOLLY LEE:

I first discovered indigenous architecture in a seminar taught by African art historian Herbert M. Cole while I was pursuing my M.A. studies in art history at the University of California, Santa Barbara. For a symbolic anthropologist, the rich correspondences between Yoruba house form and culture—the topic of my seminar paper—opened up a new and unexpected avenue of research.

During my second year at the University of California at Berkeley, Peter Nabokov, one of my fellow graduate students, taught the Native American architecture course through the Native American Studies Department. This 1985 class was the true genesis of the study reported in the following pages. At that time, Nabokov and Robert Easton were researching and writing their seminal *Native American Architecture* (Nabokov and Easton 1989). Because I had already declared a circumpolar specialty for my graduate work, Nabokov asked me to do my class project on Eskimo architecture. For the research, I plundered the riches of Berkeley's vast northern holdings. How well I remember sitting day after day in my carrel on the top floor of Doe Library, surrounded by books, each older, heavier, and moldier than the last. That winter, I literally marched across the Arctic in my pursuit of every last house type, only occasionally glancing out the dormer window at the Golden Gate Bridge, its spans poking out of the fog in the distance. Compared with the daily demands now placed on me as a professor and curator, that time was a luxury, one that has served me well in my subsequent research and teaching. I require my own graduate students to make the same forced march across the Arctic, whatever their topic.

As I was completing my research, which formed the basis of the Eskimo chapter in Nabokov and Easton's book, Peter Nabokov told me about a young graduate student who was filing a dissertation on the same subject at University of California, Los Angeles, under the supervision of Wendell Oswalt. That young student was Gregory A. Reinhardt.

During the spring semester of 1986, in order to complete my research on Eskimo architecture, I took a seminar with Jean Paul Bourdier in the Department of Architecture at Berkeley. Studying with Bourdier, a talented draftsman who specialized in African architecture, made me aware that my paper lacked the drawings and photographs that would bring it to life. Some time later, having seen Greg Reinhardt's meticulous drawings in his dissertation, I called and asked if he would be interested in co-authoring an article about Eskimo dwellings. To my delight he accepted. The amount of information turned out to be too voluminous for an article, and the book, along with Greg and his wife Karen's daughter, Allison, was born. Nine years—and one Reinhardt son, Eric—later, and after many changes in my own life and latitude, we have brought the project to completion. I am grateful for the countless hours that Greg has devoted to the book, not only in contributing drawings and information, but also in rounding up endless historical photographs and illustrations. I look back with pleasure on our collaboration from start to finish. I cannot imagine an *Eskimo Architecture* without him.

GREGORY REINHARDT:

Like Molly Lee, my academic focus had narrowed to the Arctic by the end of my graduate career and four summer field seasons in northern Alaska. In 1985, while Molly Lee was taking her Native American architecture class at Berkeley, I was living in Indianapolis and working on my dissertation, the topic of which was Eskimo dwellings. Despite my archaeological experiences, I nevertheless saw (and still see) myself as a generalist in anthropology.

About 1985, I met Peter Nabokov at Indiana University, where he was giving a talk about Native American architecture, subject of the book he had in press with architect Robert Easton. As a result of our meeting and discussions of my dissertation, Peter asked me to review the Arctic chapter of his and Easton's book. When it was published, there I was—alongside Molly Lee and Nelson Graburn—in the acknowledgments although with my name inexplicably transformed into "Gotfried Reinhard." I had known of Molly Lee, of course, through her publications. The most prominent of them, to me, was her book on baleen baskets, a subject relevant to my northern Alaska research focus.

With the patient support of my wife, Karen Friss, and my mentor, Wendell H. Oswalt, I filed my dissertation in 1986. In preparation for the book I intended to publish subsequently, 90 pages of dwelling descriptions became 190, and I redrew some of my illustrations and created new ones. At the 1990 Alaska Anthropological Assocation meetings I was asked to referee Molly's article-length manuscript on Eskimo architecture for *Arctic Anthropology*. Once Molly had read all the reviews, she invited me to co-author a revised version. Eventually we realized we had a book on our hands.

At this point the project languished for several years until Molly had been hired at Fairbanks. When the Alaska Anthropological Association meetings were held there in 1996, Molly and I met face to face for the first time, and took the book to the University of Alaska Press acquisitions editor, Pam Odom, who expressed interest in the project. We submitted our first draft in July of 1996 and, after more reviews, our final draft in May 1999.

Molly and I came to *Eskimo Architecture* by different routes, but this book would have been impossible without her guidance. She breathed life into my dry architectural details, kept us going with her cheery enthusiasm, found archival materials, and edited with finesse, care, and civility. Because of Molly, this is more than just a book on indigenous architecture: it is about the people, too.

Acknowledgments—The authors wish to thank the many people who have contributed to this work in past or present form, including Nezar AlSayyad, Mary Beth Bagg, Margaret Blackman, Ernest S. Burch, Jr., Jennifer Collier, Philip N. Cronenwett, Aron Crowell, Judy Dunlop, Ann Christine Eek, Bob Finch, Nelson H. H. Graburn, Julie Hollowell, Carol Zane Jolles, Lawrence Kaplan, John MacDonald, Thomas Ross Miller, Murray Milne, Lisa M. Morris, Peter Nabokov, Pam Odom, Wendell H. Oswalt, Kenneth Pratt, David P. Staley, Kesler E. Woodward, Andreas Züst, and three anonymous reviewers. James W. VanStone advised on many relevant issues and topics, Jeanne E. Ellis produced and/or modified some illustrations, Stoney Harby drew the endpaper lamps, and Tammy R. Greene assisted with bibliographic editing. Some material originally appeared in a dissertation (Reinhardt 1986); the contributions toward that work by Wendell H. Oswalt and the rest of Reinhardt's Ph.D. committee (Rainer Berger, Clement W. Meighan, Murray Milne, and Frank H. Weirich) are gratefully acknowledged.

INTRODUCTION

In each house [the Eskimos] have only one room. . . .

One-half the floor [is] raised with broad stones . . .

whereon, strewing moss, they make their nests to sleep.

(George Best, 1577)

IGLOOS AND ACCURACY

EXPANDING THE DEFINITION OF ARCHITECTURE TO INCLUDE THE NONPEDIGREED has opened for investigation a broad spectrum of the world's building practices, including those of small-scale societies (Rudofsky 1964). Given the scholarly attention paid to indigenous[1] housing in other parts of the world over the past two decades (e.g., Bourdier and Alsayyad 1989), a comprehensive appraisal of Eskimo[2] dwellings is long overdue.

Those outside the small circle of arctic specialists, however, are sure to greet such a survey with surprise, if not dismay, for it challenges one of Westerners' most cherished misconceptions about Eskimos. Thanks to the wide dissemination of nineteenth-century accounts of travel among Canadian and Greenlandic Eskimos (e.g., Boas 1888; Kane 1856; Lyon 1824; Parry 1824; Peary 1898), the snowblock "igloo" was cemented into our collective consciousness as a key symbol of Eskimo culture. In reality, however, the domical snow house associated with that term (*igloo*, or, more properly in the Inuit Eskimo language, *iglu*, is a generic term for "house" in most Eskimo languages) was built by only a small minority of Eskimos. Four hundred years of arctic literature make clear that Eskimo architecture was anything but monolithic.

Entrenched though the igloo may be in the Western imagination, it was by no means the first Eskimo dwelling type to be illustrated or described. This honor belongs to a fanciful recreation of some Greenland summer tents adorning a map published by Olaus Magnus in 1539 (Oswalt 1979:21, figs.1–2). Neither does the earliest-known written description of an Eskimo dwelling refer to an igloo, but to a transitional autumn or spring dwelling (*qarmaq* or *qarmaŋ*).[3] In 1577, an English sailor on the Frobisher expedition wrote,

> From the ground upward [the Baffin Island Eskimos] build with whale bones, for lack of timber, which, bending one over another, are handsomely compacted in the top together, and are covered over with seal skins, which, instead of tiles, fence them from the rain. In each house they have only one room, having one half of the floor raised with broad stones a foot higher than the other, whereon, strewing moss, they make their nests to sleep on. (Best 1867:138; spelling modernized)

In the interim, countless travelers have attested to the considerable variation that is the norm in Eskimo dwelling types from Greenland to Siberia. Nevertheless, even today, when the snow house has for all practical purposes melted into the past, comic strips, cartoons, and advertisments continue to reinforce the igloo as emblematic of Eskimo culture.

SCOPE AND DEFINITIONS

THE INTENT OF THIS STUDY IS TO DESCRIBE THE VARIETIES OF HOUSES AND other buildings that constitute indigenous Eskimo architecture of the early historic period, when, we assume, it was closest to traditional, that is, the precontact built form. We use "early historic" to mean the roughly fifty-year period immediately following a group's first contact with the West, irrespective of the date that first contact occurred (Nelson H. H. Graburn, personal communication). At best, however, this is a heuristic device. It would be impossible to pinpoint the moment when Western influence first appeared in any group, particularly because in many cases Western goods, such as canvas, reached the Arctic through trade and were incorporated into local structures well before the arrival of the first non-Natives into a particular area. Moreover, not only the date of contact but also the rate of modernization varied from group to group (Reinhardt 1986:56). Since the Eskimos interacted frequently with other Native peoples before the historic period, it is also important to stress that house types of any period were by no means static. Thus the early historic period of any group is more accurately an era of accelerated adaptation, borrowing, and innovation, not the time when culture change began. For want of a more precise scheme, this overview focuses on the period between Frobisher's 1577 expedition and the first half of the twentieth century, after which Eskimo groups began replacing their indigenous dwellings with Westernized housing (e.g., Collignon 2001; Duhaime 1985).

Of necessity, this study is object oriented (Upton 1983). It seeks to describe house types rather than theorize about them. We endorse Rapoport's (1969) position that architecture evolves in response to aesthetic, spiritual, and social requirements as much as to physical needs, but taxonomy, in our opinion, must precede interpretation. Though at least one brief survey of Eskimo architecture has been undertaken (Nabokov and Easton 1989:188–208), and studies of specific features of Eskimo housing (e.g., Reinhardt 1986), and of house form in a particular Eskimo group (e.g., Ray 1960) are known, the literature lacks a comprehensive survey of built form covering the entire Eskimo area. This volume is intended to fill the gap.

Our survey concentrates on Eskimos who live above latitude 60 degrees north (fig. 1). It excludes the closely related Aleuts (e.g., Jochelson 1933), a distinction contrary to Burch's recent merging of these two linguistically separate cultures (Burch and Forman 1988). Moreover, it somewhat under-emphasizes the Alutiiq (formerly known as the Chugach Eskimo and the Koniag; e.g., Birket-Smith 1953; Knecht and Jordan 1985) because environmental conditions, Aleut and Northwest Coast Indian influence, and lack of adequate ethnographic details set these groups apart.

We begin by discussing geography, climatology, and ethnography as they relate to Eskimo architecture, and then address housing in four geographic subregions. We consider the winter and summer dwellings of each subarea, briefly mention transitional-season dwellings (those of spring and autumn) and special-use structures and, finally, summarize certain beliefs, rituals, and customs as they relate to architecture. In the concluding chapter, we classify Eskimo dwellings along systematic lines and suggest future avenues of reserach. The appendix compiles data on floor area and numbers of occupants for selected Eskimo dwellings.

FIGURE 1

The Eskimo cultural area.

After Damas 1984b:ix; courtesy of Smithsonian Institution Press, Washington, D.C.; produced by Robert Drozda.

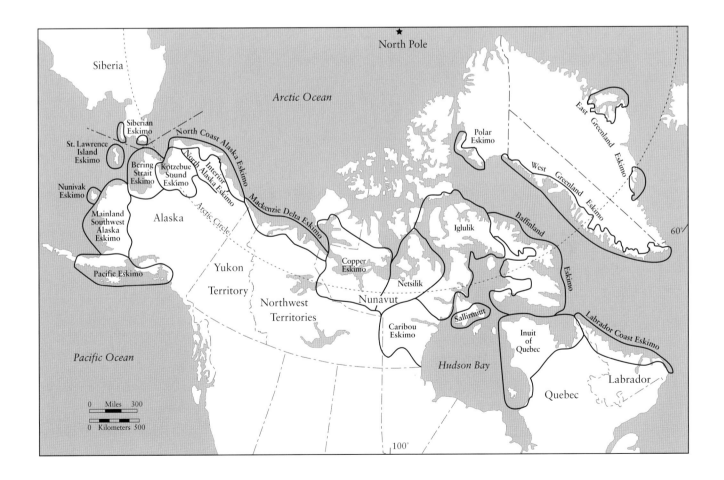

PHYSIOGRAPHY, PREHISTORY, AND SEASONALITY

THE ESKIMO HOMELAND STRETCHES EASTWARD FROM EAST CAPE, SIBERIA, through northern Alaska and Canada to Greenland, and southward along the Alaska coast to Prince William Sound (fig. 1). The north is a region of intense climatic contrasts. During deep winter, which lasts from October to February, the sun does not clear the horizon. At midwinter sunshine disappears altogether for some 70 days in north Alaska and West Greenland, over 100 days in northwest Greenland (Steensby 1910:285), yet not at all in places south of the Arctic Circle. Nevertheless, in winter daytime north of the Arctic Circle, the brilliance of stars, reflection of light from snow and ice, the circling moon, and the sun's noontime glow from below the horizon create perpetual twilight more than profound darkness. In January, the average minimum daily temperature at Iqaluit (Frobisher Bay) in Canada's Northwest Territories is −30.6° C (−23.1° F).

Arctic summers are brief but intense. During May, June, and July, the sun never dips below the horizon, allowing plants to flourish from round-the-clock photosynthesis while animals fatten themselves on this extravagant bounty. Because of the sun's low slant, however (in July, it is only somewhat higher in Iqaluit than in New York at midwinter), the maximum average temperature at Iqaluit rises to only 11.6° C, or 52.9° F (Dawson 1983:22; Ekblaw 1927–28:163–164).

The Arctic coastline was settled as early as 3,000 B.C., although an uninterrupted linkage between those pioneer populations and modern Eskimos is a matter of conjecture. The immediate progenitors of today's Eskimos were the Thule people, who perhaps migrated across the Bering Sea about A.D. 1000 and worked their way eastward, reaching Greenland around A.D. 1200. With respect to house form, archaeological evidence suggests that features characteristic of indigenous Eskimo architecture—southerly or seaward orientation, semisubterranean house floors, raised sleeping platforms, cold-trap tunnels or passageways, domed snow houses, and tents—derive from a Thule base (McGhee 1983). Through time, Thule peoples in the eastern and central Arctic changed their winter house designs from small sod/stone/wood houses, to snow houses and autumn stone/bone/turf houses (*qarmaq*s), and finally, in East and West Greenland and Labrador, to multifamily homes (Schledermann 1976a).

Their broad geographical spread notwithstanding, Eskimos enjoyed a remarkable degree of cultural homogeneity (Schweitzer and Lee 1997). In this generally treeless environment, they used for building material whalebones, caribou antlers, even narwhal tusks, and, where they could find enough of it, driftwood. Eskimos were seminomadic and semisedentary peoples with an estimated precontact population of about 50,000 (Oswalt 1979:341 ff.). They exploited both sea and land animals during the seasonal round of subsistence activities, moving from site to site according to the availability of food sources. Unlike the diets of most forager societies worldwide, Eskimo subsistence relied overwhelmingly on animal protein and fat, whereas plant-food consumption was notably insignificant (Reinhardt 1986:56–164).

The classic Eskimo settlement pattern shifted seasonally between concentration and dispersion. According to Mauss and Beuchat (1979:56), "The movement that animates Eskimo society is synchronized with that of the surrounding life." In winter, groups congregated in communal dwellings. The dark, cold days were a time of visiting, ritual, ceremony, dancing, and story telling—activities regenerating the cooperation vital to group survival. Late winter was also the season of greatest food stress. Among the Polar Eskimos, for example, except in a few very favorable animal-kill locations, families were often forced to vacate their winter-house sites after a single season because of the dire depletion of nearby game. Ordinarily they would not return for two years or more (Peary 1898:2:273).

By contrast, in summer, groups splintered into nuclear families, living mainly in skin tents, and roaming coastline and river, lakeshore and muskeg, mountain and tundra in search of game. Indeed, seasonal alternation was the organizing principle of the Eskimos' material, social, and ceremonial existence. "This opposition between summer life and winter life profoundly affects ideas, collective representations and, in short, the entire mentality of the group. [These oppositions] are like two poles around which revolves the system of Eskimo ideas" (Mauss and Beuchat 1979:60–62). House form supplied a major idiom of this pattern. Steensby, for instance, notes that "summer and winter bring very different modes of livelihood [to the Eskimos]. We might indeed speak of a summer culture and a winter culture. The summer culture is characterized by the kayak, kayak hunting and the summer tent, whilst the winter culture is characterized by the dog-sledge, hunting on ice and the winter-house" (Steensby 1910:284).

The switch from winter house to summer tent constituted a major demographic shift. Most Eskimos did not regard houses as private property and felt no obligation to return to the same winter settlement year after year (Birket-Smith 1924:135). At summer's end, families who had camped and hunted near each other also had frequently cached their food communally and spent the winter together. By springtime, when group members had wearied of each other's company, they split into nuclear units, each going its separate way (Ekblaw 1927–28: 156, 160, 165; Goddard 1928:194; Jenness 1922:74). Thus, residence pattern was as much a product of sociocultural forces as environmental considerations.

This winter/summer organizing principle had a purely practical side. As winter turned to spring, days grew warmer, the ground began to thaw, and many forms of winter housing turned into dripping bogs. During the transitional season, inhabitants in the Eastern and Central Arctic removed most or all of the substantial turf-covered roof, replacing it with a makeshift skin cover. This allowed them to air their dwelling and make it habitable until the weather was warm enough for them to stow their newly made tent cover in a skin boat or on a dogsled (or pack it on their backs) and begin their summer travels (Ekblaw 1927–28:166). When summer arrived they tore away even the skins, exposing the whole interior to the elements.

To summarize, this text is meant as a general introduction to Eskimo architecture of the early historic period. Because there is no comprehensive survey of this topic, the following four chapters are largely descriptive. Drawing on a literature that is the most extensive for any indigenous people anywhere (Riches 1990), we will survey built form among the Eskimo peoples from Greenland to Siberia. We will argue that the seasonal alternation of winter and summer dwelling more accurately characterizes Eskimo housing patterns than does the widely held stereotype of the snowblock igloo normally associated with them.

INTRODUCTION NOTES

1 We use "indigenous" here much as Rapoport used "vernacular building," to mean an architecture characterized by the "lack of theoretical or aesthetic pretensions; working *within* the site and micro-climate; respect for other people and *their* houses . . . and working within an idiom with variations" (Rapoport 1969:5). In other words, we focus on dwellings and other structures made by local design and of predominantly local materials.

2 Today, "Eskimo," because of its strong connotations of the colonial period and the incorrect assumption that it means "eaters of raw flesh;" (see Damas 1984b:5–7), is no longer universally accepted among the Eskimo/Inuit people. There is, however, no general agreement on a replacement. Many Alaskan Eskimos still use the term, but often prefer regional designations such as *Yup'ik*, *Inupiaq*, or *Alutiiq*, to give a more precise indication of their language group. Canadian groups call themselves *Inuit*, and Greenlanders want to be known as *Kalaallit*. Loosely translated, these terms mean "people" or "real people," except for *Kalaallit*, whose origin is uncertain (Lawrence Kaplan, personal communication to Lee 1996). To further complicate the issue, the Inuit Circumpolar Conference, a political body representing the totality of Eskimo peoples, has adopted "Inuit" as a collective replacement. Because this term is meaningless in the Yup'ik/Yupik languages of Alaska and Siberia, it is widely accepted only in the political sphere. For want of a better alternative, we shall use the term Eskimo here as a collective label but will employ the terms preferred by the various subgroups whenever possible (Schweitzer and Lee 1997:29).

3 This may seem rather tent-like, due to its skin cover. However, the raised stone platform at the rear and the bone structure described here are very similar to features of nineteenth-century Eskimo autumn dwellings from the Canadian Arctic (Boas 1888:547–549).

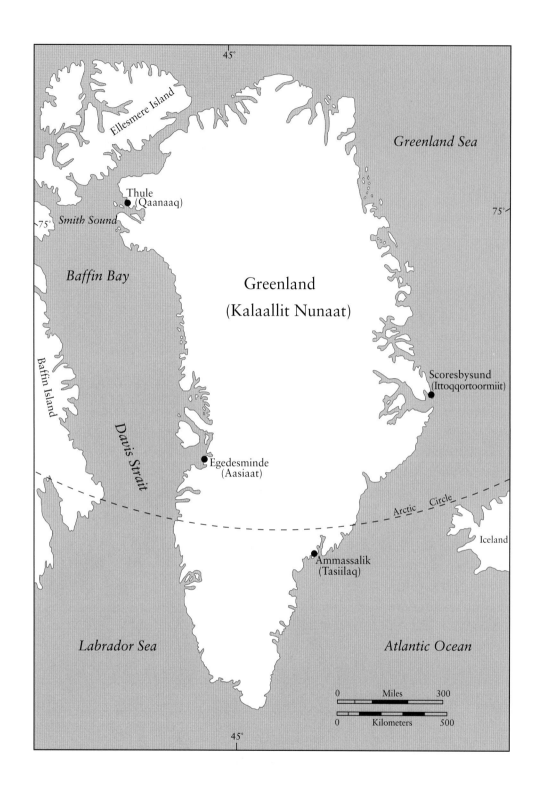

FIGURE 2

Map of Greenland.

Produced by Robert Drozda.

1

GREENLAND

The Eskimo lamp literally created

culture, transforming dark into bright,

cold into hot, raw into cooked.

GREENLAND'S ABORIGINAL POPULATION STOOD AT ABOUT 9,000 (OSWALT 1979). The Greenlandic Eskimos, or Kalaallit, clustered in three geographical areas, southeast (Ammassalik), southwest (West Greenland), and northwest (Polar, Thule, or Smith Sound). The Ammassalik and Polar Eskimos were confined to relatively small stretches of coastline compared to West Greenland Eskimos, whose numbers were markedly larger and who were more widely dispersed than their eastern and northern co-ethnics (fig. 2, map). Ironically, the earliest and latest dates of historic contact between European explorers and an Eskimo group occurred in Greenland (even excluding Norse settlers in southwest Greenland ca. A.D. 1000). In 1585 the Davis expedition first sighted West Greenlanders but Holm did not see an Ammassalik (East Greenlander) enclave until 1884 (Oswalt 1979:37–38, 142).

WINTER HOUSES

THROUGHOUT GREENLAND THE MOST PRESSING CONSIDERATION FOR locating winter settlements was the proximity of fresh water (usually ice from a lake or pond). Also, to take advantage of leads in the sea ice for hunting, settlements tended to be near open water (figs. 3–4). Protected south-facing hillsides were ideal; southerly orientation was a long-standing and deep-rooted custom both here and in the Western Arctic (Murdoch 1892:79), not only to maximize light and shelter but also because elevation was important for spotting the sea mammals on which the Eskimos depended for food. A related consideration was smooth, solid, snow-free sea ice. Predictably, the best

FIGURE 3

Detail from a "View of Lichtenfels," West Greenland. Nine summer tents stand near six communal winter houses, all close to the shore, while a European mansard roof building rises farther inland.
Frontispiece to the 1820 edition of Crantz 1767.

FIGURE 4

"A summer-encampment" by the sea, West Greenland. Four women with topknot hairdos stand between two sealskin tents, while men lounge by the other. Below, women row an umiak as a man in his kayak hitches a ride. Note the many individual seal pelts that go into constructing each tent cover.
From Rink 1877:opp. 178.

locations had long since been identified, and these were inhabited year after year; it was more practical to refurbish an existing house than construct a new one (Ekblaw 1927–28:156–9). For all the Greenlandic populations the use of interior space, materials, and construction techniques were much the same, but winter houses in the three subareas differed as to size and shape.

EAST AND WEST GREENLAND STONE COMMUNAL HOUSES

The communal houses of East and West Greenland (fig. 5) stand in marked contrast to the snug, small-family dwellings of the Polar Eskimos described below. Archaeologists suggest that communal houses evolved at least in part as a response to the quick alternation of warming, cooling, and warming trends from A.D. 800–1850. During this period, economic pressures (such as

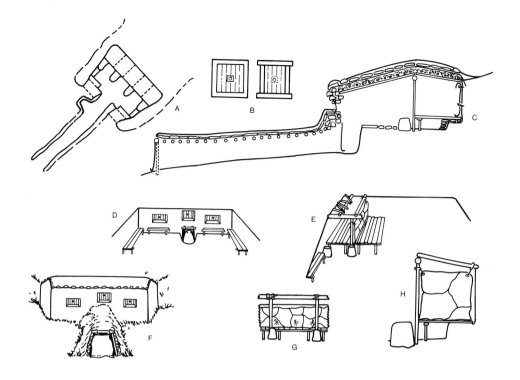

reduced whaling prospects owing to sea-ice changes) led people to adapt with communal responses in getting and sharing food and fuel (Birket-Smith 1924:144–148; Frederiksen 1912; Mathiassen 1936:114–122; Schledermann 1976a).

Nearly identical on both coasts, East and West Greenland winter communal houses (sometimes referred to as long houses in the literature) were large, rectangular or oblong semisubterranean communal dwellings usually accommodating four to six families (twenty to thirty persons), or sometimes as many as eight to ten families (fig. 5A). A West Greenland house (*igdlo/illu*) might be as large as twelve by seventy-two feet, while one Ammassalik (East Greenland) example (*itte*) measured thirty-three by thirty-six feet (Crantz 1767:1:139; Thalbitzer 1914:353). With four walls arranged in a rectangular to trapezoidal floor plan, East and West Greenland houses were built either as free-standing structures (fig. 3; Thalbitzer 1914:fig. 64), or with the back end dug into a hillside. When excavated into slopes overlooking prime ocean hunting grounds, the top edge of a house's back wall often stood flush with the slanting ground surface (fig. 5C; Holm 1914:35, fig. 29). Because of this slant, the front end of the main chamber required little digging, but the side and front walls and the tunnel walls sometimes had to be built up (fig. 5A, F). Residents reached the living area by crawling upslope through a three-foot-high stone-and turf-walled tunnel, which ran perpendicular to the house's long axis (fig. 5A, C, F; Crantz 1767:1:139; Nansen 1894:80; Thalbitzer 1914:356). Tunnels always penetrated the front wall of the house (fig. 5A, F), sometimes breaching it off-center (Thalbitzer 1941:fig. 167).

Rows of hardwood[1] or whale-rib rafters, and loosely arrayed, smaller wooden crosspieces held up the roof (figs. 6–7). Each row rested on a continuous

FIGURE 5

Idealized Greenlandic stone communal house for winter: (A) floor plan (kitchen on left side of tunnel, West Greenland only); (B) window with peephole (left, gut, peephole patch, and border; right, framed window as seen from outside); (C) cross section through house and tunnel—a line connecting the upper right and lower left ground surfaces would indicate the original ground slope; (D) interior, view toward door; (E) interior, view toward rear; (F) exterior, view toward front (kitchen on left side of tunnel, West Greenland only); (G) wall liner (West Greenland only) and ridgepole details; (H) lampstand, sleeping platform, and partition details.

After Crantz 1767:1:pl 4; Holm 1914:fig. 31; Ostermann 1938:fig. 19; Thalbitzer 1914:figs. 64–65, 1941:figs. 167, 224–225; drawn by Jeanne E. Ellis.

FIGURE 6

Cut-away view of a West Greenland winter-house interior. In each partitioned family space are a clothes-drying rack and cooking pot suspended over a lit lamp on a lampstand. Note arrangement of roof timbers, ridgepole, and posts to support the superstructure.

From Crantz 1767.

FIGURE 7

"Interior of a rich man's house" from the late nineteenth century. The ridgepole is absent and the stove, dish shelves, pictures, and finished timbers are not traditional, but most other details are reasonably accurate: upright posts; lighter ceiling timbers; drying racks overhead; back and side platforms; and lamps on wooden lampstands.

From Rink 1877:176 ff.

FIGURE 8

"Interior of the house of a very rich man," shows even more non-traditional items of material culture than those appearing in figure 7. Note the depth of the main platform (left) compared to the side and front benches, widespread upright posts independent of three women's work spaces, part of a window niche in the front wall (right), and storage beneath and at the back of the main platform. The ridgepole evidently runs transverse to design expectations.

From Rink 1875:frontispiece.

ridgepole, giving interiors a maximum height of about six and one-half feet inside (fig. 5C, E, H). One ridgepole was the rule in West Greenland, but in Amassalik territory the addition of a second or third ridgepole permitted expandable house-width (Holm 1914:35; Thalbitzer 1914:355). To enlarge a house lengthwise, shorter ridgepoles could be lashed together, thereby spanning greater lengths. Blocks of sod were sometimes added around the interior walls to enhance insulation.

Ceilings and outermost roof coverings for West and East Greenland communal houses consisted of old, fat-rubbed boat- or tent-skins, which were laid over the rafters. The skins were weighted with stones, then layered over with turf, earth, and more turf as insulators to form a flat or slightly pitched roof (fig. 5C). Heavy, vertical posts transmitted the roof load to a bare or stone-paved floor (figs. 5C, E, G–H, 6–8). Floorplans were rectangular to trapezoidal and wider at the back (Holm 1914:fig. 31), mostly measuring twenty-four to fifty feet long by twelve to sixteenfeet wide.

Two nearly transparent gut windows, made from scraped strips of seal-gut membrane, admitted light through the front walls of the Greenlandic communal house (fig. 5B–D, F; Egede 1745:63–64; Thalbitzer 1914:352). On occasion, builders would insert a third window, framed in stone like the others, over the inner doorway (fig. 5D, F; Thalbitzer 1914:356). In West Greenland, as among the Polar Eskimos, gut windows included a peephole (fig. 5B; Birket-Smith 1924:151).

The wooden sleeping platforms of Greenlandic communal houses, which were about six feet deep and raised a foot and a half above the floor, ran the length of the rear wall (figs. 5C, E, G–H, 6, 8). Transverse skin partitions divided the platform into an average of six separate family compartments three to five feet wide (figs. 5E, 6). Typically, these curtains draped from a floor-to-ceiling post in front and a rafter in back. By not tacking the partitions to the back wall (fig. 5H), the occupants could cross the length of a house, at the back, without leaving the platform. Sometimes the interior walls were insulated with skins (fig. 5G), improving comfort—and probably cleanliness, as the skins kept wall debris contained. Unmarried men, older boys, and guests slept on lesser versions of the main platform built along the side and/or front walls (figs. 5D, 7–8; Holm 1914:38).

Interior furnishings of Greenlandic houses were simple. Each family unit kept its own small wooden lampstand on a stone pedestal in front of the sleeping platform (figs. 5C, E, G–H, 6–9). This was the focus of women's activities indoors. Residents used driftwood boxes (and the cavities under sleeping platforms) for storage, and extra platforms were sometimes added to the fore and side walls, thereby increasing the total sleeping and storage space (figs. 5D–E, G–H, 6–9).

Minor design differences between East and West Greenland included the occasional absence of outer tunnel doors in the west (fig. 10; Crantz 1767:1:139). Skin curtains sometimes served this purpose in the east (fig. 5C–D). West Greenland house tunnels could include a tiny kitchen[2] (fig. 5A, F; Birket-Smith 1924:151). Different wall-insulating techniques are reported for the two groups. West Greenlanders used seal ribs to attach cast-off tent or boat skins, animal

FIGURE 9

"Interior of a hut. Part of the platform between two props." In front of the left post, a lamp flickers atop its stand while a pot hangs off-center above it next to scissors stuck into the post. Note the small, apparently cramped family space defined by the posts. *From Holm 1914:fig. 30.*

"Winter house," viewed from the front, showing realistic-looking stone walls, pairs of non-native six-pane windows, and a stove pipe in the roof. Boots dry on poles and fox furs hang from lines (left), as someone sits in the framed entryway to the short tunnel. The foreground is littered with (apparently) dried beheaded fish.

From Rink 1875:opp. 11.

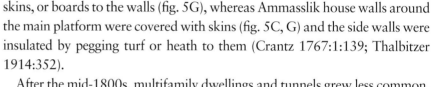

FIGURE 11

Idealized Polar Eskimo small-family, winter stone house. Top, plan view; bottom, side view.
After Steensby 1917:fig. 2.

skins, or boards to the walls (fig. 5G), whereas Ammasslik house walls around the main platform were covered with skins (fig. 5C, G) and the side walls were insulated by pegging turf or heath to them (Crantz 1767:1:139; Thalbitzer 1914:352).

After the mid-1800s, multifamily dwellings and tunnels grew less common, although people occasionally reoccupied the old communal houses (e.g., Kleivan 1984:fig. 4), and Thalbitzer mentions smaller, rectangular one-family variants in East Greenland (1914:353). In 1870, 613 out of 985 Moravian-influenced houses in West Greenland still met two basic criteria for Native-style dwellings: "flat roofs and no stoves" (Rink 1877:182). By the 1880s, European stoves were supplanting lamps for heating (figs. 7–8, 10), yet "the indispensible lamps [were] kept burning" for their light (Nansen 1894:83). Still more modern times (the 1920s to 1940s) saw communal houses abandoned in the northwest and replaced by small (generally under thirteen feet on a side) one-family homes (Birket-Smith 1924:148; Kleivan 1985:fig. 4). Even so, the household might include several additions to the nuclear family, such as daughters-in-law and grandchildren (Birket-Smith 1924:154).

POLAR ESKIMO STONE HOUSES

Prehistoric Polar Eskimo houses were rectangular in design (Ekblaw 1927–28:167), but the one- to two-family stone-walled iglu (alternatively, *qarmaŋ* or *qaŋma*) of ethnographic times was roughly pear shaped in plan (fig. 11), and measured about 9.5 by 12 feet, narrowing at the back (Birket-Smith 1936:127). Steensby describes the form as having "something of the characteristic arching of the turtle-shell, [with] the low entrance-passage [analogous to] the neck" (1910:311–312). Polar Eskimo houses employed up to three lamps—one per family—for illumination and heat, a large one on the main sleeping platform and two smaller versions placed on the narrower side platforms.

Like East and West Greenland houses, those of the Polar Eskimos sloped backward at a steep angle and were sometimes partly excavated into a hill-

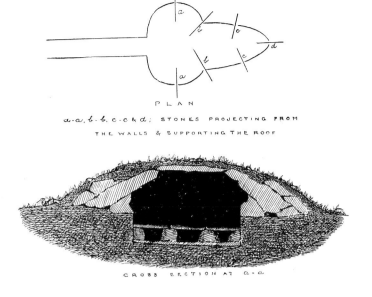

FIGURE 12

"Plan and section of Northumberland Island igloos," showing placement of supporting cantilever stones (top), center roof slab resting on cantilevers, and storage niches beneath the sleeping platform (bottom).
From Peary 1898:1:108.

side, which served as the rear wall. Built of local sandstone slabs, sea mammal bones, and turf, house walls were thickest at the base for added insulation and roof support (fig. 12). The roof consisted of rather long sandstone slabs, set at intervals atop the walls and counterweighted with boulders (fig. 13, bottom). These slabs were roofed over with broader ones. On top of the roof slabs the men would place an insulating turf layer, held down by more stones. This architectural use of the cantilever, or corbel, created a squat but dome-like roof that was evidently unique[3] to the Polar Eskimos in historic times (Holtved 1967:fig. 6; Peary 1898:1:108, 1898:2:271; Steensby 1910:314–315). The cantilevered roof could be used only in small houses,[4] which had minimal span requirements.

One entered the winter house by stooping or crawling on all fours through a low, narrow, dark, semisubterranean tunnel ten to thirty feet long (fig. 14). Sloping up toward the house, the tunnel ended abruptly at a squarish trap door (called *katak*, perhaps a reference to "falling"). The main chamber was a single room with narrow, elevated stone platforms along the side walls (fig. 11). At the rear, distinguished by a line of stones, sat a larger stone-paved platform that served as the main living space (figs. 11, 15). Layered with dry heather and skins, this platform was a work- and play-space in the daytime and at night was converted into sleeping quarters. Additional dry masonry produced small stone-lined storage niches set into the main platform's front edge (figs. 11–12, bottom).

A single window was built into the front wall, above the door (figs. 16–17). Windows were glazed with translucent gut strips sewn together and stitched into a large panel (Steensby 1910:316). Usually a small sealskin peephole, sewn to the gut, pierced the center of the window (Ekblaw 1927–28:168; Steensby 1910:318; cf. fig. 5B). Gut, the diaphanous outer intestinal lining, mainly of seals, was the normal window covering used throughout the Eskimo culture area. It had several material advantages. Collecting little frost, it did not rot. Early ethnologists who spent time in Polar Eskimo *iglu*s reported that

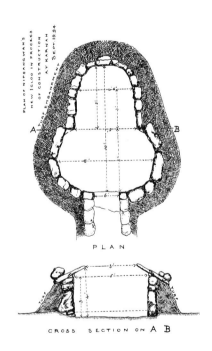

FIGURE 13

"Plan & section of stone igloo [1894]," showing dimensions of the floor (top), walls, and ceiling (bottom), and construction of the counterweighted cantilevers (bottom).
From Peary 1898:2:270.

gut was such an efficient light conductor that for most of the year it was possible to read and write inside without additional illumination (Hantzisch 1931–32:63; Steensby 1910:354). The gut window served yet another purpose: During the dim winter months its glimmer of light functioned as a beacon, guiding hunters homeward across the sea ice. Billows of warm moist air, emanating from the peephole, served as a further indicator of home and warmth (Ekblaw 1927–28:167–8).

The main platform at the rear of Polar Eskimo stone dwellings was the central living space (figs. 11, 15). Each member of the household had a specially designated place on the ledge; women sat at the outside front to tend the lamps, men at the center rear (fig. 15). The Polar Eskimos, like many other Eskimos, customarily slept with their heads toward the front wall of the house. Although the platform was used communally, it was considered the province of men (Paulson 1952:65). The front of the dwelling, where cooking and other housekeeping chores took place, was the women's domain.

Contributing to the Polar Eskimo house's bulbous floor plan, narrow at the rear and widening toward the doorway, were two indented side platforms (figs. 11–13). Each was intended as a lamp place and storage space for one family, although occasionally these were used as additional sleeping platforms. This plan thus integrates the notion of dual-family occupancy within a single house.

Before 1900, when wooden doors came into use in northwest Greenland, air circulation could be further regulated by adjusting stone slabs at either end of the tunnel (Ekblaw 1927–28:167; Steensby 1910:322). Once warmed, the stone walls and floor retained heat. In one instance, the fourteen residents of a house drove up the temperature to 90°F (Kane 1856:2:113). During historic times, Polar Eskimos added an inner envelope of skin—often worn-out tent covers or clothing—for greater insulation (Ekblaw 1927–28:168–169; Holtved 1967:14).

As with any type of vernacular architecture, the Polar Eskimo winter house was built in many variations. One design had a single tunnel off to one side of the main room and a thin wall separating two back-wall sleeping platforms (Steensby 1910:fig. 15). In another, two or three houses might be built close enough to share one or both lateral walls (Peary 1898:2:268) while apparently using separate tunnels. Even as late as the 1930s and 1940s Polar Eskimos retained the essential Greenlandic house features described above, preferring to refurbish existing houses rather than build new ones (Holtved 1967:2, figs. 9–16). Here as elsewhere in the Eastern Eskimo culture area, when families

FIGURE 14

"The Esquimaux huts," depicting a long tunnel to a small, windowless house and, nearby, a storage platform (right).

From Kane 1856:1:122.

FIGURE 15

"Life in the Esquimaux igloë," an idealistic view of household activity. The woman at left cooks over a non-Eskimo lamp, a pot dangling from the drying rack overhead. The platforms seem unrealistic, as does the great ceiling height.

From Kane 1856:2:opp. 113.

FIGURE 16

"Igloo at Little Omenak and native women." Note the window above a short tunnel (upper center), the tunnel entrance (lower center), and apparently a small storage place (right).

From Senn 1907:106 ff.

FIGURE 17

"Esquimaux hut," like figure 16, depicts a short tunnel with a square-framed window over it and a storage place or doghouse to the right.

From Kane 1856:1:60.

departed the winter house in springtime, the roof was dismantled, thereby exposing the lived-in center for the elements to cleanse. If a family did not return to the house the next fall, anyone in the group had equal claim to it (Peary 1898:2:272–273).

ALTERNATIVE WINTER DWELLINGS

Greenlanders in all three regions used secondary and infrequently occupied winter dwelling types, which we call alternative housing. Polar and West Greenland Eskimos built small but less complete versions of their stone-walled winter homes (Holtved 1967:28, 111–112; Rink 1877:182) and, in earlier times, West Greenland coastal people contrived a winter-house variant made with whale bones (Birket-Smith 1924:144–146). East Greenlanders sometimes built a smaller house of stone, without turf, when they were "unable to reach the usual wintering places" (Holm 1914:41). Even if turf were available in winter, its frozen state prevented its convenient removal and use, so builders of temporary shelters sometimes covered a structure with snow for insulation. This might have been a carryover from the prehistoric, one-family stone house (cf. Holm 1914:41–42). When traveling, all Greenland groups built small, dome-shaped houses of snow (Birket-Smith 1924:148; Thalbitzer 1914:fig. 222; cf. 1914:406–407, 1941:658–659). The East Greenland name for such houses was uttisaawt, "a place (house) where one stays for a day, or for a few days" (Thalbitzer 1941:659; cf. Holm 1914:42).

Hunters sometimes erected simple versions of the stone house while in transit (Birket-Smith 1924:149). Among the Polar Eskimos these were very small,

> about four feet by three in ground-plan, and some three feet high. In shape they resemble a rude dome. No doubt they are human habitations—retiring chambers, into which, away from the crowded families of the hut, one or even two Esquimaux have burrowed for sleep.... [T]he hardy tenant, muffled in furs, at a temperature of –60° is dependent for warmth upon his own powers and the slow conduction of the thick walls. (Kane 1856:1:122, 458)

Polar Eskimos made use of snow houses (though not the more sophisticated type made in Canada) more often than did other Greenlanders and occasionally resorted to digging into a snowdrift for shelter (Hayes 1885:243–244; Holtved 1967:31). Called *iglooyak* or *igluiya*, these hastily erected snow houses were temporary[5] (Kroeber 1900:271; Steensby 1910:287). Originally, this house type was built up from both sides of the doorway and peaked at around six feet, although it still took on a "semi-elliptical" to circular plan (Kroeber 1900:271). In 1856, visiting Baffin Island Eskimos showed the Polar Eskimos how to make the Canadian Inuit spiral-built snowblock dome (Holtved 1967:31), and at the same time introduced the subsurface tunnel to replace the shorter, covered, surface passage of earlier times (Rasmussen 1975:32).

The floorplan of the temporary Polar Eskimo winter house closely resembled that of their stone-walled houses (Steensby 1910:fig. 2). At the doorway, a large snowblock kept out the cold, but for greater circulation it stood ajar. In spring, Polar Eskimos did not cap the dome, roofing it instead with old

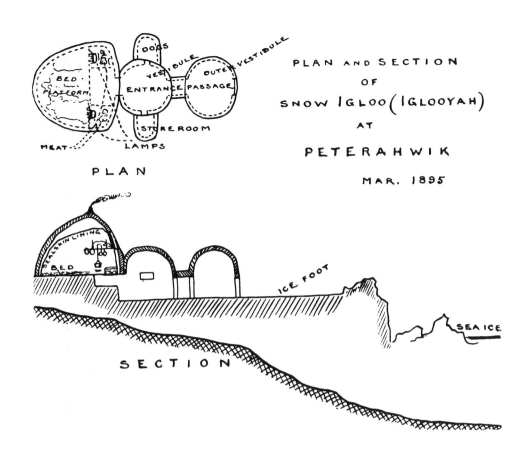

tent-furs, which they "folded and laid upon poles, then covered with turf and snow"; they preferred expendable covers whenever possible (Peary 1898:501–502 n1; Steensby 1910:287). Separate antechambers might have been integral prior to the time of the large snow house Peary commissioned (fig. 18; Peary 1898:2:431–432), and Steensby (1910:figs. 1, 2) treats them as aboriginal. However, gut (versus ice) window panels and skin linings tacked up inside the main chamber probably postdate the 1856 contact with Baffin Islanders (cf. Boas 1888:541–542, figs. 492–493; Holtved 1967:31; cf. Kroeber 1900:271).

ASPECTS OF WINTER HOUSE LIFE

Generally in Eskimo houses, heat was conserved by the relatively large number of people who inhabited a relatively small space (e.g., fig. 9). In Greenlandic communal houses, as many as three adults and six to seven children could occupy a cubicle four feet wide, although the average was four people (Holm 1914:37; Nansen 1894:79). Lamp flames, insulated walls, and body heat all combined to keep the occupants comfortably warm, if not hot. Thus, Greenland inhabitants usually wore no more than the barest underclothes indoors and regularly sat on the floor, where it was cooler (Holm 1914:35, 60, fig. 30). "Although the many lamps and the many people produce a stifling heat in the house, the air is nevertheless by no means as foul as might be expected, when one bears in mind that blubber and half-rotten meat as well as urine are to be found inside; the fact is, the low passageway ensures a good ventilation, without preventing the warmth from escaping" (Holm 1914:60). Despite the

FIGURE 18

Snow house constructed for Robert E. Peary, in design more like Baffin Island Eskimo snow houses than traditional Polar Eskimo examples.

From Peary 1898:2:427.

naturally upward ventilation flow, some of the humid household air wafted down into the tunnel, where it gradually condensed into a thick coat of ice on all sides (Thalbitzer 1914:357). Consequently, the spring thaw turned this crawlway into a sloppy, slippery passage through a fetid miasma.

From the Western perspective, Eskimo living spaces were disorderly, malodorous, and frequently stuffy (e.g., Mathiassen 1928:141), yet, in keeping with their seminomadic or semisedentary ways of life, Eskimo household furnishings were spartan. They typically included such necessities as platters, cups, bowls, and urine buckets of wood or baleen. There were also various utensils generally made from whale bone, baleen, musk ox horn, walrus ivory, caribou antler, wood, or stone; these included dippers, one or two spoons or ladles, a blubber pounder, and a skewer or fork for cooking meats (e.g., Murdoch 1892:86–109; Schwatka 1884a; Stefánsson 1914:67; Thalbitzer 1914:524–561).

The cornerstone of the Eskimo household—and indeed of life itself—was the lamp, or *qulliq* (Hough 1898a, b). Given to a girl when she married, the shallow, semilunar stone lamp, along with the crescentic woman's knife, or *ulu*, and the similarly shaped parka hood in which an infant spent the first year of life, was the ultimate symbol of femininity (Graburn 1972, 1976). There was some local variation in lamp form[6] (see endpapers) but the general features were much the same (Hough 1898b). On the straight side of the basin, a narrow ridge sometimes divided the wick channel from the reservoir for oil, usually rendered from blubber. Lamp fuel needed frequent replacement.

A lamp was easy to operate: the woman tilted it slightly forward, and either placed solid blubber (previously pounded to speed up liquifaction) on the opposite edge of the lamp basin or suspended it overhead to drip down as it was melted by a lit wick of dried and powdered reindeer moss, a lichen (Ekblaw 1927–28:169). After a lamp was lit its flame's height had to be trimmed constantly, by poking and prodding with a stick; see fig. 19 (a soapstone rod might also be used, for example, among the Iglulik [Mathiassen 1928:148–149] and Netsilik [Ross 1835a]). Above the lamp hung a wooden drying rack from which clothing, soapstone cooking pots, and snow-melting vessels could be suspended (figs. 6–9).

FIGURE 19

A woman from Cape Prince of Wales, Alaska, circa 1892–1902, trims a small lit section of lamp wick to adjust its flame on the lamp's front rim.

Ellen Kittredge Lopp collection; courtesy of Kathleen Lopp Smith.

Whether warming the air, lighting the house, melting ice for water, drying apparel, or beckoning hunters homeward, the Eskimo lamp literally *created* culture, transforming dark into bright, cold into hot, raw into cooked. Not only did the warmth of the lamp mediate between life and death; the flame's color also monitored the amount of carbon monoxide in the house. If the air was healthy the flame burned white; yellow flames signaled a need for extra ventilation. When this happened the grass or turf plug in the roof's vent-hole would be removed (Ekblaw 1927–28:169–70; Steensby 1910:320).

Female and male roles were both contrastive and complementary in Eskimo societies, and household occupations highlight the disparity. It was women who built the houses in East and West Greenland, for example, and it was they who arranged the interior and cared for the house (Giffen 1930:28, 31). "Housekeeping includes the care of all clothing (which she helps the wearer to remove and which must be dried and softened after each wearing), the cleaning of utensils, the cleaning of the house, its ventilation, the clearing of snow from the roof or passageway, and the making of any repairs necessary" (Giffen 1930:32). Women had other duties, too. Seated next to her lamp in the house, a woman could trim the wick as necessary to control its flames (figs. 6–9, 19). "Here [she sat] hour after hour preparing skins, twisting sinew thread and cord, sewing clothes and doing embroidery . . . [and looking after the children]" (Holm 1914:60). She could also cook in a soapstone vessel suspended over the lamp and monitor clothes as they dried atop a dangling rack, from which the cookpot hung (Thalbitzer 1941:figs. 224, 258). Men's roles inside the house contrasted markedly: "The fathers of families [in East and West Greenland] sit on the border of the platform with their feet on the chest in front of it, while the unmarried men sit on the window platform. . . . When the men are not working at their implements or utensils, they usually do nothing but eat, sleep, relate their hunting adventures, [etc.]" (Holm 1914:60; cf. fig. 20).

FIGURE 20

"A resting-place for reindeer-hunters on their march." Women collect fuel for the fire, cook, serve food, and prepare caribou skins and (probably) fish (left, center, and upper right) as two men sit in the turf-walled shelter and another cleans a rifle.
From Rink 1877:104 ff.

TRANSITIONAL DWELLINGS

ACROSS THE ESKIMO CULTURE AREA, MANY PEOPLE AVAILED THEMSELVES OF what we call transitional dwellings, housing used during the brief between-season periods when, for instance, it was too cold to live comfortably in a summer tent but too warm or wet to occupy the usual winter house. Transitional dwellings were often located at sites different from the winter villages. So wedded were Greenlandic Eskimos to winter stone houses and summer skin tents that even a combined list of their transitional dwelling forms is meager. Polar Eskimo hunters made a skin-roofed, one-person version of a stone winter house (Holtved 1967:31–33, 108). These may have functioned like the low, apparently turf-walled, three-foot-deep rectangular pits that West Greenland caribou hunters used in the autumn, with cooking done outside (fig. 20). Referring to West Greenland, Rink mentions spring houses, or "separate huts," built like smaller, simpler versions of winter houses in which the sleeping area of some was "nothing but stones covered with moss" (Rink 1877:182). When traveling, the Ammassalik made small stone houses without turf, covering the exterior with snow (Holm 1914:41–42).

Birket-Smith asked a West Greenlander from the Egedesminde District "to draw the ground plan" of what may be a similar transitional house (1924:144–147, fig. 111). Obviously intended for four families, its trapezoidal floor had sleeping platforms on the back and left side walls, but the right side wall's platform was recessed as a semicircular lobe. Near this odd-shaped platform was the doorway to the tunnel, which was to the right of center in the front wall such that its two windows penetrated the wall's longer left side. Still earlier, in the northern part of West Greenland, people constructed domed houses—probably single-family dwellings—using whale bones in place of stone or wood before or after moving from the winter house (Birket-Smith 1924:145–146).

The Polar Eskimos used a second kind of spring and summer stone house, the *qarmaq*. Intended as temporary shelter, this seems to resemble a shelter that Kane described as "one of those strange little kennels which serve as dormitories when the igloë is crowded" (1856:2:159). A rock- and turf-walled circle without a passageway, it had an insulated hide roof held up by stone cantilevers.[7]

SUMMER DWELLINGS

TENT IS THE APPROPRIATE TERM FOR VIRTUALLY ALL ESKIMO WARM-SEASON shelters, with only infrequent exceptions. Across the North American Arctic, however, tent frameworks varied so much that their sole consistent attribute was a skin cover (Birket-Smith 1936:130). As discussed in chapter 5, Eskimo tents fall into essentially four categories based on general shape and structure: arched, ridged, conical, or domed. The summer tents of all three Greenlandic groups shared many features and can be divided into two basic arch types. Variations on a single-arch design were common throughout Greenland, while the double-arch was reported only for the west and northwest (Birket-Smith 1928).

The best-known Greenlandic tent design, tupeq (fig. 21), had a truncated elliptical floor plan measuring ten to fifteen feet in breadth (fig. 21D). Its entryway was vertical (fig. 21C) and its roof line sloped dramatically down, leaving little headroom toward the back (fig. 21E). The door frame consisted of a tall, sawhorse-like archway: a central, slightly curved crossbar pegged (at each end) to the apex of tall, paired uprights (fig. 21A). Long tent poles met above this door frame, where they were fastened together with skin thongs in front of the crossbar, then fanned out rearward from the crossbar and down to the ground (fig. 21B; Holm 1914:42; Thalbitzer 1914:364–365, figs. 66–68). The raised sleeping platform's wooden planks rested on stone and turf foundations, and some tents had stone and turf bases for steadying and leveling the poles (fig. 21B–D).

West Greenland Eskimos occasionally added a simple entryway windbreak (fig. 21E). Its framework consisted of either a smaller version of the entrance archway (fig. 21E, left) or lashed bipods with a crosspiece resting in their crotches (fig. 4). The upright members were placed near the main arch and connected to it by two down-sloping poles set atop both frames (fig. 4). This outer area acted as "a kind of porch, where they [could] place their stores as well as their dirty vessels" (figs. 22–24; Crantz 1767:1:142). The West Greenland tent (*tupinaq*) also differed from Ammassalik ones in having a pair of stone lamp-bases, one near each side of the archway, and an edge-upright board at the foot of the curtain, used as a threshold (fig. 21C–D). East and West Greenland tent fronts evidently varied in shape: some were essentially vertical and flat (figs. 4, 21–22), some were in-curved below the peak (figs. 3, 23, 26), and others were flat-faced but pitched forward (fig. 25).

FIGURE 21

Idealized East and West Greenland arched tent: (A) entrance arch and gut curtain details; (B) tent frame, rear view; (C) interior and exterior details; (D) floor plan (hatched circle = pole placements); (E) windbreak details and simplified side view.

Reinhardt and Lee 1997:1804, courtesy of Cambridge University Press; after Crantz 1767:1:Pls. 3–4, 1767:2:Pl 9; Holm 1914:figs. 23–24; Thalbitzer 1914:figs. 66–70, 1941:fig. 173.

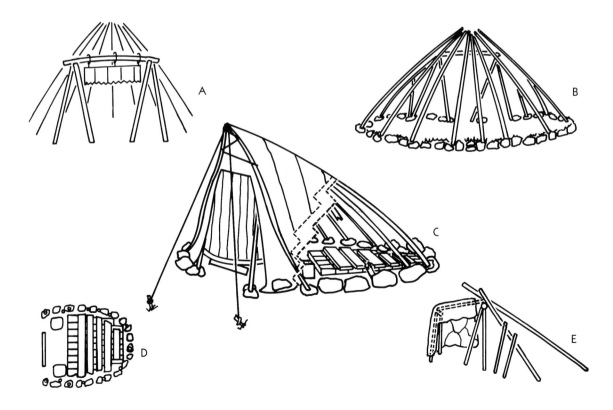

FIGURE 22

An Ammassalik "tent complete. In the foreground a man [using bow drill and mouth bearing is] about to drill a hole in a harpoon shaft." Note the sheltered space within the doorway but in front of the striped curtain. *From Thalbitzer 1914:fig. 70.*

FIGURE 23

West Greenland tent depicting a forward curve to the front and a small fore-space in front of the inner curtain. A woman with *ulu* (knife) and traditional wooden bucket prepares to butcher birds, while a baby (who should be shown inside the mother's parka hood) clings to her back. *From Crantz 1767.*

Over the tent frame were stretched two covers: an outer layer of depilated, oiled sealskins and an inner layer, also of sealskin, with their glossy fur facing inward. These covers were laced shut at the tent's opening, then pulled taut and weighted at the base with stones, turf, or other heavy objects. An abbreviated anteroom was added by pulling down and weighting the covers with stones[8] some distance forward of the doorway. To set off this little "forechamber" from the rear sleeping area, a curtain was fastened to the crossbar (figs. 21C, 22–23). Alternating winter- and summer-tanned seal intestine strips produced this artful curtain of light and dark stripes (figs. 22, 24).[9]

The double tent coverings deserve further elaboration (fig. 21C). A water-repellent outer cover of sealskins was either turned skin-side out, or was depilated and then rain-proofed by rubbing blubber into its surface. Inner covers had hair facing the interior for greater insulation. Each double tent cover, which the women of a household made, required as many as fifty to sixty sealskins (fig. 4; Birket-Smith 1928; Graah 1837:69–70; Thalbitzer 1914:365). The second (inner) layer of tent covering indicated prosperity, at least in West Greenland, especially if it were of caribou rather than seal (Birket-Smith 1924:157; Crantz 1767:1:141). Only coastal dwellers with umiaks could afford to transport such dual tent covers; other Eskimos reliant on dogsleds, kayaks, and backpacking could not bear this luxurious but weighty comfort.

WEST GREENLAND DOUBLE-ARCH TENTS

Single-arch tents were the norm everywhere in Greenland, but Birket-Smith describes a double-arch-framed variant found in West Greenland's northern Egedesminde District (fig. 27; Birket-Smith 1924:154–156). Presumably it was similar to a type that the Polar Eskimos borrowed from visiting Baffin Island Eskimos during their 1856 visit (Holtved 1967:29–30; cf. Reinhardt 1986:83). The double-arch tent, called erqulik ("the one with the rear") or igdlerfiusaq ("that which resembles a box"), looked like "a sugar loaf" (Egede 1745:117). This type had an arched entrance similar to tents erected farther south and in East Greenland, plus a smaller yet otherwise identical frame that raised its back end (fig. 28). The front-arch frame consisted of two near-vertical side poles connected to a horizontal crossbar. From the crossbar's center, poles sloped downward and rearward, where they were cut flush and probably lashed to the sides of the shorter and narrower rear-arch frame (Holtved 1967:27, 29; Kroeber 1900:271–272). Both layers of tent cover consisted of skins with the hair left on. Another deviation from single-arch tents was a separate seal fur panel (erqut) not sewn to the main tent cover, closing off the back end (fig. 29; Birket-Smith 1924:157). Sometimes a gut window transmitted light through this rear panel.

Besides weighing down the tent cover all around, "there was sometimes quite a wall of sods and stones at the base" (fig. 27; Birket-Smith 1924:156). People slept along the side walls on a bed of heather (Cassiope tetragona, another Cassiope species, or generic woody plants) covered with furs. Lampstands and a rear sleeping platform paralleled the arrangement seen in winter houses, although women usually cooked outdoors over a hearth. The advantage of this design over single-arch tents is extra headroom toward the back.

FIGURE 24

"A man kindling fire by drilling [with toggle-handled drill cord], assisted by a woman [holding a two-handed fire-drill bearing], in the front room of a tent." The fire-drill shaft is seated in a wooden hearth-hole in which friction generates an ember that will be nurtured into a flame. Note the dark-and-light striped curtain behind the Ammassalik couple, and the relative roominess between curtain and outer doorway.
From Thalbitzer 1914:fig. 69.

FIGURE 25

East Greenland tents, the two on the right with guy lines, indicating a pronounced forward lean at the front ends, from an Ammassalik drawing. The large billows appear to be smoke from outdoor fireplaces.
Oswalt 1979:fig. 4–6 (after Thalbitzer 1914, redrawn by Partick Finnerty; courtesy of Wendell H. Oswalt)

FIGURE 26

"Women and children outside the tent [1885]." Ammassalik example of a tent with in-curving front; note the size of stones holding down the tent cover base.
From Holm 1914:fig. 21.

FIGURE 27

"Sealskin tent of *erqulik* [double-arch] type. Notice windbreak in front."
From Birket-Smith 1924:fig. 117.

FIGURE 28

Framework for *erqulik* [double-arch] tent. The lower rear arch (left) has two central uprights as well as two forward-leaning laterals, which spread the back considerably and provide support for the side-wall poles.
From Birket-Smith 1924:fig. 119.

FIGURE 29

Rear view of *erqulik* [double-arch] tent.
From Birket-Smith 1924:fig. 118.

Still, the atmosphere in a tent was less oppressively warm than inside a house, even though as many as twenty inhabitants sometimes shared it (Crantz 1767:1:142; Nansen 1894:84).

NORTHWEST GREENLAND TENTS

Two Polar Eskimo tents are known but only one seemingly had local aboriginal roots. Both appear transitional between the Greenlandic single-arched version to the south and east and the Central Eskimo ridged tents found much farther to the south and west. The Polar Eskimo tupeq qanisaling ("a tent with a front compartment") contrasts with those already described. Differing in design and name, it compares structurally with the double-arched, northern West Greenland erqulik, and so suggests a nonlocal[10] origin (Holtved 1967:29–30).

The Polar Eskimo *tupeq* (fig. 30) shows greater aboriginal affinity with East and West Greenland single-arch forms. In this territory, where wood[11] was scarcer than elsewhere in Greenland, a tent measured about fifteen feet front to back and twelve feet side to side. Lacking any designated antechamber, it had a ridgepole that dropped to the ground at the back. Other poles leaned against this ridge rather than having all the poles flare out from the crosspiece (fig. 31; Birket-Smith 1928; Ekblaw 1927–28:162). Stone slabs delineated sleeping and side platforms, which replicated those found in winter houses designed for two families, while a translucent doorflap or a borrowed house window (in more recent times) brightened the inside.

As of the early twentieth century, Greenland groups were changing over to European-style, A-frame ridge tents, which they covered with canvas in the south and with sealskins farther north. A thong functioned as the ridge connecting upright front and rear poles (Birket-Smith 1924:160). By this time, small iron stoves supplied most heat, which led to the use of smaller-sized lamps necessary only for illumination (Birket-Smith 1924:162).

ASPECTS OF SUMMER TENT LIFE

Women played a central role in Eskimo culture with regard to tents as well as winter houses. Most important, Eskimo women were in charge of skin preparation and sewing the cover.[12] Sealskin, because of its fatty texture and the low temperatures at which it is used, does not require extensive tanning. After being soaked in the householders' (usually children's) urine, skins were scraped and staked out on the ground to dry, then worked again with a scraper and softener. Next they were cut with an ulu and sewn with a bone needle, usually made from the leg of a gull or arctic hare. For this, women used the blind stitch, a sewing technique that only partly perforated the skins' thicknesses, creating waterproof seams. They made sinew thread by shredding caribou, seal, or, in parts of Greenland, narwhal tendon. Moreover, women were the engineers in Eskimo societies: It was they who erected these shelters upon arrival at each new summer encampment, setting up the frame, stretching the tent-skin over it, and securing the cover's skirt with stones against inclement weather. When the summer camps were abandoned, women usually dismantled the tents (Ekblaw 1927–28:161, 174–175; Holtved 1967:134–136, 140–141).

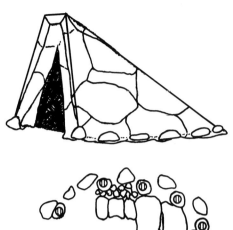

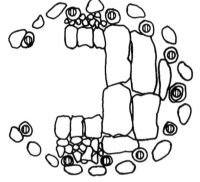

FIGURE 30
Idealized Polar Eskimo arched tent.
After Holtved 1967:fig. 20; Steensby 1910:figs. 17–20, 22.

FIGURE 31
"A friendly 'tupic' and its inhabitants," probably a small version of the Polar Eskimo single-arch tent. Note that the tent-cover sides do not droop toward the center.
From Diebitsch-Peary 1893:168 ff.

During the twenty-four-hour daylight of northern summers, interior illumination of the tent was less critical than in the winter house. Both East and West Greenlanders suspended a gut curtain from the doorframe crossbar. Polar Eskimos substituted a curtain made from the inner, translucent layer of split sealskin, or membranes from walrus penis or gullet (Birket-Smith 1928:84; Holtved, 1967:140–141; Thalbitzer 1914:364).

Interior space in summer tents reflected the same basic pattern seen in the winter houses. Lamp platforms stood within the doorway, either on both sides (figs. 21D, 30) or centered (fig. 32). The elevated, sod-and-wood, or stone-paved sleeping and living platform took up the rear in a space demarcated by either wood or stones. The West Greenland *erqulik* had additional, narrow platforms along the sides (Birket-Smith 1924:154–158).

"A tent...when warmed with lamps, makes a very pleasant place to live in" (Holm 1914:42). In fact, the attraction of the tent was so great that Eskimos sometimes vacated their winter houses sooner than was safe:

> When the people of Angmagsalik moved into tents in the spring, they were erected on the snow. In fact some people said that the first night after they had moved into tents they had literally frozen...as the platform was raised only six inches above the ice. When we hear that at this time it was 10 degrees below zero [Celsius, or 14°F] at night, and that the natives notwithstanding this stripped to the skin as usual, although the lamps had not warmed up the tent in the day time, we cannot help wondering at the hardiness of these people. (Holm 1914:42)

SPECIAL-USE STRUCTURES

IN CONTRAST TO *DWELLINGS*—OR HOUSE FORMS TYPICALLY USED FOR sleeping and living activities—*nondomestic special-use structures* are defined here as ceremonial buildings, most windbreaks, and any built space *not normally intended for sleeping* (Reinhardt 1986:38). The ceremonial men's house (*qagsse*)[13] is the most important of these. Common to most Eskimos, the ceremonial house had disappeared from Greenland before Danish colonization. Thalbitzer (1941:656–658) hypothesizes, however, that the windowless, long-passaged "summer playing house" reported by his Ammassalik informants may have been based on the prehistoric *qagsse*. No historic-era Greenlanders built a *qagsse*, instead engaging in *qagsse*-related activities in their regular houses (figs. 33–34). However, Birket-Smith (1924:135, 144) notes prehistoric examples from West Greenland, spatially associated with summer camps rather than winter villages. The Ammassalik sometimes constructed small replicas of winter dwellings, complete with miniature lamps, outside their dwellings for their children's amusement (Holm 1914:41). Curiously, the name for this playhouse, *(n)erteelät*, is synonymous with a meeting house (hence, a *qagsse*), variously intended for whale hunters or for sexual liaisons between young people (Thalbitzer 1941:656–658).

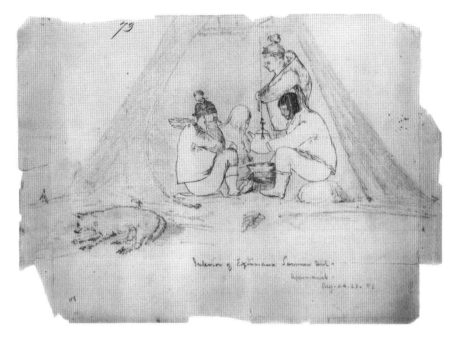

FIGURE 32

"Interior of Esquimaux Summer Tent, Uppernavik. Aug. 24–23–51" [*sic*], reproduced in Kane (1854:431) as "Interior of a Native Hut." In this tent American explorer Elisha Kent Kane "superintended the manufacture of a dish of coffee" (1854:432). A dog sleeps near the entrance, uninterested in a seal's ribcage before the doorway. Resting on its low platform, the traditional stone lamp heats a Western coffee pot as well as a man (squatting, right). A woman (seated, left) scratches her head, perhaps, while another (standing, right) warms her hands as a baby rests in her parka.

From Kane 1854:431; courtesy of Andreas Zust.

FIGURE 33

"Building a wind-break." Six Polar Eskimo men cut and set the snowblocks; the third man from left and the right man hold snow knives.

From Whitney 1910: 288.

FIGURE 34

"Wind-break of snowblocks." Three Polar Eskimo men (left, center, and right) wear traditional pants of polar bear fur (of the three other, one is reclining out of view and evident only by his boot soles). Note snow knife stuck in a snowblock (left), a bottle and cans as litter (foreground), and a dogsled and part of its stanchion (right).

From Whitney 1910:93.

Kaalund notes that small tents were occasionally erected for childbirth, one in the bow of an open skin boat, or umiak (Kaalund 1983:166). The Ammassalik Eskimos lacked a separate birth hut,[14] but, when weather permitted, a pregnant woman was expected to leave the house or tent during delivery or even beforehand (Holm 1914:61–62).

Greenland Eskimos assembled snowblock shelters: windbreaks for Polar Eskimos (figs. 35–36), huts for Ammasslik ice fishing and (possibly) workshops, and huts for fox trappers and windbreaks for seal hunters among West Greenland Eskimos (Crantz 1767:1:72; Holm 1914:42; Holtved 1967:27, 31; Ostermann 1938:25; Porsild 1915:132).[15] Polar Eskimo windbreaks sheltered people or protected their cooking fires outdoors. If storms persisted, such a semicircular wall might be expanded into a snow house. Greenlanders sometimes slept directly on the snow in milder weather (Holtved 1967:27, 31; Steensby 1910:287). One Ammassalik structure was a dome-shaped "dog kennel" (Thalbitzer 1941:fig. 222).[16] Among the more durable special-use structures were "large store houses of stone" used in East Greenland as fish caches (Ostermann 1938:25). One or more additional structures could be found in association with Polar Eskimo houses. "Small stone rooms" (Ekblaw 1927–28:172), or auxilliary caches, for "skin clothing, tools, and the like" (Holtved 1967:26) were often built nearby (figs. 16–17). (Another choice was simply to widen the house passage's outer entryway into a storage space.) Polar Eskimos also erected "stone pedestals for the protection of meat" (Kane 1856:2:159). These pillars were roughly three feet wide and five feet high, putting their tops beyond the reach of dogs. Blubber drippings further solidified the structure over time (fig. 14; Steensby 1910:311).

Some writers refer to special-use structures built for hunting. Polar Eskimo hunters made use of unmodified caves and cliff niches (Holtved 1967:33; Steensby 1910:287–288). Another ancillary structure type occurred among West Coast hunters, who built seal-hunting blinds of sod and turf after rifles became available (Birket-Smith 1924:321–322, fig. 233; Porsild 1915:138). These allowed hunters to kill seals from shore, a method that would have been impossible with aboriginal harpoons.

ASSOCIATED RITUALS AND BELIEFS

GREENLANDIC ESKIMOS HAD MANY RITUALS AND BELIEFS ASSOCIATED WITH housing. Kaalund (1983:54) reports that [unspecified] Greenlanders recited a ritual formula on moving from the summer tent into the winter house: "The skin of my face have I covered and I am wearing a mask."[17] Kaalund also illustrates a house mask (representing tutelary spirits) that East Greenlanders placed on the wall of a dwelling to prevent strangers from seeing household members when they entered (Kaalund 1983:56–57). Moreover, among some Greenland Eskimos a raven skin—complete with head, beak, and claws—might be attached to a house wall or tent to ensure good hunting or to protect against sorcery (Kaalund 1983:19).

Still other Greenlandic beliefs associated with housing centered around death. In the Egedesminde district of West Greenland, people smeared the house ridgepole with lamp black to prevent the death of a family or its members (Birket-Smith 1924:149). Polar Eskimos reportedly deserted a house or tent as quickly as possible if one of its occupants died, believing that the house had been contaminated with evil (Gilberg 1984:587; Steensby 1910:308).[18] To prevent symbolic pollution of their normal entrance-exit route, house residents either jostled the corpse unceremoniously through a hastily punched hole in the back wall or removed it by way of the window. Upon disposing of the corpse, Polar Eskimo corpse handlers stuffed one of their nostrils with grass[19] (men the right nostril, women the left), removing the plugs only "when entering one of the huts" (Bessels 1884:877).

FIGURE 35

"This house interior (a drawing by Kaarle) shows an examination by a *qila-quercer*, a man or woman who is consulting his or her private familiar spirit (*qila*).... It is the method where the patient sits up on the platform in the neighboring stall ... with his back turned towards the room, while the consulting 'doctor' lies on his back on the inmost part (*kile*) of the platform covered by a sealskin." Apart from showing Ammassalik house-construction details and the lampstand-lamp-drying rack arrangement, this image illustrates the use of houses for shamanistic rituals (cf. fig. 36), much as the *qagsse/qaggqi/qasgiq* might assume such role in other parts of the Arctic.
From Thalbitzer 1941:fig. 224.

FIGURE 36

"An angakoq [shaman] séance developing in the hut. We see the front wall of the room facing the beach. The shaman is sitting with his face turned towards the dried sealskin hung up in front of the inner door opening (*katak*) to the house passage; over which is seen a small window (over the passage extending between the two larger ones). His hands are tied on his back; on the left his drum. On each of the two platforms by the window is seen one of the angakoq's assistants (young boys)." Like struggling with spirits while being covered (cf. fig. 35), demonstrating magical feats while hand-bound allowed shamans to demonstrate their prowess. Performing in a house arguably transformed the structure temporarily into a *qagsse* of sorts.
From Thalbitzer 1941:fig. 225.

Eskimo ideas of spiritual pollution due to death coincided with dwelling taboos and rituals adhered to faithfully. For example, Ammassalik practices surrounding death indicate the pervasiveness and seriousness of such proscriptions:

> Everybody had to take their possessions out of the house before the death; after it the house itself had to be cleaned and all those living in it had to wash their whole bodies. A man who had to attend to a corpse had to remain at the rear of the [sleeping] platform fully clad, with even his hood turned up and his face averted, for three days. This is regarded, not without reason, as a veritable torment in the oppressive [heat] of the house. (Birket-Smith 1936:158–159)

Finally, the love of hearth and home is a recurrent theme in Greenlandic Eskimo folk tales. "To the [Eskimo] his dwelling place is more than a place where he happens to carry on his trade; it is his real home. No more heartfelt hymn can be imagined than the simple legend of the hunter from Aluk, whose heart burst when once again he saw the sun rising over the sea at his own dwelling" (Birket-Smith 1928:187).

CHAPTER 1 NOTES

1   The only wood available in most of the Eskimo area was driftwood. The main source in the eastern American Arctic was the Mackenzie River, which originates in interior Canada well south of treeline. From the Mackenzie delta driftwood spread across the Canadian Archipelago and as far east as Greenland by a complex series of currents. Both hard- and softwoods from the Mackenzie were carried on these currents (Dyke et al. 1997).

2   Most descriptions of this cooking area (Birket-Smith 1924:151; Nansen 1894:82; Rink 1877:177) suggest that it was not so much a chamber as a tunnel alcove (e.g., the left-side tunnel bulge in fig. 5F).

3   Jenness reports one example of a prehistoric Copper Eskimo dwelling with cantilever construction, although it might have been of English origin (Jenness 1922:57–58).

4   Small houses were the rule among the Polar Eskimos, in whose territory sizable driftwood was in very short supply; the roofs of the larger communal houses of East and West Greenland, where wood was more plentiful, required wood in quantity.

5   Peary (1898:2:431) states that the Polar Eskimo snow house could be inhabited for up to three months, but his design (1898:2:fig. 111) seems more like Baffin Island-type snow houses (Holtved 1967:31).

6   Eskimo lamps came in different sizes and shapes. Those from Greenland to northwestern Alaska were mostly large, semilunar in top view (i.e., having a curved back edge and a straight to very slightly curved front edge), about two inches thick, and carved from soapstone. In southwest Alaska, they were small ceramic saucers, while along the Gulf of Alaska they were thick, midsized, and stone-pecked objects (see endpapers). On St. Lawrence Island and at East Cape Siberia they were mid-sized pottery basins, their outlines rectangle to ellipse shaped, with two raised lamp-wick ridges running lengthwise across the middle.

7   Holtved (1967:28, 111–112) distinguishes the *qarmaq* from a less substantial, more temporary shelter.

8   Central Eskimos arrayed poles similarly as rafters for certain stone-walled houses (Boas 1888:figs. 498–499).

9   In winter, skins and gut tanned by exposure to the elements turned white, whereas summer tanning at higher temperatures yielded darker results.

10 Two other Polar Eskimo tent types mentioned in the literature are rare, if not unique. The first, photographed by Peary circa 1898, is a ridge-type example resembling Labrador and Copper Eskimo tents (Peary 1898:2:547). Possibly the design was borrowed from the immigrant Baffin Island Eskimos (Boas 1888:figs. 504–506). The second was seen in the unusual case of an old widow who survived abandonment by her community, living alone in a tiny tent of her own devising (Steensby 1910:32–326, fig. 18).

11 Polar Eskimos often used narwhal tusks as poles because of the wood shortage in their region (Peary 1894:44).

12 Some land-focused groups relied on caribou hides but the great majority used seal hides for tent covers.

13 Called *qagsse* in Greenland, the ceremonial house was known as *qaggiq* (also *qaggi*) in Canada, *qargi* in Northwest Alaska, and *qasgiq* or *qaygiq* in Southwest Alaska. *Kashim* is a Russo-Anglicized term no doubt derived from the Yup'ik word (i.e., *qasgiq*). In southwest Alaska, on the other hand, the *qasgiq/qaygiq* served regularly as a men's dormitory. Thus, in chapter 4, some men's houses are listed under Winter Houses rather than Special Structures.

14 Death huts, special-use structures built expressly for those expected to die soon, are reported widely throughout the Arctic (Reinhardt 1986); we discuss them further in chapters 2–4 (see sections on *Special-Use Structure*). Rasmussen mentions one compelling example from the Polar Eskimos. A woman was walled up in a snow house for not having disclosed a miscarriage. People blamed her nondisclosure for a subsequent game shortage. Entombed with no food or bedding, she was in effect sentenced to freeze or starve to death. However, the game reappeared, after which her husband released her still alive (Rasmussen 1975:30).

15 West Greenland fox and raven traps consisted of stones piled up with a hole at the peak through which the fox would fall (Birket-Smith 1924:351, fig. 9; Crantz 1767:1:72; Egede 1745:62; Thalbitzer 1914:406–407; 1941:658).

16 A similarly designed building also served as a bird and fox trap. The trapper actually sat inside this cramped structure. Once the prey alighted on the translucent roof it was yanked inside the building (Thalbitzer 1914:406–407, 1941: 658–659).

17 A remarkably similar ceremony was reported at Wales, on the western tip of the Seward Peninsula, Alaska, in the early twentieth century (see Thornton 1931:226).

18 See note 14 above.

19 In other parts of the Arctic, Eskimos made nostril plugs for the same purpose from materials such as caribou fur, caribou skin, grass, cotton grass, down, etc. (e.g., Boas 1888:614; Parry 1824:325).

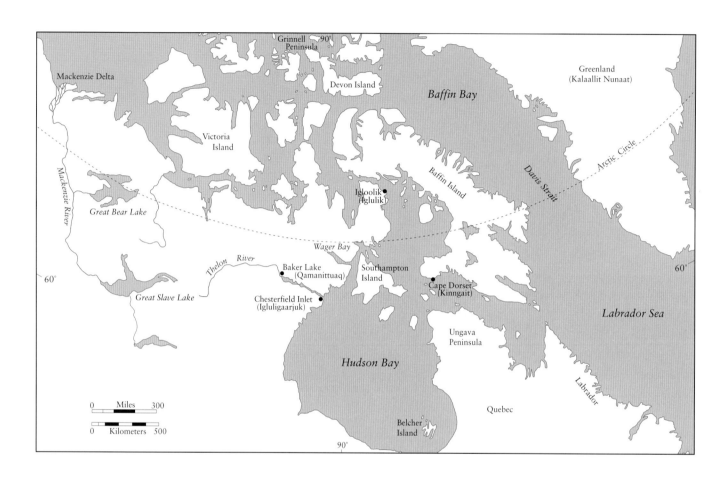

FIGURE 37

Map of Central Arctic.

Produced by Robert Drozda.

2

CENTRAL ARCTIC

Could one imagine the Lilliputs living in flat
candy jars with drumhead covers, he would have
a fair miniature representation of an ice village.

(Schwatka 1883:216–217)

THE DOMED, SNOWBLOCK IGLOO THAT IS UNIVERSALLY BUT INAPPROPRIATELY associated with all Eskimos (fig. 38) was limited as a primary dwelling type to the Central Arctic, mainly in the area of Canada between Baffin Island and the Mackenzie Delta. The designation Central Arctic is problematic,[1] of course, as this is a region of architectural transitions. On the eastern end of this cultural continuum, for example, Labrador Eskimos, like the Greenlanders, favored stone-walled dwellings over snow houses.[2] Estimates for the nineteenth-century population of the Central Arctic Eskimos range from a conservative 2,000–3,000 (Boas 1888:426; Damas 1984a:359–475; Stefánsson 1914:61) up to 9,000 (Oswalt 1979:314–315, map 1).

FIGURE 38

Meeting between the Netsilik and Sir John Ross' exploring party. Small semilunar spots in the domes are ice-pane windows; larger, lower apertures are tunnel entrances; upright poles with circles at top are probably ice scoops for fishing; and apparent "ladders" are dogsleds. The archer's bow (center, main group of people) is exaggerated in size.
From Ross 1835a:248 ff.

WINTER HOUSES

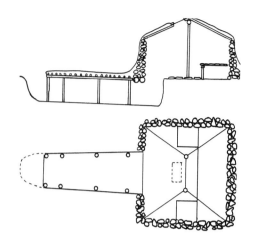

FIGURE 39

Idealized Labrador Eskimo winter stone communal house. The hip roof (bottom) and skylight (top, and dashed line, bottom) are features distinct from Greenlandic houses.
After Hutton 1912:40 ff, 308 ff, 314 ff; Taylor 1984:figs. 5–6. Reinhardt and Lee 1997:1803, courtesy of Cambridge University Press.

LABRADOR ESKIMO STONE COMMUNAL HOUSES

During the historic era Labrador Eskimos constructed a turf-covered, semisubterranean stone (or wood) communal house (iglu or igluqsuaq) of moderate capacity (fig. 39). Critical details are scarce for this structure, and our reconstruction is based on a combination of ethnographic and archaeological sources. The principal feature distinguishing Labrador houses from the Greenlandic types was their roofing, which differed in at least four ways. First, the roof of the Labrador Eskimo winter communal house tended to pitch more steeply to front and rear (figs. 40, 42); second, it sloped down to the sides as well as the front and rear (i.e., a hip roof); third, the outermost material of the roof was turf (not stone); and fourth, Labrador communal house roofs had one or two wood-framed seal-gut skylights rather than gut windows (figs. 40–42; Taylor 1984:fig. 6).

Nevertheless, these Labrador dwellings recall Greenlandic communal houses in other respects, particularly in the large number of people (an average of twenty, or about five families) they were apt to house (Schledermann 1976b:28, fig. 2–3; Taylor 1984:513). Furthermore, in contrast to the stones used for Greenland house tunnels, after historic contact at least the Labrador house had a lengthy entry tunnel made of wood or bone (fig. 41). Labrador Eskimo winter houses also had a window, possibly in the front wall (figs. 41–42; Packard 1877:68); stone floors; large sleeping platforms at the rear; smaller side platforms, central wood posts to support a ridgepole, and skin or whale scapulae over the roof (Hawkes 1916:60–61; Hutton 1912:38, 308; Taylor 1984:513–514).

Archaeological examples confirm that the Labrador communal house had a rectangular floorplan, in contrast to the more trapezoidal design of Greenlandic communal houses. Long, wide tunnels usually remained lower than the stone-flagged floor, penetrating the main chamber near the center of the front wall (Bird 1945:fig. 4, 128, 179; Schledermann 1976b:figs. 2–3, 28). The Labrador examples also had as many as five platforms for lamps and hence cooking. Each one jutted forward roughly three to six feet from a broad sleeping platform at the rear and, in one case, from the narrower side platforms. In all likelihood, inhabitants would have set simple bridges (boards or stone slabs, perhaps) between these outthrust lamp platforms, thereby converting the interstices into storage recesses. Similarly, whenever families shared a house, they likely partitioned off the sleeping platform (Kleivan 1966:27; Packard 1877:68).

Earlier precontact Labrador houses were small, round, and evidently meant for single families, but probably because of socioeconomic stress about A.D. 1700 this house type expanded into a rectangular multifamily structure (Bird 1945:figs. 3–4; Kleivan 1966:26; Schledermann 1976b:31–32, 36; Taylor 1984:513). The Labrador communal house evolved immediately before the influx of Euro-American pioneers and missionaries and therefore was short-lived (Bird 1945:fig. 4, 128, 179). Soon after, the Labrador house shrank back

FIGURE 40

"Old Tuglavi's iglo. It is a gloomy little hut of turf and stones, floored with trampled mud." A 1900s-era house probably with a turf-covered surface passage (darkened entrance on right, between two children). The house itself (left) has a turfed-over hipped roof, with a skylight, all held down by stones; exterior wall stones are roughly assembled.

From Hutton 1912:40 ff.

FIGURE 41

"Old iglos at Hebron." This late 1800s-era turf-covered house (center), with modern window frame (but formerly glazed with seal gut) in its front wall and a stove pipe, has a semisubterranean passage with wooden superstructure.

From Hutton 1912:308 ff.

FIGURE 42

"An elaborate snow porch [right]. As soon as winter comes the Eskimos build snow porches to their doors to keep their houses warm." Early 1900s-era house (left) has a framed window in a side wall and a stovepipe; such porches were no doubt more modern innovations.

From Hutton 1912:314 ff.

FIGURE 43, A–Q

Steps in constructing a snow house, photographed during the Stefánsson-Anderson Canadian Arctic expedition. Women and children are absent from this group.

Rauner Special Collections, Dartmouth College Library.

A, B: Cutting and placing snowblocks.

C, D: Diagonal cut through part of first course, allowing start of upward spiral.

E: Setting first blocks of second-course spiral.

F: Continuing spiral to third "level."

G: Trimming a block with the snow knife.

H: Cutting doorway.

to its former one- or two-family size (possibly because of the Protestant missionaries' culture-bound concerns about promiscuity; see Kleivan 1966:34). As of 1914, these habitations had become "gloomy little huts" of stone, mud floored and "indescribably dirty" (Hawkes 1916:ix, 61). By then the low tunnel had long since evolved into a surface windscreen or porch (figs. 40–42), sometimes with a door, clearly a response to missionary complaints about cramped crawlways (Kleivan 1966:33).[3] Apparently at least some tunnels had an attached antechamber or porch (fig. 42). In Northeast Labrador, "the old Eskimo tribes" (early contact era?) used whale bones in houses similar to their communal houses, but later switched to snow houses as their primary house-type (Hawkes 1916:61–62), whereas the more recent all-wood walls recall missionary modernity.

CANADIAN ESKIMO SNOW HOUSES

Four interrelated environmental circumstances led most Canadian Arctic Eskimos of the ethnographic-era (i.e., the late 1500s to early 1900s) to live in snow houses. First, they had to be near their food supply (usually seals), which meant they needed to live on or near the sea ice. Second, hunters found it efficient to cooperate in simultaneous hunts and to share the resulting food. Third, due to an easily exhausted food supply, people often had to move every few days to weeks. Finally, snow houses normally required little time and effort to build, which made them easy to abandon when the inevitability of the next move presented itself.

The antiquity and origin of the snowblock igloo is uncertain (Birket-Smith 1936:30; Kuznetsov 1964:239) and hard to trace archaeologically because

C

D

snow, the abandoned building material, disappeared with the next spring thaw (Savelle 1984). In the early historic period, the Central Eskimos made stone-and-sod winter houses like those of their Thule forbears. By the mid-nineteenth century, however, all but the Labrador Eskimos had adopted the snow house (Boas 1901).

West of Canada's Mackenzie Delta the spiral-built technique (described below) was unknown, though some Alaskan Eskimos made rectangular snowblock houses when traveling (Brown 1956:n.p.; Stefánsson 1914:61). It is certainly no accident that snow houses developed in the localities where driftwood is scarcest. The merit of this creative adaptation cannot be overemphasized: "Without the snow house, winter traveling in [the Central Arctic] would be practically impossible; that the earlier [English] discoverers up there were so immobile in winter is principally [because] they had not learned to build snow houses" (Mathiassen 1928:118).

Site Location and House Construction—By late November or early December enough snow had settled to make snow house building feasible. In areas where they proliferated, Eskimo winter settlements would hold as many as sixty-four people (Ross 1835a). One Iglulik community consisted of "five clusters of huts, some having one, some two, and others three domes, in which thirteen families lived, each occupying a dome or one side of it" (Lyon 1824:115). People usually established their villages—sets of domed structures—on the sea ice after freeze-up. To avoid the dangers of snowdrifts the villages were situated out of the prevailing wind on east- or south-facing slopes. Proper snow conditions always limited house locations; if the snow was too solid it

G

H

I

J

FIGURE 43 (continued)

I, J: Proceeding toward center of dome; second man (right) fills cracks with snow chunks.

K, L: Setting steeper in-curving blocks.

M, N: Completing passage (left), and setting last overhead blocks.

O: View of passage (left), yet to be finished.

P: Shoveling snow against exterior.

could not be properly cut, if too soft it would fall apart. Snow from a single snowfall was ideal. For determining its consistency men generally used a long, slender probe made of steam- or heat-straightened caribou antler (Birket-Smith 1929:1:76, 78; Schwatka 1883:218; Stefánsson 1944). However, the Sallirmiut (of Southampton Island in Hudson Bay) "often simply stamped on the snow to test its firmness" (Mathaissen 1927a:270).

After probing for snow of the proper feel (a fairly deep drift, not too powdery, not too icy), which could take several hours (Schwatka 1883:218), the first step in raising a snow igloo was to inscribe a circle for its perimeter with a snow knife of bone, ivory, antler, wood, or baleen. House building ideally required two men, one to cut blocks, and the other to position them (fig. 43). The cutter, who might wear specially made flexible gauntlets for this purpose, sometimes worked inside the house, removing the snow in sections (approximately 30 by 20 by 6–8 inches) from what would become the floor. Cutting the blocks from within had the advantage of creating a floor below the snow surface level. Consequently, once the house was completed, the floor was lower than the sleeping platform, keeping cold air below that main activity area.

The builder worked from either inside or outside the structure (fig. 43A, B). Blocks were cut on edge if possible and had a slightly curved shape. Upon cutting each one, the cutter stomped on its surface to work it loose, then, removing it, handed it to the builder, who placed the first row side by side along the inscribed circle (fig. 43C, D), trimming the blocks so that each tightly abutted its predecessor (fig. 43E, G).

M

N

K

L

Once he finished the first circular row, the builder went back and cut down a part of it diagonally, facilitating the upward, in-curving spiral to follow (fig. 43C, D). In Labrador, men built the principal dome spirally from east to west, or "as the sun goes down" (Hawkes 1916:59). Caribou Eskimos built their domes upward counterclockwise, but left-handed men followed the sun's path (clockwise). By contrast, Copper Eskimos did not always build spirally, especially when they began their house by digging into a snow drift (Jenness 1922:59, 61; Stefánsson 1914:63). As the igloo rose in its winding ascent and, as the dome neared completion (fig. 43H–M), the builders sometimes cut larger and larger blocks, some weighing as much as thirty pounds (Steltzer 1981). Snowblocks were trapezoidal in outline, except for the final one, which was multisided and beveled so that its smaller inner surface would be held up by all the opposite-beveled blocks ringing it. The man inside first pushed this block sideways through the hole in the top, then rotated it overhead, trimmed it with his snow knife to suit the aperture, and lowered it horizontally into its seat (fig. 43N). This was not a true keystone block, as the dome could stand without it (Birket-Smith 1929:1:81; Kroeber n.d.).

Upon setting the last block in place, the team cut out an air vent near the dome's crest and removed a section from its side for a temporary entrance (fig. 43H). As soon as the women had crawled through with their lamps and other household possessions, this entrance was sealed to trap heat as they set up housekeeping. Lamps not only warmed the space but also glazed the dome's interior surface with a windproof shell of ice. To maximize protection from

O

P

FIGURE 43 (continued)

Q: Finished snow house, probably built in one hour.

the cold, the men sometimes did not cut the door—an oval aperture in the bottom tier of blocks—until they had completed the tunnel (fig. 43L, Q). They also cut another oval hole higher up and inserted the precious window of freshwater ice, removed late the previous autumn and hauled along by sled from camp to camp all winter long.[4] Ideally, windows faced south, to maximize sunlight, and were fitted in over the entryway (e.g., fig. 38).

Finally, while someone inside stomped down the floor and indented or built up a platform and others outside built a tunnel, women and children chinked any remaining holes in the walls with scraps left from block-cutting (fig. 43I, J). The dwelling was further insulated by shoveling snow against its exterior (fig. 43M–Q). Once the lamp was lit the snow house stood "dazzlingly bright" (Hutton 1912:37) and ready for use.[5]

The speed with which a snow house rose is astounding. Two accomplished workmen took forty-five minutes to an hour to build a snow house eight feet in diameter, housing five to six persons. The literature suggests that, overall, main dome diameters were commonly larger, twelve to fourteen feet, and generally high enough to allow a six-foot-tall man to walk upright within them (Hawkes 1916:59; Hutton 1912:36). One striking exception was the very low-domed Netsilik house. This configuration speeded up heating the interior and also conserved heat by enveloping less air volume within (fig. 44).

Snow House Design Variations—Tunnels were the last structural part added to a snow house. Some were domed like the house proper (figs. 45–46), while others employed two straight walls about three feet across and four to five feet high, horizontally roofed (fig. 47). They were not always below the snow surface level but could slope downward from the outside entrance, then up again to the house's low entryway (fig. 46). Two or more connected sleeping domes might share a common tunnel, or side-by-side domes might have either parallel or converging tunnels (Jenness 1922:65–79). People sometimes reduced drafts by constructing the tunnel as a series of progressively smaller antechambers leading to the main dome or domes (fig. 46). At other times, they put up a snowblock windscreen to divert cold blasts from the tunnel

FIGURE 44

Cross-section of a Netsilik snow house, illustrating an unusually low dome and high platform, compared to the more vaulted design of most Eskimo snow houses (dashed lines indicate higher dome and lower platform). *After Schwatka 1884b:fig. 4.*

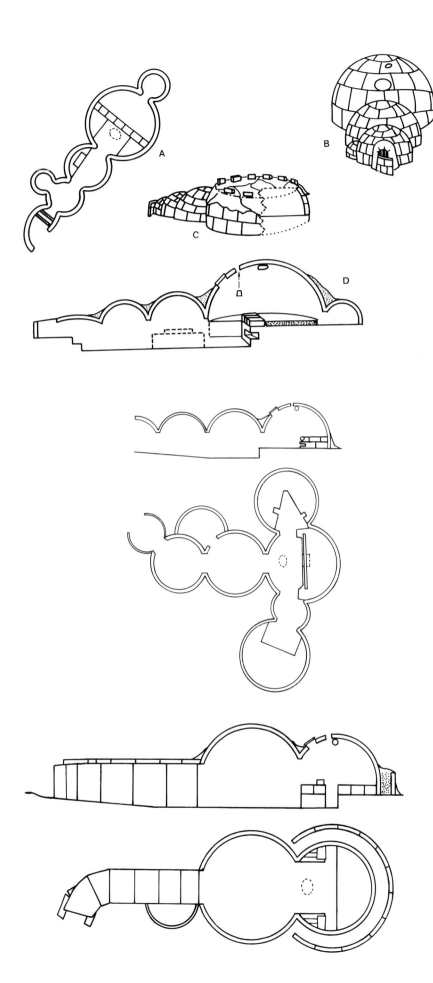

FIGURE 45

Idealized Caribou Eskimo snow house: (A) floor plan (dashed line indicates window overhead); (B) exterior front view (vent hole near peak, elliptical window below it)—snowblocks in foreground are smaller than they should appear; (C) skin roof over dome walls, held down by snowblocks (springtime option); (D) cross-section through house and tunnel, showing positions of window, vent hole and plug, and snowball at peak to absorb drips (kitchen dome is left of sleeping chamber; sleeping platform is raised with snowblocks and shoveled snow).

After Boas 1888:figs. 491–492; Franklin 1823:267; drawn by Jeanne E. Ellis. Reinhardt and Lee 1997:1795, courtesy of Cambridge University Press.

FIGURE 46

Idealized Iglulik snow house . Note pole edge along front of central sleeping platform, storage niche below it, and other two-family sleeping platform and lamp platform alternatives. A snowball "sponge" absorbs water near the vent hole (top).

After Boas 1888:figs. 492 and 495–497, 1901:fig. 140; Mathiassen 1928:fig. 77.

FIGURE 47

Idealized Copper Eskimo snow house. The larger central dome is for communal dances; the smaller one for two families' daily activities. Lamp platforms and sleeping platform are raised above snow surface-level by means of snowblocks, and a snowball "sponge" soaks up water near the vent hole (top).

After Jenness 1922:figs. 12–25, Pls. 3A–B; Stefánsson 1913:pls. opp. pp. 170, 256.

entrance (figs. 45, 48–49), while a snowblock door kept wind out of the sleeping chamber. Copper Eskimos even angled their tunnel entrances 90° leeward (fig. 47), or they diagonally offset the tunnel by about one tunnel width (for three feet or so near its opening), to baffle the wind (Jenness 1922:fig. 19). Caribou Eskimo doors made of boards, which were used to block main dome entrances (Birket-Smith 1929:1:83), are presumably a modern feature.

Frequently, residents appended small anterooms for storage and other uses (figs. 45–47), but Caribou Eskimos are the only Central Arctic group known traditionally to have had a kitchen outside the main snow-house dome (fig. 45). Sleeping platforms and smaller storage spaces also diverged in their designs. For example, Labrador builders cut and removed snowblocks from the floor area, thereby creating raised platforms for sleepers and lamps, whereas the Iglulik sometimes stacked the back and side platform areas with one to five tiers of blocks, leaving the floor at the original surface level (fig. 46; Mathiassen 1928:122; Nourse 1879:73; Rasmussen 1929:15). Caribou Eskimos built their main platforms with both blocks and loose snow (fig. 45), and an optional pole in Iglulik houses sometimes reinforced sleeping platform edges (fig. 46).

Sometimes two Iglulik families shared a dome such that their sleeping platforms virtually faced each other, and the edges of both were cut out to divide a tiny lamp zone (near the chamber doorway) from the sleeping spaces (fig. 46, top of lower illustration; Mathiassen 1928:fig. 78). Copper Eskimos kept goods in the gap between their lamp and sleeping platforms (fig. 47), capping the space with a board when necessary (Jenness 1922:61). Alcoves, which were larger than niches, were easy to install and attach to existing domes. Caribou Eskimos reportedly used their alcoves to separate the types of things stored there, e.g., house sweepings, offal, food, etc.

The longevity of a snow house depended in part on the temperature inside and out; in the coldest part of winter it could last a month to six weeks. Adding a skin lining, which trapped cold air and formed an extra layer of ice on the dome, could prolong the igloo's life expectancy to an entire winter (figs. 48, 50). This technique was used mainly by Baffin Island Eskimos (Birket-Smith 1936:126), although the Polar Eskimos had adopted the idea by the end of the nineteenth century and the Iglulik by the 1920s (Boas 1888:543–544; Hayes 1885:243–244; Mathiassen 1928:128; Mauss and Beuchat 1979:fig. 4). Another means of extending the usable life of a snow house was the addition of low external walls, which kept winds from eroding the more vertical (i.e., the more severely buffeted) aspects of the dome. Copper and Labrador Eskimos, for example, buttressed their main domes with a row of snowblocks, packing the interstices with shoveled snow (fig. 47). Of course, shoveling snow about the base of an igloo afforded still simpler protection (figs. 43Q; 45D; 46, top; 49); this diverted the wind flow upward with ever-decreasing erosive effect as it blew over the domes.

Snow houses are strong and stable enough to support much weight (fig. 41). Except during spring thaws, when the domes weakened, people could even dance on the rooftop if they cared to (Mathiassen 1928:124; Parry 1824:148, 410). The structural integrity is easy to explain, inasmuch as one sharp rap

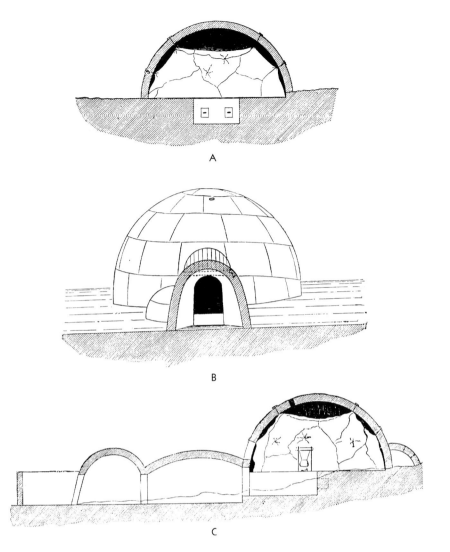

A

B

C

FIGURE 48

"Snow house of Davis Strait [Baffin Island], sections." Note storage niches (front edge of the sleeping platform—top and bottom), vent hole and window (center; apparent gut-strip panel probably *should* appear as an ice-slab window—cf. fig. 50) and vent hole (center); skins lining the interior (black space above skins is cold air—top and bottom); and curved snowblock wind break at outer end of tunnel.

From Boas 1888:fig. 492.

FIGURE 49

Netsilik snow houses, King William Island, 1904–1905. Note leeward-curved wind-deflecting snowblocks at entrance to tunnel, and pole tools or weapons stored upright next to domes.

Photograph by Roald Amundsen or someone of his crew, courtesy of the Ethnographic Museum, University of Oslo.

FIGURE 50

"Section and interior of snow house" of Baffin Island design. View toward the front half of the main dome. Observe the lamps, pots, and drying racks—and their supporting structures—on both sides of the fore-space (leading to the tunnel), the skin liner held in place with large toggles (outside the dome) tied by thongs to smaller toggles within, and a gut-strip panel to transmit daylight through the ice-pane window (cf. fig. 48, center). Dark space at top of dome is unheated air outside the skin liner.

From Boas 1888:fig. 493.

FIGURE 51

Four men, standing on a snow house, demonstrate its strength.

Probably photographed during the Stefánsson-Anderson Canadian Arctic expedition; courtesy of Dartmouth College Library.

FIGURE 52

"Kuk. House ruin III with the fallen-in roof removed [during archaeological excavation]." One slightly elevated lobe, or family area, within the house appears here, plus the lower, stone-lined entryway (center foreground) and an apparent storage niche (center, left).

From Mathiassen 1927a:fig. 75; cf. fig. 53; courtesy of the Arctic Institute, Danish Polar Center.

fixes each block hard against its neighbors: "each blow instantaneously melted the ice crystals at the point of contact through pressure and this momentary creation of water immediately froze again to cement the two blocks together" (Graburn and Strong 1973:149). Friction from the blows also adds vertical strength, an effect enhanced by gravity's added force on all blocks below.

The ability of a snow house to withstand external pressure is also the result of its unique shape. Most domed structures are hemispherical; consequently, their ring stress subjects them to collapse. The steeper-sided catenary arch of Eskimo snow houses, like an eggshell's long axis, prevents caving in and bulging, thus enhancing the structure's stability (Handy 1973:276–277). The catenary arch is the only kind not requiring an external scaffold during construction (Kroeber n.d.:2).

SALLIRMIUT STONE HOUSES

The Sallirmiut of Southampton Island, whose cultural patterns deviated markedly from most other groups, built a winter house that seems to have been unique in the Eskimo culture area. Many of their winter houses, which they usually planned for two to four families, incorporated whale bone extensively and "had the unique feature of supporting pillars of limestone slabs" (Damas 1984b:396). The walls for each rounded sleeping area consisted of upright stones and, sometimes, whale skulls. With the exterior turfs removed, they looked something like a miniature Stonehenge (figs. 52–53).

Sallirmiut houses evidently had two to three stone-covered sleeping areas, each about sixteen inches higher than the paved floor and each boasting two lateral lamp platforms. Floor plans with three sleeping spaces sometimes resembled a clover leaf (fig. 53). Slabs set on edge alternated with horizontally laid ones, producing shallow storage niches around the house perimeter; larger ones occurred under the platforms. The roof, doubtless sealed with turf except at the vent hole, was made of supporting materials such as whale skulls, jaws, ribs, baleen, and vertebrae, as well as caribou antlers and more limestone slabs.

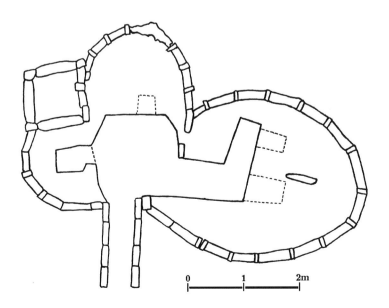

0   1   2m

FIGURE 53

"House Ruin III; Kuk." Plan view indicates two larger sleeping platforms with niches below (top and right), a presumed storage space (upper left), a smaller platform (center left), and a stone-lined passage (bottom left). *From Mathiassen 1927a:fig. 76; cf. fig. 42.*

A few central pillars supported these roof beams. Roughly square storerooms abutted some of the sleeping platform walls (fig. 53, upper left). Without their ice-slab extensions in winter, which could be six feet high, stone-sided tunnel entrances were only about six feet long. Finally, for more light there was an animal-membrane or ice-pane window over the doorway (Mathiassen 1927a:227–229, 253, 269, figs. 74–76, 82).

ALTERNATIVE WINTER DWELLINGS

From Labrador in the east (Taylor 1984:514; Turner 1894:225) to Victoria Island in the west (Jenness 1922:60, 64), Central Eskimos occasionally built smaller snow houses for themselves as individuals, for hunting parties, or for their whole families. They used these dwellings only as short-term protection when traveling between snow house settlements. Figure 54 demonstrates how simplified the Caribou Eskimo travelers' shelters might be, compared with their more elaborate long-term dwellings (cf. fig. 45).

More southerly Labrador Eskimos constructed snow houses only when they traveled. Temporary snow houses of the Caribou Eskimos ordinarily lacked a passage but could have a sleeping platform (Birket-Smith 1929:1:83, 84). In Iglulik construction, the transient snow house's size was diminished and, when built by men journeying alone, sometimes it had no platform. Neither separate storage alcoves nor windows figured into the design, and a wall replaced the tunnel (Mathiassen 1928:129). Less elaborate still were Sallirmiut snow houses, which lacked a doorway and often had no raised platform (Mathiassen 1927a:270). Copper Eskimo travelers' snow houses had a very short tunnel (almost an awning) and they lacked the low protective outer wall circumscribing more permanent domes. Instead, they relied on loose snow tamped against the dome's base and seams (Jenness 1922:60, 64).

ASPECTS OF SNOW HOUSE LIFE

Until lampblack sooted the glistening, sugar-like interior of an igloo's main chamber, some sun- and moonlight penetrated the snowy dome and shone a bit more brightly through an ice pane over the doorway (figs. 55–56). Those illumination sources, coupled with lamplight and the dome's reflective white interior, meant that seeing indoors was seldom a problem. Nor were snow houses as damp as one might imagine. Moisture escaped through the vent hole (*qiŋaq*) of the house (figs. 45B, D, C; 47, top; 48b–c; Mathiassen 1928:129) by the same ventilation principles as in Greenland houses.

As lamp tenders, Central Eskimo women were forever seeking an equilibrium between oxygen-rich fresh air (always cold), and the ideal level of oil in the lamp (otherwise the flame burned too high or low); and worked constantly to maintain a balance between a dome thinly glazed with ice and one that was melting. If an existing vent hole proved inadequate to the task of controlling the dripping from an overheated ceiling, and if an impromtu second hole (punched through the dome) failed, someone might mold a snowball,[6] touching it to the wet spot until it froze into place. This created a temporary sponge (figs. 45D, 46 and 47, top). When these sponges failed, the drip-points might be chipped away

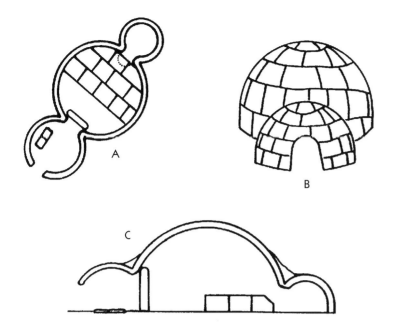

FIGURE 54

Idealized Caribou Eskimo travelers' snow house: (A) floor plan; (B) exterior view; (C) cross-section through house (left, kitchen dome; center, sleeping chamber with raised platform; right, storage niche).
Drawn by Jeanne E. Ellis.

FIGURE 55

Small snow-house settlement with five domes showing assorted orientations and sizes of ice window. Two passages (left) consist of multiple, descending domes that end at in-curving upright walls built as wind deflectors.
C. M. Cato photograph f21, #162, the British Museum.

FIGURE 56

"Ig-loos or snow village at Oo-pung-ne-wing," illustrating daily life in a winter village. Note people and dogs around the village, dogsleds and kayak stored atop igloos (left and upper center), the close spacing of main domes (and consistent orientation of their ice window panes), evidence of successful seal hunts (foreground), and walrus skulls stored on house passageways (lower center and far right).
From Hall 1864:269.

FIGURE 57

"Interior of an Eskimaux snow-hut. Winter Island 1822." A face-tattooed Iglulik woman nurses her child while sitting on furs on the platform (left) as another woman (tattooed arm and hand at upper right, partially obscured by wooden pole) stirs food cooking in a large, rectangular hand-carved soapstone pot. Semilunar lamps on wooden stands (below the carved pots) are tipped at an extreme angle but show how sea mammal fat (lamp centers) renders into oil. Bentwood or bent baleen vessels rest on the platform, and webbed drying racks rest above the pots. An ice-sealing harpoon leans against the right rack, supported by another harpoon inserted into the dome wall, while one upright for the other rack is a caribou antler.

From Parry 1824:160 ff.

to redistribute the melt-water so that it flowed down the dome walls; such chipping eventually pitted a dome's interior (Jenness 1922:63).

Without a lamp, body heat could still raise indoor temperatures typically to 24° or 26°F if enough snow was shoveled against the dome outside, but as outside temperatures lowered to –20 to –50°F the air inside would be only ten degrees warmer (Birket-Smith 1929:1:92–93). Between floor and ceiling in lamp-lit houses, temperatures could vary as much as 70°F, at times rising above 100°F if the space was crowded and a skin lining was in place (figs. 48, 50). Even without such a lining, the people, dogs, and lamps could increase the heat inside to temperatures of around 37 to 39°F for a while without weakening the dome. Toward the walls, temperatures dropped by fifteen degrees. This is still significantly warmer than the temperature outdoors (Jenness 1922:70; Lyon 1824:124; Mathiassen 1928:131; Parry 1824:412). Birket-Smith says of the impressive temperature gradient in an igloo: "[I]t is actually possible to experience all the climatic belts of the world at once: at the feet temperature is still arctic, waist-high the surrounding air is almost temperate, and the head sometimes projects a good way into the tropics" (1936:126–127).

The configurations of a snow village expressed in material form the social structure of a community at a given moment. A single dwelling could, and often did, stand alone, but just as regularly the igloo served as the basic unit of a larger complex of structures conjoined by a central domed space with a common passageway to the outdoors (e.g., fig. 46). Iglulik houses might have four or more such chambers spread as satellites around a central anteroom. As group size waxed and waned throughout the winter social season an existing igloo wall could be cut through and a new dome added, or the doorway could be closed off with minimal effort (Jenness 1922:63; Mathiassen 1928; Schwatka 1883).

Short passages made it possible to link an entire settlement with a network of domes (figs. 38, 49, 55–56, 45; cf. Hawkes 1916:58–60; Mathiassen 1928:fig.

FIGURE 58

Netsilik snow house interior, King William Island, 1904–1905. Note the vertically-set snowblock platform edge, the side lamp platform, and arrangement thereon of lampstand, lamp, and strut-supported drying rack with mittens and clothes on it. Two pairs of snow goggles hang from the rack's right edge.

Photograph by Roald Amundsen or someone of his crew, courtesy of the Ethnographic Museum, University of Oslo.

79), shaping them into a changeable, fluid "little hive of human beings comfortably established below" the drifting snows of winter (Parry 1824:147–148). Glowing ice-pane windows here and there might be the sole means of distinguishing such a community from natural landscapes in the arctic night. In fresh-built domes, winter's dim light shone through "in most delicate hues of verdigris green and blue" (Lyon 1824:111).

Spatial arrangements inside the Central Arctic snow house replicate those of Eskimo winter houses everywhere (figs. 57–58). The platform occupied about half the floor of a dwelling and frequently had cut-outs underneath to provide additional dry, above-floor storage (figs. 45D, 46, 48; Birket-Smith 1929:1:83; Boas 1888:545). For warmth, platforms were covered with such materials as stones, paddles, tent poles, and whale scapulae, and then insulated with a mattress of baleen strips or birch (*Betula* sp.) and heather (*Cassiope* sp.) sprigs and covered with layers of skins (Mathiassen 1928:142, fig. 85; Parry 1824:411). Families used side platforms (figs. 45–47, 50, 58) for storage and lamps (Birket-Smith 1936:126; Jenness 1922:61; Schwatka 1883:304). Wooden pegs or poles, antlers, etc., might be driven into the floor and walls to provide additional hanging storage (fig. 57). For their lamp shelves, Copper Eskimos inserted an L-shaped board into the house wall between snowblocks during construction (Stefánsson 1914:67). Above the lamp, the ubiquitous cooking pot and drying rack either hung from poles set into the ceiling or rested on supporting frameworks (figs. 50, 57–58). The only exception to this pattern is the Caribou Eskimo habit of cooking over a brush-fueled fire in a kitchen-like antechamber just outside the main dome (fig. 45A, D) and of using lamps for light only (Birket-Smith 1929:1:83; Franklin 1823:265–267; Rasmussen 1930:45).

Snow houses are no longer made for habitation although the knowledge of how to construct them is still part of Inuit culture. In the 1950s the Inuit of Cape Dorset experimented with the weathering capacities of styrofoam igloos (Dickie 1959:117). During the winter of 1987, in the same community, Nelson

FIGURE 59

A small snowblock doghouse, built at Cape Dorset in 1986 for a bitch and her puppies, indicates continuity of the snowhouse tradition into modern times in the Canadian Arctic.

Photograph courtesy of Nelson H. H. Graburn.

FIGURE 60

"Plan and sections of qarmang or house made of whale ribs." Cross-sections *ab* and *cd* indicate the roof vaulting that curving whale ribs made possible. Note the low floor relative to the platforms at side and back of house.
From Boas 1888:fig. 502.

Graburn and Molly Lee photographed a tiny igloo built to shelter a litter of newborn puppies (fig. 59), and, in April of 1990, residents of Igloolik erected the largest snow house ever reported, built to celebrate the signing of the Tungavik Federation of Nunavut agreement-in-principle (*Inuit Art Quarterly* 1990–91:cover and p. 6). Nor has the versitility and drama of the snow house been lost on non-Native outdoors enthusiasts (e.g., Browne 1946): It was— and remains—*the* Eskimo icon.

TRANSITIONAL DWELLINGS

BEFORE ADEQUATE SNOWDRIFTS HAD ACCUMULATED IN AUTUMN, AFTER THE ice had begun to thaw in spring, or when tents had been cached at some distance, Central Eskimos lived in transitional houses called *qarmat*. The Iglulik inhabited theirs from late September to late December, once the chill drove them from tents but before snow had formed drifts deep enough for them to make snow houses. Witnesses describe two types of *qarmaq*.

CENTRAL ARCTIC STONE/BONE/TURF AUTUMN HOUSE

The more common qarmaq form was a semipermanent, small, family-sized structure with walls of stone, turf, and whale bones, a stone platform, a skin roof, and a gut window framed with whale rib (figs. 60–61). Usually, these were used for several years, so that the people merely cleared, cleaned, and reoccupied them intermittently. They had either straight or slightly inward-spiraling walls three feet high and an elliptical to circular floor plan upwards of twelve by fourteen feet (Ross 1835a:389), although one report mentions a rectlinear-plan house (Parry 1824:230, 290). Birket-Smith hypothesizes that the Central Eskimo qarmaq derived from the Thule-type prehistoric winter house (Birket-Smith 1945:136).

Descriptions of early travelers give us some details about the *qarmaq*. Whale half-mandibles or ribs presumably acted as rafters, thereby giving the roof a bowed or rounded appearance (fig. 60; Dawson 2001). The skin-covered roof admitted some light, which was enhanced by a gut window. Occupying one-third to one-half of the house's rear was a sleeping platform paved with flagstones and raised by turf blocks about two feet above floor level. A lamp platform no doubt sat on either side. When two or more families shared a

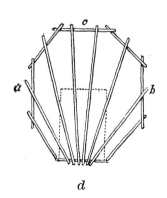

d

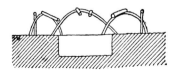

ab

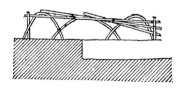

cd

qarmaq, they divided the sleeping platform using sealskins pinned to the ceiling. Stones formed a short, low, turf-covered entrance tunnel about ten feet long and two feet high (fig. 61), the bottom of which was typically littered with bones and other refuse (Parry 1824:230). Sometimes an ice-slab extension or antechamber was attached to the tunnel's entrance.

IGLULIK AND NETSILIK ICE AUTUMN HOUSE

Far less common was the qarmaq made with large, rectangular fresh-water ice-slab walls (fig. 62). These were set vertically and cemented with a snow-and-water slush; smaller slabs produced a flat-roofed tunnel. An ice house required few building blocks, but it could not be worked as easily as snow because of the weight of the blocks and the difficulty of trimming them to fit. Slabs had to be cut from bodies of fresh water and hauled by dogsled to the village. Given the requirement for flat, limpid ice slabs from ponds or lakes, the need to live near the sea to hunt seals, and the location of fresh water pools on land, this house-type probably was built mainly on land but near shore.

An ice-slab *qarmaq* required a skin or fur roof (fig. 62) because an ice roof, despite its integrity, would have been much riskier to live under, due to the warmth that could concentrate inside. Before attaching the cover, builders grooved the walls high up at the points where joined ice slabs met. Now the skin could be spread over tent poles or fish spears stuck into the wall slabs, with the excess cover draping down the walls. People then cinched the cover tight, into the wall grooves, using a sealskin thong wound around the upper walls (not shown in fig. 62), the same idea used in constructing Eskimo tambourine drums. Gravel was scraped and heaped toward the rear of the house to form a low sleeping platform and presumably side platforms, too. Flagstones substituted for the gravel at times (Mathiassen 1928:138–140, fig. 83).

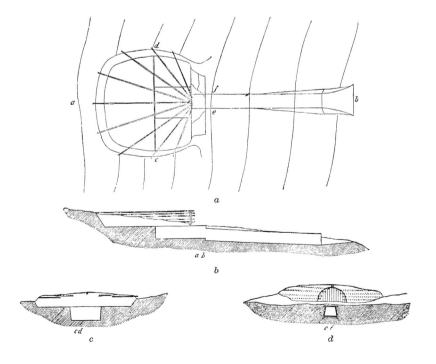

FIGURE 61

"Plan and sections of qarmang or stone house." This design lacks whale ribs, relying exclusively on poles (or possibly whale mandibles cut lengthwise) for the roof superstructure. Note the flat roof (b–d), the long, low tunnel (a–b), and the step-downs (b) from sleeping platform (left) to tunnel entrance (right).

From Boas 1888:fig. 498.

FIGURE 62

"Eskimaux house, built of ice. Igloolik 1822." The structure of an octagonal-sided house and square-framed passage are made of ice slabs (center), as are kayak rests (upper center and right) and a doghouse (center right). Note the slightly rounded skin roof over the house. A child with dog-whip and tether cows one of the dogs near a dogsled (foreground).

From Parry 1824:358 ff.

The ice *qarmaq* had an octagonal floor plan and a room arrangement similar to that of snow houses. However, because of its transparency, increased by the glare from snow and ice during this season, it needed no windows (Birket-Smith 1945:82; Boas 1888:551; Jenness 1922:77, 79; Mathiassen 1928:138–139). According to Schwatka (1883:216–217), before snow blanketed an ice *qarmaq*, the structure was practically transparent. The glow of lamplight from a *qarmaq* settlement at night, he notes, was "one of the most beautiful sights I have ever witnessed. Could one imagine the Lilliputs living in flat candy jars with drumhead covers, he would have a fair miniature representation of an ice village" (Schwatka 1883:216–217).

Another kind of dwelling, possibly late prehistoric but likely not earlier than the 1700s, was reported from an abandoned village on Prince Albert Island in the northern Canadian archipelago (Belcher 1855:1: 94–96). This house form seems comparable to the *qarmaq*, although it might have been a winter dwelling. Its floor, dug some three feet below ground level, was stone-paved, elliptical, and about ten by twelve feet across. Particularly unusual was the wall lined with stone slabs, within which was a second ellipse of slabs (the space between the ellipses being "filled in with fine clay and gravel"). Piercing one end of the house's double-wall was a stone-sided tunnel, which descended away from the house. The tunnel's inner doorway had a stone-slab lintel, which spanned the wall and created an opening only three feet wide by two and a half feet high (Belcher 1855:1:95).

Another recurring theme in Central Eskimo transitional housing is adapting domed snow houses to the warming weather in early spring, roughly April to May. Groups such as the Netsilik (Ross 1835a:384) and Caribou and Labrador Eskimos (Birket-Smith 1929:1:84; Graburn 1969:43) elected to stay in a snow house—despite its dripping, weakening, or even collapsing roof—because snow walls insulated better than single-layer tents covers. These groups compromised in favor of comfort, removing the crest of the snow dome and replacing it with tent skins as a roof (fig. 45C). To keep the pliable skins, which inevitably had soaked edges, in place, householders weighed them down with snowblocks stacked around the cut-back rim of the dome. Copper Eskimos, on the other hand, held up their tent skins with poles to create either flat or gable roofs (Stefánsson 1914:66). Until the crown of the dome actually caved in, however, the odd melt-hole here and there might be stuffed with fur (Turner 1894:226).

Finally, Iglulik hunters sometimes assembled a shelter of stones and covered it with furs, and they built into the back end an elevated headrest. This was typically an overnight arrangement, seemingly like the Sallermiut *qarmaq* (Mathiassen 1927a:270). Its floor shape could be either curvilinear or rectilinear (Mathiassen 1928:129).

SUMMER DWELLINGS

IN A PATTERN THAT EXISTED ACROSS THE ARCTIC, EACH CENTRAL ESKIMO household made the decision to move into its summer tent independently from the rest of the community; the date depended on weather conditions (Jenness 1922:77). Like winter settlements, summer encampments usually conformed to natural features of the landscape rather than any prescribed order (Birket-Smith 1929:1:74). One consideration was the proximity of heather, the preferred fuel for summer cooking (Stefánsson 1914:71). As a protection against unfriendly Indians, Copper Eskimo summer settlements were frequently located on hilltops, where the hair-out skin tent covers—often bicolored and randomly patterned—blended with the rocky landscape, providing a natural camouflage so convincing that the tents could not be detected from as little as one-quarter mile away (Stefánsson 1914:71).

RIDGE TENTS

Central Arctic Eskimos used tents (singular *tupiq*) of two basic types, those with a ridge and those shaped like a tepee. Ridged examples generally consisted of a raised horizontal piece (either a thong or pole) that connected standing poles at the front with varying upright arrangements at the rear. Some groups employed two pairs of socketed, obliquely slanted legs; others might opt for a wood-saving single pole at each end of the tent. Most Central Arctic Eskimos used a conical arrangement of several poles fanned out at the back and, sometimes, at the front, which added vertical and horizontal space and gave the tent an apsidal or bell-like plan view. Tent pegs were rare; usually stones, snow, or other weights spread and anchored the tent skirt.

Labrador Thong- or Pole-Ridge Tents—Labrador Eskimos began their tents by lashing two poles into a rear bipod and sometimes a front bipod (fig. 63). If there was only one front pole, it fit into a pocket sewn in the tent cover, but in either case the tent needed a guyline to hold up the front end. Either a thong

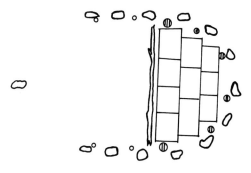

FIGURE 63

Idealized Labrador Eskimo thong-ridged tent.

After Hawkes 1916:Pls. 11B, 12; Hutton 1912:pls. opp. pp. 60, 254; Taylor 1984:fig. 5, right; Turner 1894:Pl. 37.

(fig. 63) or a pole (fig. 64) formed the tents' median ridge by connecting these uprights at their peaks. Other poles, stacked against the rear uprights and along the pole-type ridge, reduced sagging by bolstering the sides. This spreading arrangement resulted in a near-apsidal ground plan, with a conical back and parallel sides. The tent cover consisted of two parts, one made of fur, the other of translucent depilated skins (see Saladin d'Anglure 1984:482); the two sides were laced together horizontally, starting from the back, then overhead along the ridge line. A door flap was made of another fur or skin. Loose skins were thrown over the first layer to seal any gaps (Turner 1894:226–227). Covers were made from caribou, seal, beluga, or salmon, depending on the preferred or available local medium (Taylor 1984:514). Inside the Labrador tent, a stick or pole created a symbolic division between the raised-earth or -turf sleeping platform at the rear and the space at the front (fig. 63), where other activities took place. Guests or distant relatives might occupy sleeping places along the sides of the tent (Turner 1894:228). A similar Labrador tent had a rectangular outline, bisected into nearly square halves, with each half open on one side (Hawkes 1916:pl. 11B).

There is some disagreement in the literature about how Labrador Eskimo tents were heated. Some sources state, or imply, that the traditional oil lamp was used exclusively (Hawkes 1916:fig. 11, 1A; Hutton 1912:32; Kleivan 1966:39). However, Turner (1894:228) claims the tent's "central portion is reserved for a fireplace for cooking and heating."[7]

Ungava Peninsula (Québec) Ridge Tents—Tents of this region occurred in two varieties. Coastal ones evidently were similar to the ridged Labrador tents with apsidal plans. Ten to fifteen skins of bearded seal (*Erignathus barbatus*, a large species) went into making their covers, which incorporated sides made from thinned, translucent skins that increased the lighting inside. Where bearded seals were lacking, women sewed their covers from the skins of ringed seals, beluga whales, or even salmon (Saladin d'Anglure 1984:482).

Baffin Island Pole-Ridge Tents—Tents from Baffin Island varied in design details but essentially employed a half-cone arrangement of poles at the back and a pole bipod at the front. The islanders probably used a single ridgepole (fig. 65) more often than two poles (fig. 66). Another conspicuous difference in construction is that in some tents the rear poles extended above the cover (figs. 65–66) whereas in others they did not (fig. 67). As reported elsewhere, sleepers lay at the back, an area set off by a log (fig. 65).

Iglulik Ridge Tents—Smaller than other Central Arctic ridge tents, the Iglulik (fig. 68) designs had a center pole with a short, stout crossbar on top and a thong or pole ridge. However, they lacked accessory rear and lateral poles. A bipod held up the fore end while a single vertical pole on a stone footing elevated the back. When wood was scarce the Iglulik and Netsilik ingeniously assembled center poles from sections of antler (softened by soaking, then straightened), wood or bone, broken spear shafts, or narwhal tusk (Lyon 1824:229; Rasmussen 1927:168; Taylor 1974:122). Given the short ridge thongs and small tent openings that Parry depicts in one settlement (Parry 1824: 271 ff; cf. fig. 73), the front area in Iglulik tents seems to have been inconsequential compared to the front of Labrador and Copper Eskimo

FIGURE 64

"Eskimos of Great Whale River, Labrador. Taken 1896" shows a horizontal ridgepole projecting from the tent's front support poles. *From Hawkes 1916:189.*

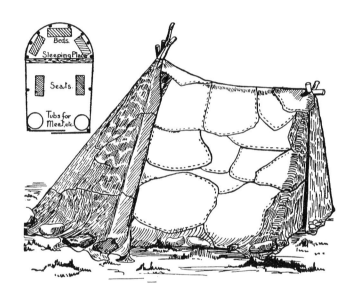

FIGURE 65

Baffin Island pole-ridged tent, possibly with de-haired sides. The ground plan suggests raised sleeping spots for three (rear), and the two "seats" of like size might have doubled as extra sleeping places. *From Bilby 1923:73.*

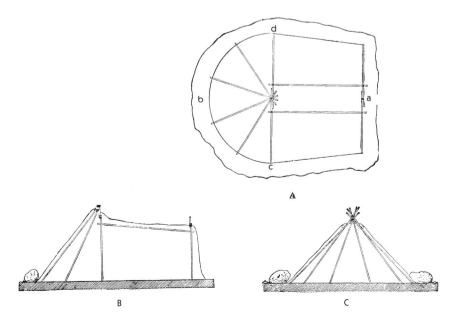

FIGURE 66

"Plan and sections of tupiq or tent of Cumberland Sound." This tent from eastern Baffin Island had a wider floor area and broader center, overhead, due to the dual ridgepoles, which must have been lashed to the front and rear lateral uprights. *From Boas 1888:fig. 504.*

FIGURE 67

Side view of a ridge tent, probably with one ridgepole, from eastern Baffin Island. Note the overlapping arrangement of hair-on seal furs (left and right), apparently de-haired skins (center), and the breadth of the back end (right). A cleaned fish dries near the entrance (left), next to a harpoon that leans against the side.

Courtesy of The Field Museum, negative #CSA66425, from the Rawson-MacMillan expedition, 1927–28.

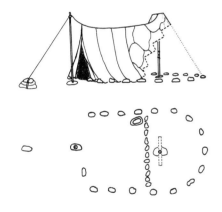

FIGURE 68

Idealized Iglulik thong-ridged tent with "T" center-pole. The tent cover rear consists of seal furs, turned hair-side out, the front of de-haired hides (admitting more light).

After Boas 1888:fig. 505; Mathiassen 1928:figs. 80–81 and 84; Parry 1824:pl. opp. p. 271; Rasmussen 1929:fig. opp. p. 225. Reinhardt and Lee 1997:1796, courtesy of Cambridge University Press.

specimens. The crossbar formed a T that spread the cover laterally. This slightly increased head and shoulder room within the tent.[8]

At certain Iglulik sites a low rock wall, sometimes set up in a collapsed *qarmaq* depression, substituted for the usual stones or gravel that weighted a tent's edges (Parry 1824:73, 300–301). Inside, the sleeping area was distinguished by a stone border. Inhabitants slept on either the hard ground or on heath (*Ericaceae* family, *Cassiope sp.*, or generic woody brush), warmed by a bedding of furs (Parry 1824:223). To stop drafts, they might stuff openings in the tent cover with bunches of feathers (Lyon 1824:233). Just inside the entryway was a general housekeeping section where a lamp and other cooking accoutrements mingled with the remains of daily butchering, blubber scored and rendered for lamp oil, bones, feathers, and other meal debris.

Netsilik Ridge Tents (probably more modern)—Turn-of-the-century photographs indicate that at least some Netsilik Eskimos had come to favor pole- and thong-ridged tents (figs. 69–70; Eek 1998:fig. 8). It may be that both ridge designs used only a single pole or bipod to support the front and back ends of the cover. Netsilik ridge tents seem much like Iglulik ones in construction details.

Copper Eskimo Pole-Ridge Tents—Among Copper Eskimos, men and women erected tents cooperatively (Jenness 1922:78). Their tents began as a pair of tripods or bipods, stacked subsequently with more poles to round out a conical rear section, so that the floor plan was semicircular at the back and rectangular in front (fig. 71). Bridging these uprights was a wooden ridgepole, with lighter side poles placed against them. As many as five more poles splayed out from the rear support, and six or seven others angled diagonally to the ground from points along the ridgepole, thus supporting the sides (Jenness 1922:fig. 26). A pair of tent-cover sheets, pieced together from caribou or sealskins, met and were laced along the ridge. Little care went into securing this cover tightly against rain, although pliable objects at hand (e.g., skin

scraps, mittens) could be stuffed into the cover's ridge seam. Unlike the carefully sealed Iglulik tent (above), the Copper Eskimo version sometimes left its ridge line and the apex of its rear poles exposed.

CONICAL TENTS

Every ridge tent mentioned above is a modified cone with a ridge that draws out the circular floor plan in one direction (figs. 63–67). Arguably, then, conical tents might be the more basic Central Arctic form. These tents resemble North American Plains Indian tepees in general features, including a half-round covering and sizable poles, some or all of which extended far above the peak of the tent, hence the term long-pole conical tent. In contrast, short-pole conical tents have poles of more uniform length that do not erupt beyond the cone's apex.

At least the long-pole conical tents may have been borrowed conceptually from the Central Eskimos' Algonkian Indian neighbors (Klutschak 1887:137; Rasmussen 1929:79). Unlike Plains Indian tepees, however, conical Central Eskimo tents were comparatively wider and more squat in outline and more constricted at the apex of the poles. This narrow opening at the top not only minimized drafts, but Stefánsson gives another reason why this design would have been advantageous: in the bug-ridden arctic summers "one of the best points [about the tepee shape] is that the draft [from the fire] sucks in mosquitos and sends them up with the smoke—likely scorched but at any rate expelled" (Stefánsson 1944:208).

Québec Eskimo Long-Pole Conical Tents—On Belcher Island (southeast Hudson Bay), Québec Eskimos made an unridged tent: a broad version of tepee-style tents, called *nuirtaq*. Here the covers consisted of hair-on seal furs, while interior Eskimos on the mainland used dehaired caribou skins in theirs (Saladin d'Anglure 1984:fig. 2, 482). These low structures seem very much like the Caribou Eskimo tents detailed below.

FIGURE 69

(*above left*) Netsilik pole-ridged tent, King William Island, 1904-1905. Rather small and seemingly not well made, this caribou fur tent uses a bipod to support the front (the back is not visible). The doorway is off-center, even if the doorflap is folded back (to the right).

Photograph by Roald Amundsen or someone of his crew, courtesy of the Ethnographic Museum, University of Oslo.

FIGURE 70

(*above right*) Netsilik thong-ridged tents in sparse arctic terrain, Gjoahaven, King William Island, 1904–1905. Moored is probably the ship Gjoa, viewed from a camp of at least two tents—likely with sealskin covers.

Photograph by Roald Amundsen or someone of his crew, courtesy of the Ethnographic Museum, University of Oslo.

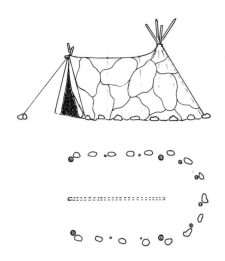

FIGURE 71

Idealized Copper Eskimo pole-ridged tent.
After Jenness 1922 figs. 26–30 and 55, pls. 4A, 4C; Stefánsson 1913:pl. opp. p. 266.

FIGURE 72

Idealized Caribou Eskimo long-pole conical tent: (A) floor plan (circles indicate pole placements); (B) cutaway view; (C) detail, lacing of tent cover.
After Birket-Smith 1929:1:figs. 15–18 and 108; drawn by Jeanne E. Ellis.

Caribou Eskimo Long-Pole Conical Tents—In summer, Caribou Eskimo women erected a large conical tent, or *tupeq* (fig. 72). To raise a tent, two women first hoisted a bipod (either poles or sled runners, lashed together) while others in the family positioned several loose poles in the crotch of the bipod and fanned them out to make a circle. The bipod had to incline rearward, because its poles marked the sides of the tent's entrance. In order to stabilize this frame, they then wrapped the bipod's lengthy thong a few times around the apex, where the poles converged. Next, a caribou-fur tent cover was drawn over the tent frame; its doorflap could be closed when needed. Two skin strips, pierced with eyelets and sewn as reinforcement into the cover's front edges, helped cinch up this sheet about the frame (fig. 72C; Birket-Smith 1929:1:84–87, figs. 15–18). A circle of stone tent-cover weights and a separate door flap completed each tent's complement of essentials.

These tents were often structures of considerable size, requiring as many as thirteen caribou skins (Gabus 1961:108). Tent covers had the fur left on, except at the very front, where the hair was removed to allow more light through the hide. In daytime or in breezy weather, a short upright pole might prop open one flap to increase ventilation[9] and lighting (fig. 72B).

Netsilik Short-Pole Conical Tents (probably more traditional)—Just west of the Igluliks, the Netsiliks made tents that were simpler in design, "raised into a conical form by means of a central pole, from which lines are extended, and surrounded at the base by circles of stone" (Ross 1835b:23; see also Parry 1821:283). Because no poles erupted above the tent's apex, we call this a *short-pole conical tent*. Presumably, each radiating line (thong) originated near the tip of the pole and terminated in a loop around an anchoring rock. The Netsilik configuration resembled a very drooping cone (given that they lacked poles to support the sides of the cover), with the addition of a short door thong attached to a pole outside (fig. 73). While this dwelling might be

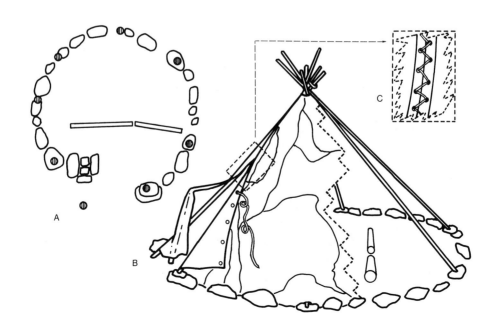

considered typologically a thong-ridge tent, it seems more conservative to call it essentially *conical*. The fore area seen in larger Central Arctic ridge tents also seems to have been absent from Netsilik examples (see Balikci 1970:26). In any case, the floor outline was more circular than apsidal. Missing from Ross's description is the T-forming crossbar that topped the pole, which appears in an early 1900s Netsilik tent (Taylor 1974:122). That modification (fig. 68) appears to have been borrowed later from the Iglulik (Balikci 1970:26).

SALLIRMIUT DOUBLE-ARCH TENTS

Mathiassen's reconstruction of the Sallirmiut double-arch tent type is superficial but it clearly demonstrates, as in the case of their winter houses, that Sallirmiut architecture deviated from that of other Central Eskimo groups. The whale-bone supports for this structure "consisted of two four-sided, upright frames, connected by two horizontal cross pieces [overhead?]." As Mathiassen describes the tent, it appears that the entire frame described all but two connected edges of a cube. However, this description seems partly nonsensical, inasmuch as the tent must have had a shed roof, probably with a pitch to the rear and some pole reinforcement of the roof's center (cf. West Greenland Double-Arch Tents, chapter 1; Siberian Eskimo Double-Arch Tents, chapter 4). Otherwise, as Murray Milne points out, in wet weather the occupants would have lived inside a large animal-hide water filter because the roof center would sag with rain and soon drain water onto the floor and people below (Milne, personal communication to Gregory Reinhardt, 2001).

A sealskin cover, hair side out, draped over the frame, giving it a flat roof and, compared to other Central Arctic tents, adding head room within. When families conjoined two tents, they entered from one long side (presumably in the middle), and skin partitions separated the left and right halves. A line of stones delineated the unelevated sleeping areas inside from the rest of the floor

FIGURE 73

Netsilik-style conical tent with short poles. *Anonymous 1825:22, based on a drawing of an Iglulik tent in Parry 1824: 271 ff.*

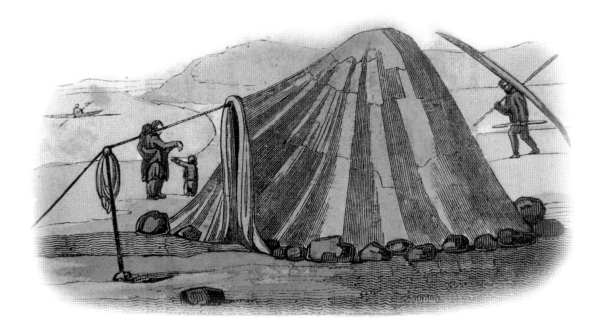

(Mathiassen 1927a:270). Whether the tent had vertical, box-like sides, or needed guy lines (two would be suitable, four even more stable), is unspecified. Flat vertical sides would more readily catch the wind than diagonally spread out, weighted-down sides (in contrast to the northern West Greenland *erqulik* design), but the relative stability of a solid, cubical framework might compensate adequately for that.

ALTERNATIVE SUMMER DWELLINGS

Hawkes (1916:63) describes the Labrador Eskimos' long-pole conical tent, or qanak ("tent pole"), as "more modern," so we do not consider it to be the primary indigenous type for Labrador. An ivory comb excavated from a Sallirmiut archaeological site (fig. 74) is of long-pole conical—rather than double-arch—form. Mathiassen thought it "strange to find pictures of such tents on an old comb on Southampton Island" (Mathiassen 1927a:260). Of course, physical location is not the same as cultural ascription: The comb may have originated elsewhere or might depict another Eskimo (or even Indian) group's tents.

Copper Eskimos, the westernmost of the Central Eskimos, typically used ridgepole tents, although the short-pole conical tent with no smoke hole (characteristic of coastal Eskimos farther west in Canada and Alaska) was known there (Birket-Smith 1929:1:79; Jenness 1922:79–80; fig. 27). A tripod of wood poles provided the central frame; for further stability a number of other poles rested in the three crotches and rounded out a circle. This conical tent variation, described in the next chapter, differed from the squat hide cones found dotting the Central Arctic tundra.[10]

For summertime protection while traveling, Copper Eskimos assembled a skin-covered lean-to (fig. 75). To form the basic wind break, a canted row of poles was anchored in the ground, then furs or a tent were draped over them. A sturdier alternative required two bipods or tripods set some distance apart. Slender ridgepoles, resting on the lateral uprights as well as medial bipods, were positioned between these yokes. Long sticks leaned against this crosspiece to complete the framework, across which the same kinds of siding were hung (Jenness 1922:58, 131).

Compared with ridge and conical tents, other summer options from the Central Arctic seem meager and slipshod. For instance, the simple Labrador Eskimo shelter used by those "too poor to own a skin tent" (Turner 1894:226) consisted of a caribou blanket over a few wooden supports, and it might compare with the Copper Eskimos' "triangular shelter" (Stefánsson 1914:66). As its name indicates, this pyramidal Copper Eskimo structure consisted of tent-cover furs wrapped around a tripod, quadripod, or some other simple frame (Jenness 1922:58, 80, 134). Still more destitute Labrador Eskimos slept behind stone windbreaks (Turner 1894:226), which may equate with "camping houses" that also served as hunting blinds (Hawkes 1916:62–63). Caribou Eskimos had a short-term shelter "erected in the form of a wind-screen of skin supported by three or four poles" (Birket-Smith 1945:191); perhaps it was a lean-to. Traveling Iglulik hunters built similar retreats with round to rectangular floor plans (Mathaissen 1928:129). Additionally, Copper Eskimos made an emergency shelter from caribou furs covering a space between rocks, and one old woman built a rude, fur-covered rock structure for herself (Jenness 1922:59).

In Copper Eskimo territory Stefánsson (1914:228) spotted a round or square tent-ring (i.e., stone outlines remaining after people pull up their tents and depart) with a diameter of eight feet. That is, the design did not reflect a typical ridge tent. Among a different series of elliptical tent-rings at an abandoned encampment was one measuring nine by ten feet that had been cross-cut by a line of stones—probable evidence for a sleeping area border (Jenness 1922:82, fig. 29). Hawkes (1916:fig. 11.1)—and Packard (1885:557) also mention abandoned circular tent rings in Labrador.

ASPECTS OF CENTRAL ESKIMO TENT LIFE

Central Eskimo women, who made the tents and usually erected them, sewed tent covers from the skins of commonly hunted animals, normally either caribou or seal. The number of skins required varied according to size. For instance, seal-hunting Labrador Eskimos needed ten to fifteen sealskins to house "a good sized family" (Turner 1894:227). Some tent covers, such as those of the Iglulik, combined different types of skin. For example, at the back a cover might be made of fur for warmth and, for transmitting light, the front might employ a split walrus hide or other depilated skins (fig. 68). At times, people made double-size tents by "joining the mouths of two single ones, and making the opening on one side" (Lyon 1824:229), so that two families could share them. In such instances, the entrance was in the center of one long side (Jenness 1922:81, 85, 131, fig. 30; Lyon 1824:229). Boas illustrates tandem tents from southeast Baffin Island that are joined near their separate entryways so as to share about half of one tent-side apiece between them (1888:553, fig. 506), an economical adaptation.

One major determinant of regional variations was the availability of wood. For example, the so-called "summer tent" of the Iglulik and Netsilik appears to be a simplified version of their ridge tents but using less wood (Damas 1984a:405; Jenness 1922:80-81). In the event of shortages, whale bones or narwhal tusks could be substituted for the crosspieces (T-bars) or spliced

FIGURE 76

"Prince Albert Sound—spring house, sled, and dogs" presents a Copper Eskimo tent reinforced with snowblocks, including a carved doorway.

From Stefánsson 1913:300 ff.

together into uprights, and a heavy thong or whale bone might act as the ridge (Boas 1888:551–552). The size of ridgepole tents varied accordingly. Ridgepoles for Copper Eskimo tents were five feet above the ground and seven feet long, extending the floor's effective length to about nine feet (Stefánsson 1914:66). Iglulik tents had seven-foot tent poles and ranged in size from ten to fourteen feet across for round to oval floor plans, or seven to nine feet wide by seventeen feet long for rather apsidal plans (Lyon 1824:229; Parry 1824:271).

Arctic tents must have been cold in early spring.[11] Paradoxically, however, snow could be used to lessen the dwellers' discomfort (fig. 76). When the snow was still deep enough Copper Eskimos sometimes cut snowblocks and fashioned a foundation of them, seating the tent cover's skirt on this platform. More blocks created an encircling barrier against windy weather, the interstices between wall and cover being filled with loose snow. Near the typical doorflap entryway, an ice pane lit up an added-on surface passage of snowblocks. Snow also served to make sleeping platforms and side platforms during this period (Jenness 1922:76, 78–79, fig. 27).

For seminomadic peoples such as the Central Eskimos, a heavy tent cover was usually the most burdensome piece of equipment to move; thus, they devised endless methods for transporting it. Caribou Eskimos did not use dogsleds in summer, so they had to carry the single-layer cover and the dozen or more poles on foot, whereas the East and West Greenland tents, though much heavier, remained practical because those campers hauled their dual-layer covers and many poles by umiak. The eastern Netsilitk showed even greater ingenuity in solving the transportation dilemma. Following freeze-up, the tent cover could be transformed into a sled by cutting it in two, wetting each cover-half and rolling it around frozen fish, quickly sculpting the rolls into sled runners as they froze, coating the undersides with moss and ice to prevent erosion of the runners when in service, and lashing ladder-like slats (bones, antlers, etc.) to their top sides (Balikci 1970:48–49; Faegre 1979:127; Hantzisch 1931–32:63).

As with countless other dimensions of Eskimo culture, house construction encoded seasonal and gender complementarity (Giffen 1930). Men built *iglu*s; women pitched *tupik*s. Here again, the procedure was much the same everywhere across the Arctic. The first step was to lay out large, flat anchoring

stones in the shape of the intended floor. (Anything else of mass might be substituted: snowblocks, gravel, wood, turf, etc.) Next, the cover was spread out and adjusted. For ridge tents, the rear section was secured and crosspieces inserted through pockets (if any) sewn to the inside of the cover. Any additional pieces to the frame were added, and the guylines drawn taut. The cover was then weighted with the stones. After this, the crosspieces were raised and the ridgepole inserted into sockets at the apex of the crosspieces. Poles at the front were then fanned out and positioned, along with any additional pieces or supports to the frame. Finally the cover was laced to the ridgepole, then tightened, anchoring it with the ring of stones on the ground, which would thereafter indicate an earlier settlement (Jenness 1922:78; Low 1906:154; Mathiassen 1928:135).

Ways of pitching conical tents or the conical portions of ridge tents could deviate in some respects. When tents relied on a lone centerpole, a stone footing for it was usual. Women might lean all additional cone-forming poles against the rear bipod or tripod before raising the cover, the halves of which some groups tied to poles at the rear. To prevent sagging at the midpoint, ridgepoles could be propped up with an extra bipod (fig. 77, left tent; Birket-Smith 1929:1:84–86; Turner 1894:227).

Setting up housekeeping in a tent differed from group to group. A raised platform usually sat at the rear, lamps at the front, and sometimes a fireplace at the front but more often outside (fig. 77, center tent; Birket-Smith 1929:1:86; Leechman 1945:39). Again, a physical divider usually separated the two spaces, front from rear; poles (figs. 63, 65, 72) or stones (fig. 68) were typical separators. In Labrador Eskimo tents, piled turf approximated the raised sleeping platform of winter houses (fig. 63). Copper Eskimos even used snowblocks for the same purpose at times. Occasionally they stacked them to form low walls outside—or tunnels leading into—their tents (fig. 76), as noted above, but they did not use any platform in warmer weather (Jenness 1922:79, fig. 27). For similar walls, the Iglulik built up a few courses of stone onto those anchoring the tent covers (Parry 1824:90).

Despite the tent's darkness, Eskimo women across the Arctic sat inside during the day sewing without the annoyance of ubiquitous mosquitoes.

FIGURE 77

"A summer camp on the prairie, Copper Eskimos." A bipod supports the left tent's ridgepole at its midpoint, the center tent appears to have a windbreak to its right (possibly protecting a hearth just right of the standing figure), and, beside the right tent, meat strips (caribou?) dry on a low thong or pole(s).

From Stefánsson 1921:opp. 371.

Men, too, carried out "various small tasks" indoors (Birket-Smith 1929:1:75). On entering some tents, the first thing one would encounter would be a stone hearth lying just inside and next to the family cooking equipment.[12]

SPECIAL-USE STRUCTURES

LESSER STRUCTURES

In the Central Arctic other structures coexisted with the principal snow dwellings. An example is the Iglulik children's miniature snow house, possibly like Ammassalik playhouses. One can presume its similar use because a child "[would beg] a lighted wick from her mother's lamp to illuminate the little dwelling" (Parry 1824:434). Copper Eskimo children built miniature snow houses, too (Jenness 1922:115). These tiny structures, however, may have been more comparable to the toy dollhouses of Western children.

Associated utilitarian structures in Iglulik winter villages included separate little snow houses built to store equipment, house dogs, and serve as latrines (Mathiassen 1928:129), plus ice slabs or snowblocks (stood on end) to keep kayaks and dogsleds above the reach of dogs (fig. 62; Birket-Smith 1929:1:75). Smaller ice slabs were also cemented into cube-like doghouses (fig. 62). The Sallirmiut built limestone salmon caches and other storage structures, the latter being short, conical, and looking like "tower traps" (Mathiassen 1927a:225). Stone stacks were probably universal, wherever stones were accessible, for storing kayaks and sleds out of dogs' reach. Finally, many Central Eskimos built fish weirs, or dams, to trap migrating species such as salmon and char as they swam upstream to spawn.

Stone and skin "camping houses" in Labrador also "served [the hunter] as a blind" (Hawkes 1916:62–63). Circular structures with rock walls were constructed in high places as lookouts, windbreaks, and shelters. These or related structures were also employed by Copper Eskimos (Stefánsson 1914:71) and by populations as far away as the Bering Sea (Hawkes 1916:62). The Iglulik, Netsilik, and some Caribou Eskimos turned snowblocks into windbreaks while they waited to hunt seals at their breathing holes (Parry 1824:172 ff). Crouched out of the numbing airstream, men sat patiently on a small snowblock seat (Parry 1824:143), probably with a pad of fur underfoot (Birket-Smith 1929:1:128). Hunters would "sometimes sit ten or twelve hours in this manner, at a temperature of 30 or 40 degrees below zero, without hearing a seal" (Lyon 1824:331). In summer, windbreaks of skins or bundled brush, which eventually became fuel for the fire, shielded women against the wind as they sat or cooked outside their tents (Birket-Smith 1929:1:75, fig. 10; Mathiassen 1928:135).

BIRTH, MENSTRUAL, AND DEATH HUTS

Less common special-use structures include those related to taboos; we call them birth, menstrual, and death huts (after Reinhardt 1986). Birth and menstrual huts generally were used for sleeping and therefore technically qualify as a type of dwelling, but because of their association with ritualized restrictions we feel they are better classified as special-use structures. All three hut forms are more common in the Western Arctic, but do appear in the Central Arctic (e.g., Boas 1888:610; 1901:159). Postpartum Sallirmiut women had to stay indoors until they were "clean." During menstrual periods a woman was "not to go out through the same door as the others but had her own opening in the tent;" if in a house at that time, she could not leave it at all (Mathiassen 1927a:282). A sort of mourning tent—perhaps atypical—sheltered one Copper Eskimo woman whose child had died recently (Jenness 1922:164 n2).

The Iglulik built a death hut, the term we use to define special-use structures meant to house those seen as especially sick (Boas 1888:610) or terminally ill. One snowblock example had a ten-foot tunnel and a dome six feet broad by four to five feet high (Lyon 1824:357, 389–390; Parry 1824:408–409); inside, a weak lamp lit this windowless chamber. With the hut closed tightly, the lamp's flicker, at first smoky and choking, may have bestowed a humane end by carbon monoxide suffocation. A Copper Eskimo song suggests that death huts occurred in their territory, too (Reinhardt 1986:115):

> Here I lie, recollecting
> How stifled with fear I was
> When they buried me
> In a snow hut on the lake....
> A block of snow was pushed to ...
> That door-block worried me... (Rasmussen 1932:136).

On the other hand, Jenness (1922:174) states that the bodies of Copper Eskimos who died in winter were surrounded by snowblock windbreaks to protect them from the elements. Clearly, some confusion remains. Does the song refer to a true death hut, into which a dying person is sealed, or does it refer to a corpse recalling some other postmortem burial chamber?

CEREMONIAL HOUSES

Outside Greenland the Eskimo *qaggiq/qargi/qasgiq*[13] was virtually ubiquitous in the historic period. Among the Central Eskimos it served both genders (for ceremonies and more secular dances) and was usually nonresidential in any real sense. Boas (1888:597, 600–603) refers to the qaggiq as a "singing house," and a place for feasting and dancing as well. Taylor (1990) has constructed a thorough account of the Labrador qaggiq complex, which had all but disappeared by the nineteenth century. The Labrador Eskimo snowblock qaggiq had a tunnel that led from an antechamber and adjoined the main dome (Hawkes 1916:59). On Baffin Island, light was provided by one or more lamps, which sat on an ice pillar (fig. 78; Bilby 1923:217–219), and by a window of ice in the side of the dome.

Every Caribou Eskimo *qaggiq* was "merely an ordinary snow house built on a larger scale" (Birket-Smith 1929:1:269–270); one seen near Iglulik territory was twenty-five feet across and twelve feet high. A Labrador *qaggiq*, or "pleasure-house," built in 1777 stood sixteen feet vertically and, astoundingly, seventy feet diametrically (Packard 1885:478)! Among other Central

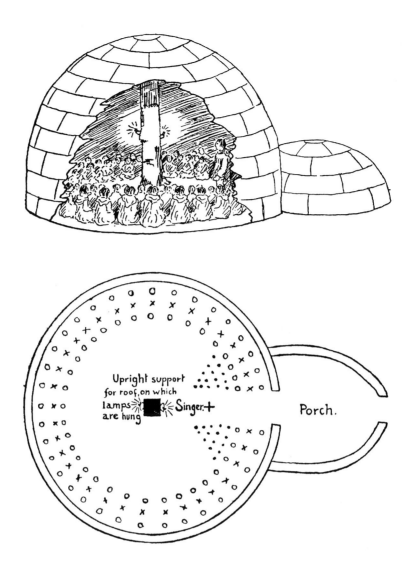

Upright support
for roof, on which
lamps
are hung   Singer. +

Porch.

FIGURE 78

"A kagge or singing house [side and plan views]," with an entrance passage or tunnel. This Baffin Island structure had a central roof-supporting pillar on which celebrants placed lamps at varying heights.
From Bilby 1923:218–219.

Arctic groups the courtyards of snow house settlements were domed over to become dance houses. This architectural approach to satisfying community needs had an economic advantage as well: It conserved energy—labor as well as lamp fuel. The Baffin Island *qaggiq* (fig. 78) was

> generally built upon the usual round plan of the *igloo*, sometimes three being grouped together, apse and transept fashion, with a common entrance (nave). The company disposes itself in concentric rings round the house, married women by the wall, spinsters in front of them, and a ring of men to the front. Children are grouped on either side of the door, and the singer or dancer, stripped to the waist, takes his stand amid them and remains on the one spot all the time. (Bilby 1923:217–218)

On a single night one dual-domed Copper Eskimo house-with-*qaggiq* accommodated twelve dogs and twenty-five young people, then sixty people during a festival (Rasmussen 1932:129; Stefánsson 1914:62, 65). Obviously temperatures would skyrocket in such circumstances.

The Copper Eskimo *qaggiq* was "never a separate structure standing by itself" (Jenness 1922:112). As few as two Copper Eskimo families would build a dance dome, ordinarily placing it between the tunnel exit and the smaller sleeping-chamber dome(s) (fig. 47, large dome in center). Stefánsson mentions a Copper Eskimo dome measuring ten yards across and holding a hundred people for a celebration (Birket-Smith 1936:126). Another *qaggiq* sheltered forty party-goers and still left a five-foot circle open in its center; peak heights of nine to ten feet were not uncommon (Rasmussen 1932:129; Stefánsson 1914:62). The Iglulik sometimes required two snow domes for their *qaggiq* activities (Mathiassen 1928:131; Nourse 1879:90). At a prehistoric Iglulik-area site with fifteen abandoned dwellings stood a stone edifice, very likely a *qaggiq* related to whaling ceremonies. Its walls (large limestone slabs) were about three feet high and its floor was some fifteen feet in diameter. Slabs, polished through use, formed a concentric bench within this circle, and in the center sat another bench-like stone (Lyon 1824:448; Parry 1824:362–363).

ASSOCIATED RITUALS AND BELIEFS

CENTRAL ESKIMOS OBSERVED RITUALS IN CONNECTION WITH SNOW-HOUSE building. For instance, to ensure good luck for their children, they removed from the house any chips left over from fitting the blocks together. For the same reason the initial sloped block for a new tier had to be cut out from the snow (rather than poked loose), and the softest end of the dome's final, overhead block had to face the rear of the house. When a family hoped for a son, they believed this last block should be made larger than the block preceding it (Birket-Smith 1929:1:82). If a child was born in the winter house, its afterbirth had to be removed through a special hole in the wall and a new house built within five days (Rasmussen 1931:505). Around western Hudson Bay, new mothers could "re-enter the hut a few days after delivery, but must pass in by a separate entrance" (Boas 1888:611), and they could not enter another house for two months.

Nonempirical factors were major determinants in the placement of Eskimo settlements (e.g., Burch 1971). Birket-Smith points to one such example, an island in Baker Lake that would have made an ideal summer site. Caribou Eskimos avoided the spot, however, because it was thought to be inhabited by spirits—several people had disappeared there in the past (Birket-Smith 1929:1:73).

In the Central Arctic the dwelling figured in many rituals and beliefs associated with death. According to Boas, for example, when a death occurred "everything that had been in contact with the deceased must be destroyed" (1888:610); this explains the isolation of the terminally ill in a special death hut. As another example, mothers of recently deceased infants could not enter a house until all the men had first withdrawn from it (Boas 1888:612). According to Netsilik custom, furthermore, no frost could be scraped from the window for several days after a death. Finally, to ensure that game animals would not leave the vicinity, platform bedding was not to be rearranged during periods of mourning (Rasmussen 1931:505; cf. Boas 1901:147).

Folk beliefs also linked dwellings with other occupations. Killing seals required some gesture of respect, thus when a seal carcass was dragged into a house the women could do no other work until it was butchered. Related taboos governed the consuming, storing, and handling of sea mammal meat indoors when caribou meat was present (Boas 1888:595). Another ritual linked to dwellings was the prohibition of sewing winter clothing in a summer tent. This taboo was hard to enforce in a year when winter came late, because sewing needed to begin before there was enough snow for winter house building. The Netsilik solved the problem by erecting a transitional *qarmaq*, an acceptable substitute because it had a base of snowblocks and not an earthen (summer) floor (Rasmussen 1931:503). This belief also "[forced] them to look for the earliest snows of the fall," at which spot they would shovel together enough to build a rudimentary house until heavier snowfall produced drifts from which to cut proper snowblocks (Rasmussen 1926:409). Another reported belief was that a pair of caribou antlers could be put over the doorway of a house as a sign for travelers of good hunting in the region (Rasmussen 1931:328 ff.). Also, for hunting luck, house occupants would clear bones from the floor before abandoning it and, if traveling far, would bury some clothing. Furthermore, when many people moved from a village, those who stayed would build fresh snow houses (Boas 1888:596).

Both winter houses and tents (and household equipment such as lamps) appear prominently in string figure games (e.g., Jenness 1924:75, 78, 83, 110), and the Iglulik word for rainbow, *kataujak*, literally means "entrance to an igloo" (MacDonald 1998:159). The Iglulik have one story about a snow house that could fly off with its inhabitants on dark nights (Rasmussen 1929). Nevertheless, Eskimos, unlike other native North Americans, lack any charter myths to account for the origins of house form (Boas 1904).

CHAPTER 2 NOTES

1   Even the notion of geographic divisions of Eskimo societies varies. For example, Oswalt (1979) refers to Greenlanders as "Eastern Eskimos," to most Canadian groups as "Central Eskimos," and to Canada's Mackenzie Delta Eskimos and all Eskimo peoples in Alaska, the Bering Sea and Strait, and Siberia as "Western Eskimos." In contrast, Burch (1988) simply divides the Eskimo culture area in half, Greenland and Canada (east of the Mackenzie Delta) subsumes "Eastern Eskimos" and, west of there, all are "Western Eskimos."

2   At the western end of this region, the Mackenzie Delta Eskimos (Inuvialuit) built small snowblock houses when hunting on the ice (Smith 1984:349) but made their *primary* winter dwellings of cribbed logs (allying the Inuvialuit stylistically with the Iñupiaq Eskimos of Northwestern Alaska).

3   Oddly, as early as the 1890s, local Eskimos could not explain the reason for having abandoned the traditional subterranean tunnels (Turner 1894:228).

4   "According to Ross . . . [the Netsilik] make the [ice] slab by letting water freeze in a sealskin" (Boas 1888:542).

5   Snow-house construction is also described by Birket-Smith (1929:1:78–83, 1936:125), Boas (1888:540), Forbin (1926), Gabus (1940, 1944:60–73, 1947), Gibson and Comack (1940), Jenness (1922:61–62, 64, 76), Mathiassen (1928:120–123), Michea (1957), Rowley (1938), and Wulsin (1949:4–9).

6   Snowballs also served as venthole plugs.

7   Hearths and lamps need not be mutually exclusive, though. One may provide mainly heat (and mosquito-repelling smoke), the other one light.

8   Hall observed a different type of Iglulik tent, made with many poles, at a site between Chesterfield Inlet and Wager Bay (Nourse 1879:68–69). It seemed to drop to the rear as if lacking the rear-end structure of ridged tents.

9   Birket-Smith (1929:1:86–87) treats this arrangement as a windbreak, yet it would not have been as effective as lowering the flap.

10 Labrador Eskimos also raised conical tents, much like Caribou Eskimo examples, though they evidently borrowed the idea from nearby Indians (Hawkes 1916:63; Saladin d'Anglure 1984:482).

11 According to Jenness: "a tent in which the flame of the lamp extended about eighteen inches [of wick length, not flame height] gave a temperature of 43 degrees F . . . though the thermometer outside stood at zero" (Jenness 1922:79).

12 Weather permitting, however, women preferred to cook outdoors (Birket-Smith 1929:1:fig. 10).

13 See chapter 1, note 13 for a discussion of the varied Eskimo spellings of the ceremonial house.

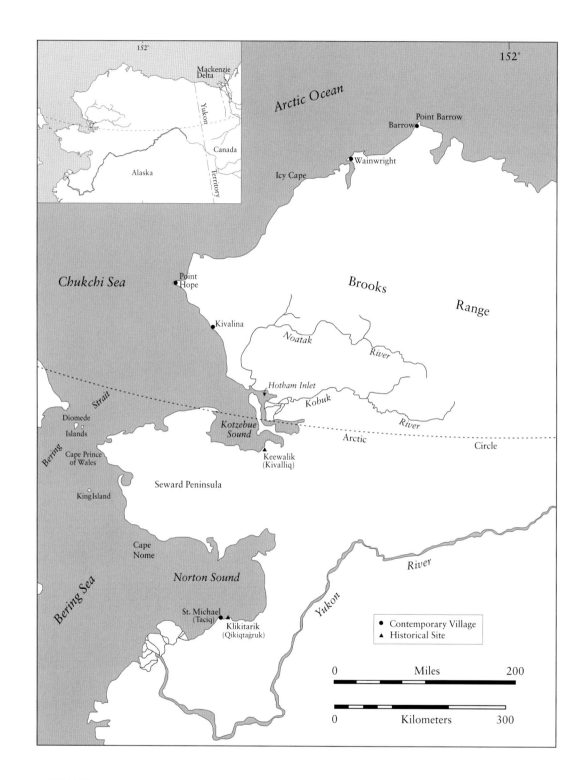

FIGURE 79

Map of Northwest Arctic and Bering Strait.

Produced by Robert Drozda.

3

NORTHWEST ARCTIC AND BERING STRAIT

The [skin tent] was built of willow poles . . .
the warmth inside had caused the buds on [their]
tiny twigs to leaf out a soft pale green. . . .

(Oliver 1989)

THE NORTHWEST ARCTIC AND BERING STRAIT, HOMELAND OF INUVIALUK-Iñupiaq speaking Eskimos, extends westward from the Mackenzie Delta in Canada to the southeastern part of the Seward Peninsula in Alaska; it also includes King Island and Little and Big Diomede Islands in Bering Strait (fig. 79). Compared to the populations of the Eastern and Central Arctic, the region-wide aboriginal population here was high, approaching 13,000 (Oswalt 1979:314 ff).[1] Sometimes called the Western or Northwestern Arctic, this region differs from the Central and Greenlandic Arctic in its seasonal surfeit of driftwood. As a result, wood replaced the snow, bone, and stone that were standard building materials farther east.

WINTER HOUSES

BY AND LARGE, NORTHWEST ARCTIC AND BERING STRAIT ESKIMOS constructed three types of turf-covered, semisubterranean winter house: (1) cross-shaped dwellings of the Mackenzie Delta; (2) rectangular dwellings in the vicinity of Barrow and Point Hope; and (3) farther southwest, pole- or timber-built variants[2] of the rectangular plan with central fireplaces, differently placed sleeping platforms, and shorter tunnels and/or passageways.

MACKENZIE DELTA WOODEN HOUSES

As North America's second-largest water course, the Mackenzie River supplied Eskimos of the Mackenzie Delta and, indeed, much of the western Arctic coast, with abundant driftwood from forested riverbanks south of treeline,

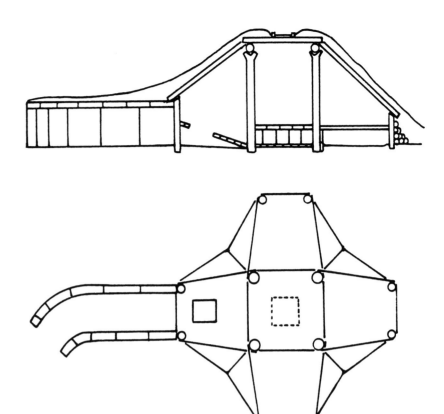

FIGURE 80

Idealized Mackenzie Eskimo winter wooden house (Reinhardt and Lee 1997:1798, courtesy of Cambridge University Press). A snowblock winter passageway leads to a hole in the pitched "floor" at the entrance to the house itself (left wing, bottom). The three remaining wings or alcoves (bottom) would have accommodated one to two families each.

After Petitot 1970:figs. 28–29; Stefánsson 1914:figs. 87–88.

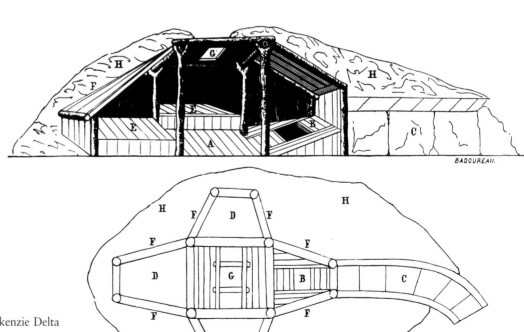

FIGURE 81

Side and plan views of a Mackenzie Delta wooden house.

From Petitot 1876:14; 1970:164.

deep in Canada's interior (Dyke et al. 1997). Few Eskimo populations could boast comparable access to wood, although this important building material becomes more available as a whole from the Mackenzie River westward. In this area, the winter house dates back some 400 to 500 years (McGhee 1974:93) and has an uncommon cross-shaped floor plan (figs. 80–82).

Mackenzie Eskimo wooden *iglu*s were reached through a curved, surface-level snowblock passageway (figs. 80–81) rather like the tunnels of Copper Eskimo snow houses immediately to the east (fig. 47). Ethnographic and archaeological assessments conflsealkinether the house floor was excavated much below ground level (fig. 80; McGhee 1974:23; Petitot 1876:13; Stefánsson 1914:160). The squarish focal room was made of logs and planks, and four tall forked posts rose from its corners. In the crotches of these posts lay four short rafters, which shouldered horizontal roof boards and a cribbed central roof. Old drawings of a Mackenzie Eskimo house (figs. 81–82) show posts with large, perfectly Y-shaped forks, but people also made do with inverted tree trunks. In the middle of the roof was a skylight that consisted of either an ice pane (only in very cold weather) or an oiled membrane made from gull necks, sealskin, polar bear intestines, or beluga stomachs (e.g., Petitot 1970:160; 1981:31; Stefánsson 1922:133).

An important feature of the Mackenzie house was its four roof wings. They projected at right angles from the central roof, slanting down to rest on stringers, which sat in the crotches of paired posts. These shorter posts marked the two back corners to each alcove of the house (fig. 80). At the foot of the descending roof wings were probably poles, planks, or scrap wood, stacked vertically against the back wall stringers to form the four low, rear alcove walls of the building. It appears that the structure had very little vertical back-wall height except behind the doorway (contrary to figure 82), and there, perhaps, only because occupants needed extra headroom for entering. Between each alcove, logs simply leaned from the ground up against the slanting roof-wing edges, creating diagonal side walls for that alcove (fig. 83). Consequently, the stringers that run from the center posts to corner posts in Petitot's depiction (fig. 81) were likely superfluous (cf. fig. 80; Mauss and Beuchat 1979:fig. 3). Men finished the interior surfaces of crib-roof logs and floor and wall planks using stone- and, later, steel-headed adzes.

FIGURE 82

"Interior of the igloo of Noulloumallok." Stylized view of one sleeping area within the house, indicating leaned timbers for the back wall. Heavy Y-shaped posts uphold part of the frame (inaccurately drawn) supporting the central roof (with skylight). Note the slightly raised sleeping platform, soapstone lamps (also misdrawn) on lateral wooden stands (with drying racks—evidently floating—above them) that sit on the central floor, and a general clutter of utensils, vessels, and weapons about the house.

From Petitot 1887; 1981:40.

FIGURE 83

"Mackenzie River house in summer. The doorway to the forty-foot alleyway is at the left of the picture." Note the rude stacking of timbers, some vertical, others horizontal.

From Stefánsson 1913:60 ff.

Three alcoves of the house served as family areas. According to Petitot (1876:15; 1981:40) one family would occupy one side of each low (only slightly higher than floor level) platform. This suggests that a wooden iglu normally housed six families (Stefánsson 1914:166).[3] Each family's lamp sat on a small stand (rather than a sizeable lamp platform) composed of a stone or of sticks somehow arranged to elevate the lamp slightly (fig. 82). Occupants occasionally used the trap-door entryway (the fourth alcove) for additional living space. In the middle of the house, lower than the platforms, was a square communal floor (figs. 80–82). The interior room measured about ten feet deep and twelve feet wide. Simple logs functioned as subfloor joists to level the floor boards (McGhee 1974:31). To the right of the door stood a small platform for an extra lamp, and, to the left, another platform "on which is a recipient serving an all together different purpose," as Petitot delicately described the wooden urine bucket (Petitot 1970:168).

People came and went by means of a low entryway about two feet in height. This doorway could be either a squared aperture (figs. 80–81) or a pair of thick boards, which, when juxtaposed, left an oval opening between them (Stefánsson 1914:159–160).[4] Above the trap door was an ice window set into this wing of the roof. Exactly how the builders of this fourth wing achieved this angled floor, supported it from beneath, and made it articulate with the vertical front wall remains unclear (fig. 80).

With the wooden structure completed, men blanketed the entire building in turf (cut sods), then banked both passageway and house with a mixture of earth and snow cemented together with water. Once enough snow was available they assembled from snowblocks a passageway, with an exit that curved away from the prevailing wind (Murdoch 1892:77; Petitot 1970:160–168). In early spring the passage gave way to a tepee-like addition (*itsark*), which served as both kitchen and dog kennel (Petitot 1970:fig. 18). When snows deepened, the skylight in the roof became the house entryway.[5]

In an arctic wooden house, comfort depends significantly on the warmth-retaining qualities of wood, but the insulating properties of the enveloping turf is equally if not more valuable. Fortunately turf is flexible enough to conform to most house contours. When that fails, blocks of turf can be stacked like bricks in a wall. To retain heat further in Mackenzie houses, people mixed water with moss, lichen, or clay as a caulking compound and forced it into ceiling or roof crevices. Earth or gravel smothered the turf, and over this came an insulating coat of snow.

One early twentieth-century house type in the Mackenzie area deviates from the norm in a number of ways. For one thing, it had a stone-lined hearth. More peculiarly, ice windows had been inserted into its walls. These inch-thick panes could stay frozen, although the thermometer read 70°F inside, because it was −30°F outdoors. Comparatively warm days forced the residents to curtain off the windows to prevent their melting. Another feature that might have been equally modern (or at least a simplification of the cook tent) was a kitchen with a snowblock chimeny in the passage that stood about five feet high (Stefánsson 1914:125–126, 175). Also, Smith (1984:fig. 2b) shows a house from 1914 that seemingly has a short surface passage instead of the half-submerged entrance alcove.

Several variants on these general designs appear in the literature. In 1906, Stefánsson saw a long and narrow house with a long sleeping alcove at the back, a small auxiliary side platform with a dog-kennel alcove opposite, and no entrance alcove whatsoever (Stefánsson 1914:fig. 87). Finally, Rasmussen reports for the Mackenzie area the substantial house of an important man, which had "an elegant log cabin very like a villa," with a "living room" measuring twenty-three feet long, sixteen feet wide, and ten and a half feet high (Ostermann 1942:33).

NORTH ALASKA COAST WOODEN HOUSES

West of the Mackenzie River, around Point Barrow, as the days shortened and families returned to the coast from summer fish camps inland, they pitched their tents among the sunken houses in the settlements until freeze-up, when the dwellings were no longer damp and soggy.[6] Before the snow flew, these semisubterranean houses were visible as randomly placed grassy mounds bulging from the ground. Come winter, the mounds would be completely concealed by snowdrifts. Then the only noticeable traces of a settlement were the elevated storage scaffolds erected behind every dwelling (figs. 84–85).

FIGURE 84

"Native house at Point Hope, Alaska." This house mound rises slightly above the surrounding terrain. Scattered about its tunnel entrance (left) are whale half-mandibles, which also constitute the scaffold posts (right); underneath this structure is the sod-covered semisubterranean house, with logs and short posts evidently stabilizing the exterior. *From Merrill 1889:46 ff.*

FIGURE 85

"Scene in Uglaamie [Barrow]." Three houses, marked by adjacent storage scaffolds, the left of which shows how sods were stacked outside the house (behind wooden scaffold) and sloping tunnel entrance (left of scaffold), and how walrus mandibles were attached as hooks for holding horizontal crosspieces (whale bone scaffolds, right; wood scaffolds, left). An umiak lies on its side (foreground). *From Ray 1885:42 ff.*

One or two North Alaska Coast Eskimo, or Tagiugmiut, families occupied each dwelling (fig. 86). As is typical of most Alaskan Eskimo winter homes, these semisubterranean houses had a rectangular main chamber connecting with a deeply dug entrance tunnel. Unlike Greenlanders, Western Eskimos generally excavated downward instead of tunneling horizontally into hillsides because the Alaska coastal terrain was so flat. Tagiugmiut builders made their central residential room entirely from hewn planks or split logs, as did most other Western Eskimos. From Barrow to Point Hope, though, people sometimes used whale mandibles as storage rack posts (figs. 84–85, 88–89; Hooper 1881:38) and struts for tunnel rafters (fig. 86D–E). Whale bones were particularly plentiful in Point Hope houses, inside and out (figs. 84, 87–89). The house floor was rectangular (fig. 86), and reportedly measured twelve to fourteen feet long, eight to ten feet wide, and five to seven feet high (Murdoch 1892:73–74; Simpson 1855:931). However, in the archaeological record smaller examples are even more common (see Appendix).[7]

House construction in the Point Barrow vicinity differed considerably from that of Mackenzie Delta dwellings to the east. Four wall sills bordered the floor of a house (fig. 86D, F). The length of available logs, usually trimmed at the ends so that their corners met at right angles, often determined floor size [Smith (1990:fig. 10–10)]. Deeply grooving or splitting out a lengthwise quarter-section from each sill log (by means of maul, wedge, and adze) provided a flat surface on which to stand upright wall planks or split logs (below right wall plank, fig. 86D, F; Slaughter 1982:145, fig. 4b). These walls rose vertically, giving the roof its only supportive framework. To prevent collapse, the structure relied on two natural agencies, vertical and lateral stablilty. Gravity transmitted from the turf envelope of the house, by way of its roof and walls, provided vertical stability to the walls and sills. For lateral stability, the wall and roof timbers relied on permafrost, which enabled them to freeze firmly against the turf blocks and the subtending soil enclosing them. The floorboards of the dwelling lay either directly on the ground within the sills or upon floor joists (transverse logs) installed to level them (fig. 86F).

The roof of the northern Alaska coast house responded to local environmental conditions and cultural preferences. Tipping from a ridgepole about six to seven feet high, its off-center gable formed two flat planes, usually with a north and south pitch. Mounted in the longer and lower south-facing roof slope, the square skylight stood out both literally and figuratively from other Eskimo window and skylight designs, most of them flat (e.g., fig. 88). The two-foot-square Tagiugmiut model was "Covered over by thin, transparent [w]hale [m]embrane [or seal gut], [k]ept up in an arched form by two pieces of [baleen] bent upwards from opposite corners, and crossing in the center" (Bockstoce 1988:114), making it rather like a squat, rounded pyramid (fig. 89). Under the longer and lower south pitch of the gable roof (fig. 86B–D), a sleeping platform, about thirty inches high and four to five feet deep, filled the north (back) end of the room (fig. 73D, F). It sloped backwards slightly, and occupants slept with their heads toward the door (Murdoch 1892:72–75). The vacant floor space beneath it served as storage for bedding and clothing, or could be used as a sleeping spot for extra guests (fig. 86F).

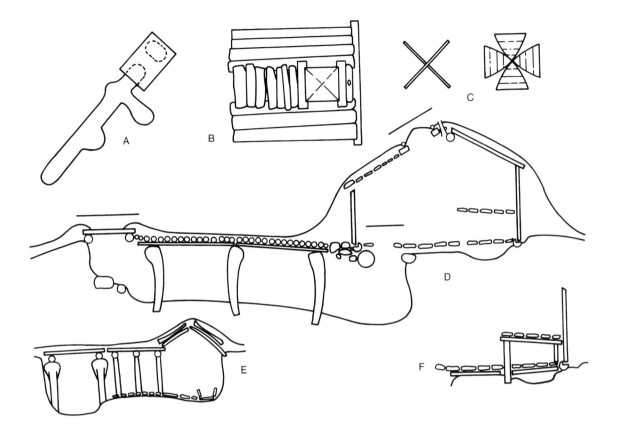

People entered the tunnel into the house by dropping down a short, square-framed shaft at its outer end (fig. 86D). A whale skull on the tunnel floor, below the entrance, sometimes acted as a step. Roofed with wood or whale ribs, the tunnel descended gradually toward the dwelling (fig. 86D–E). It narrowed and ended abruptly beneath the house floor, further discouraging drafts. The circular entrance (*katak*) from the tunnel into the sleeping chamber consisted of two very wide boards, each with a half-circle cut from it (Ford 1959:fig. 25; Reinhardt and Dekin (1990:figs. 4–3 to 4–5). To get into the house itself, people had to hoist themselves straight up and onto the floor, apparently without the aid of a step.

Many houses from the Barrow vicinity had slightly excavated storage spaces directly beneath the sleeping platform (fig. 86D, F). A gap between two floor boards, created by setting the two weight-bearing posts for the sleeping platform into the ground below, granted access to this space (Crowell 1988:fig. 247; Reinhardt 1983; Reinhardt and Dekin 1990:40–46, pls. 4–2, 4–5; cf. Spencer 1984a:fig. 3). Southwest of Barrow, at the Pingasugruk site and in the Point Hope area, a cavity in one house-wall may have substituted for the subfloor pit (Reinhardt, unpublished field notes; VanStone 1977:56, 84).

Excavations of prehistoric houses from Barrow and Pingasugruk have revealed yet another concept of inside storage. Niches between wall planks along the sills were used to hold small articles (Reinhardt, n.d.; Reinhardt and

FIGURE 86

Idealized North Alaska Coast winter wooden house from Pt. Barrow: (A) floorplan (long tunnel has storage recesses on both sides, kitchen off to right, and leads to rectangular floor); (B) details of south pitch to roof (ridgepole at right, vent hole in adjacent board, and square skylight); (C) skylight (left, baleen crosspieces; right, possible layout of gut strips before final sewing); (D) longitudinal cross-section through house and tunnel; (E) transverse cross-section through tunnel and kitchen; (F) sleeping platform, floor, and subfloor details. (Reinhardt and Lee 1997:1798, courtesy of Cambridge University Press)
After Murdoch 1892:figs. 9–12; drawn by Jeanne E. Ellis.

Dekin 1990:46, 73, pls. 4–3, 4–4). Outside the main chamber, larger food- and gear-storage recesses were scooped out from tunnel walls (fig. 86A, E; Murdoch 1892:72–75; Simpson 1855:931).

The Taġiuġmiut added one feature uncommon to the basic northern Alaska Eskimo design: a separate kitchen (fig. 86A, E). Raised slightly above the tunnel floor and at right angles to it, this tiny subterranean alcove had bare earth walls and a conical wooden or whale-scapula roof (Polglase 1990; Simpson 1855:931). Women would cook here rather than in the main chamber, as was typical among Eskimos east of the Mackenzie Delta, and used locally made jar-shaped pottery vessels, instead of the soapstone pots of Canada and Greenland.

Another feature differentiating Taġiuġmiut kitchens from those of more eastern Eskimos was their use of wood to fuel kitchen hearths (Murdoch 1892:63). Some archaeological kitchens from Barrow contained assorted storage niches and a large rock used as an anvil for pounding blubber and processing foods (Polglase 1990; Sheehan 1990). As one approached the main chamber by crawling through the tunnel, the kitchen usually was on the right (fig. 86A), but it could be off to the left, especially when two houses stood side by side (Reinhardt, unpublished Pingasugruk field notes).

Providing the main chamber's heat and light was a large, semilunar lamp. These carved soapstone basins were imported from the east and measured up to a remarkable four and a half feet long.[8] They rested on pieces of flat board toggled into the walls of the house, usually to the left of the *katak* as one entered from the tunnel (Simpson 1855:931). Above the lamp dangled a ladder-like wooden clothes-drying rack made up of several tenoned slats that fit into two mortised side pieces. A skin funnel or a hollowed whale vertebra vented spent air through a roof hole near the ridge, while walrus hides, wood, a snowblock or ice closed the tunnel hatch and house entrances (Rainey 1947:261; Simpson 1855:931–932). From outside, a wooden (or hide?) shutter might shroud the skylight in the dead of winter, preserving warmth within. A scrap of paper tipped into Murdoch's original artifact catalog indicates the level of warmth indoors during winter: "Temperature in Eskimo igloo/ On floor 46.5 [degrees F]/ On bed platform 52.5 [degrees F]/ 3 persons in house" (Murdoch n.d.).[9]

POLE-AND-TURF HOUSES

INTERIOR NORTH ALASKA HOUSES

The mountain-dwelling interior north Alaskan Eskimos, or Nunamiut, are the only Eskimo group to have lived away from the coastline year round since before European contact. With a population estimated at 300 in 1900 (Gubser 1965:20), the Nunamiut pose a challenge to Eskimo architectural studies be- cause they had two radically divergent forms of winter habitation. As a result of their winter mobility, which increased through time (Hall 1976:129–134), the late prehistoric Nunamiut seem to have adopted a tent as their primary year-round house type, but in earlier times they had built more permanent turf-covered dwellings (Corbin 1976). Reversing his earlier opinion, Reinhardt (1986:135) now argues against classifying the turf house as the primary

FIGURE 87

Interior of a Point Hope house (looking toward the entrance passage), occupied until 1942–43 by the Tooyak family. Andrew Tooyak, Sr., was born in this house in 1927. Virtually all structural members are whale half-mandibles; shallow passages such as this one (rather than subterranean tunnels) are a twentieth-century Western-influenced phenomenon (cf. fig. 173).

Photograph by Molly Lee, 1997.

FIGURE 88

"Native house at Point Hope, Alaska." Rare photograph of a skylight showing the general pitch of the sod-covered gabled roof and a close-up view of a whale-mandible scaffold hung with various objects. Lower edges of the roof sods are reinforced with wood and whale bones, using similar posts as retainers. A modern cask rests on a dogsled near bentwood vessels and other artifacts (lower right).

From Healy 1889:20 ff.

FIGURE 89

"Native House, Point Hope." Rare photograph of a pyramidal skylight (left), in this case under a high wooden scaffold (as compared to the whale bone scaffold, right). People congregate between the high combing to the tunnel entrance (right) and a conical tent (center). Note the extensive use of bones (and stones?) to stabilize the sods about the combing; this implies sandy soil, which has a poor "grip."

Thetis Album, Accession #66–46–10, Archives, Alaska and Polar Regions Dept., Rasmuson Library, University of Alaska Fairbanks.

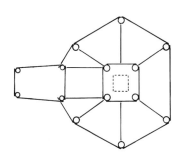

FIGURE 90

Idealized old-style North Alaska Interior winter pole-and-turf house.

After Ingstad 1954:160.

Nunamiut winter residence. Even so, if turf houses had also been built in recent times, as the Nunamiut claim, they should be included here. For consistency's sake, however, we describe Nunamiut tents in the section on summer dwellings.

The old-style Nunamiut winter house (*ivrulik*) embodied simplicity of construction, which consisted of a willow-pole framework built on heavier, forked uprights. Although lacking the heavier driftwood logs and planks found along the coast, these buildings bring to mind Mackenzie Eskimo wooden houses (fig. 90; cf. fig. 80).

Shared by all Nunamiut house design variants (Ingstad 1954) were four forked center-post uprights, cut from spruce trees found to the south and connected (once set in place) by horizontal stringers (fig. 90). To set the poles, builders would position them upright, place stringers on adjacent pairs of posts, "shove soft snow and dirts" around each post's base, and then wait overnight—evidently for the foundations to consolidate by freezing (Campbell 1998:pl. 17). Floors took shape according to how the builders arranged an outer set of shorter forked posts, also topped with stringers. The sloping roof consisted of long poles that stretched between the lower and upper stringers. Shorter poles leaned inward against the lower set and rested on the ground, thereby creating a slightly flared wall, hence a rather rounded overall shape to the building. An abrupt surface passage built in similar post-and-stringer fashion provided storage space and completed the structure, which was then sheathed with turf or frozen moss (Gubser 1965:71; Ingstad 1954:159–160). A square gut skylight (made from bearded seal traded from the coast) covered the middle of the flat central roof (fig. 90). Directly below, the occupants cooked over an open hearth in the floor (Gubser 1965:71; Ingstad 1954:158–159; Larsen 1958:575–576), a trait linking them to Eskimos farther south and west in Alaska. After closing the skylight at night (left open earlier in the evening to let out smoke), the latent fireplace heat kept a house warm until morning (Campbell 1998:pl. 16).

Entering a Nunamiut house through the fur door flap that covered the portal, one walked quickly through the passage into a central room (Campbell 1962:50; Ingstad 1954:158–159). It may be that a horizontal stick tied to the the door flap (outside, at middoor height) served as a sensible door handle (cf. Campbell 1998:pls. 16, 20). The ubiquitous Eskimo sleeping platform was absent from Nunamiut houses; instead, the shallowly excavated floor was paved with rocks and comfortably spread with moss and willow boughs. Householders also used flagstones or cobbles to line the family fireplace (Corbin 1976:162).

Ethel Oliver, who took the first Nunamiut census in 1947, vividly described construction and heating of the *ivrulik* as well as an unanticipated result of the heat and moisture in the dwelling:

> Frank [the pilot who flew with Oliver] pulled aside the bear skin, and I stepped down into the long narrow room. It seemed quite large in comparison to [Simon Paneak's] compact tent, although it was only about eighteen feet long and no more than ten feet wide. It too, was built of willow poles. They came together at the top like an inverted V. A series of these inverted V's were held

together with horizontal poles lashed to them at intervals, forming small squares. The squares were packed solidly with sod and moss. Since the green poles had not been barked, and the igloo newly built the previous fall, the warmth inside had caused the buds on the tiny twigs to leaf out a soft pale green and spring fragrant (Oliver 1989:4).

Ingstad (1954:158) illustrates three distinctive floor plans for old-style Nunamiut houses, each with its own name. The two with polygon-shaped floors had passages to their octagonal *akiḷḷigii* (fig. 90).[10] Passages in the stretched-out hexagonal *sivunmuktaq*, however, broke through one apical end of the house. The third and smallest floor plan, the *iglupiaqtalik*, was rectangular and asymmetrical inasmuch as its passage breached the left side of one long wall. Despite these variations, the components and construction were apparently alike for all three designs, which had sleeping areas along the sides (only on one side in *iglupiaqtalik*s), rather than at the back.

KOBUK RIVER HOUSES

Up the Kobuk River from Kotzebue Sound, the Kuuvaŋmiut constructed a house (ukiivik) that strongly resembled the old-time Nunamiut type (fig. 91). In historic times, the Kuuvaŋmiut built these houses only for early winter, leaving to pursue subsistence acitvities elsewhere as soon as the ground froze enough to facilitate travel.[11] Between Kuuvaŋmiut and Nunamiut house forms, material disparities are minor (spruce instead of willow poles), but construction differences are more pronounced (cf. fig. 90). Unlike the Nunamiut house, a Kuuvaŋmiut house had a truly semisubterranean main chamber and descending tunnel (not a surface passage) overlaid with turf, then moss or earth (fig. 91).

Most singular about Kuuvaŋmiut houses was their means of construction. The ground was frozen some one to two feet deep before people ever started a house (sometimes by mid-October; they abandoned it in February or later). Ingenious excavation then preceded actual construction. To start, men mapped out the house floor, marking a rectangle on the ground and starting a fire at one side of it. After that patch of earth thawed, spruce logs were used to lever up the soil, block by block, and set it aside. Leverage continued until all but a central block remained. Shoveling smoothed out this house pit and its three-to-five-foot-high edges (Giddings 1956:29–30).

Once the pit had been dug the four center posts of the house were embedded in a long rectangular pattern, paralleling the tunnel's axis. House floors were wider than they were long, relative to this axis. Four corner posts, which were nearly as tall as the center posts, shouldered stringers like those connecting the central uprights. Completing the superstructure of a Kuuvaŋmiut house were willow poles, set between the upper stringers, that spanned the width of the center rectangle. This arrangement created a broadly flat-topped hip roof with an uncovered, square opening in the middle (i.e., a skylight). Diagonal poles ran between the medial and lateral stringers to form three equal pitches (on the roof's front and side edges) and a sharper-rising rear pitch. Finally came poles that stood on the floor-pit's rim. These leaned almost vertically against the lateral stringers. When the house was finished, people then packed

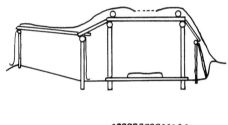
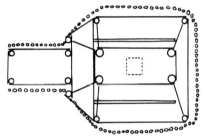

FIGURE 91

Idealized Kobuk River pole-and-turf winter house.

Reinhardt and Lee 1997:1797, after Giddings 1952:figs. 6–7; Stoney 1900:pl. opp. p. 40; courtesy of Cambridge University Press.

all the earthen blocks removed earlier, moss side down, against the exterior. Finally, the residents pulverized the large remaining block of soil within the house, heaving the debris up through the roof hole so it would cascade over the whole house, presumably for added insulation.

Each Kuuvaŋmiut winter house had a caribou-gut skylight measuring four feet on a side and framed so it "could be removed or tilted" to double as a smokehole (Giddings 1961:126). Underneath the skylight, a log crib or stones bordered the sleeping area on both sides of the house. At the outer entrance to the tunnel, fur or a few logs kept out the cold; a separate skin hung at the inner doorway. People did not use these in-sloping tunnel floors for storage. Rather, that part of the house floor opposite the doorway was devoted to storing the family's effects. The sleeping areas had a willow-withe covering demarcated by poles (fig. 91) and overlain with a soft bedding of willow boughs and caribou fur; the remaining floor surface was bare.

Like most northwestern Alaska Eskimos in the interior, the Kuuvaŋmiut used pottery (or occasionally sandstone) lamps rather than soapstone. These were small, hand-molded saucers, about six to eight inches across, that had shallow basins and only an encircling edge to support a wick (see Oswalt 1953). Because fireplaces were integral to their houses, people did not need the long ribbons of lamp-flame to heat the interior, as was common to northern and eastern Eskimos' comparatively gigantic lamps. Women used stone-boiling as the general cooking method. This technique involved heating the contents of birch-bark or bent-sprucewood containers (or bear stomachs "in ancient times") with red hot stones (Cantwell 1889b:87–88; Curtis 1907–1930:208).

Cantwell's first impression of Kuuvaŋmiut houses, in 1884, typifies Westerners' disdain of Eskimo housekeeping: "All the clothing of these tribes, and, in fact, everything they wear or use capable of harboring life, abounds in vermin. Their houses are so filled with [lice] that after one sad experience I never entered a winter habitation" (Cantwell 1889b:84). However, he transgressed the next year when he inspected a vacated house and reported on the efficiency of the fireplace: "We set fire [in the hearth] to a few dry sticks, and the smoke shot up in a straight column through the opening in the roof, showing that defective flues are a source of annoyance not yet known to the natives" (Cantwell 1887:26). Once abandoned, a Kuuvaŋmiut house slowly returned to nature, "and when deserted for a year or two, and overgrown with grass and mosses, looks like a mound, identified as having been a human habitation only by some tumble-down fish-racks on the river bank near by. . ." (Townsend 1887:86).

Variants in early Kuuvaŋmiut floor layout are known from archaeological investigations. Earlier sleeping areas consisted of a slight mounding of earth, certainly no more than two feet high (Curtis 1907–1930:208; Giddings 1952). Houses tended to have two sleeping areas, one on each side, although sometimes there might be one, or, less frequently, three. Tunnels in houses of the early historic period were generally one to two feet lower than house floors in prehistoric times. In plan view, however, Kobuk River houses changed little over the last seven centuries, the most notable difference being that earlier tunnels occasionally diverged into a small chamber or side passage (Giddings

1952). Upriver, Giddings measured fifteen mid-eighteenth-century houses averaging sixteen feet side to side, and eleven feet from entry to rear, with tunnels about nine feet long (Giddings 1952:14–19).

KOTZEBUE SOUND WOODEN HOUSES

Not far from Kuuvaŋmiut territory, and downriver, the Malemiuts of Hotham Inlet in the eastern part of Kotzebue Sound erected yet another wooden house type (Oswalt 1967:97). Simpson (1855:930) was the first to describe and illustrate the Malemiut house, showing both plan and isometric views (fig. 92). The attributes might be seen as a blend of other Northwestern Arctic mainland Eskimo house types. Like Mackenzie Eskimo houses, the Kotzebue Sound wooden house had three sleeping areas (two lateral, one rear), four-center-post construction with a cribbed central roof and square center-hole, roof-wings pitching in four directions, wooden floors, and a forward entryway (cf. fig. 80). However, among the distinguishing features of the Malemiut house was a floor hole (a trap door, leading to an underground tunnel) akin to North Alaska Coast houses (fig. 86). The Kotzebue house also had a central floor area, containing a hearth, a movable skylight that doubled as the smokehole, canted walls, and no sleeping platforms, traits found in Kuuvaŋmiut and Nunamiut houses (cf. figs. 90–91). Beyond this, it also compared with Kuuvaŋmiut houses in that it used logs, not only as headrests but also to delineate sleeping and cooking spaces (cf. fig. 91).

FIGURE 92

"Ground Plan [and] Interior of Esquimaux Winter Hut at Hotham," near Kotzebue Sound.
From Simpson 1855:930.

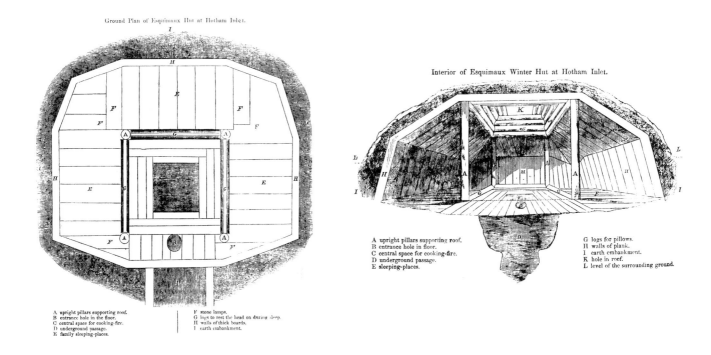

Ground Plan of Esquimaux Hut at Hotham Inlet.

Interior of Esquimaux Winter Hut at Hotham Inlet.

A upright pillars supporting roof.
B entrance hole in the floor.
C central space for cooking-fire.
D underground passage.
E family sleeping-places.
F stone lamps.
G logs to rest the head on during sleep.
H walls of thick boards.
I earth embankment.

A upright pillars supporting roof.
B entrance hole in floor.
C central space for cooking-fire.
D underground passage.
E sleeping-places.
G logs for pillows.
H walls of plank.
I earth embankment.
K hole in roof.
L level of the surrounding ground.

FIGURE 93

Wooden houses surround a canvas wall tent, circa 1899–1900. The two largest structures (left and right of tent) are likely anterooms, connected to the house proper via a tunnel or passage. Main chambers are probably beneath the storage scaffolds.

USRC Bear Collection, Accession #95-264-31N, Archives, Alaska and Polar Regions Dept., Rasmuson Library, University of Alaska, Fairbanks.

FIGURE 94

House from Wales, Alaska. A large antechamber with person on top (upper center) precedes a passage/tunnel leading to the house proper (upper right, with scaffold above it). Note use of vertical posts, with some diagonal bracing, to hold together horizontal exterior wall logs.

Ben B. Mozee Collection, Accession #79-26-180, Archives, Alaska and Polar Regions Dept., Rasmuson Library, University of Alaska, Fairbanks.

FIGURE 95

Frost collects overhead inside an anteroom, looking down the passage toward the house entrance. Extensive array of stored goods includes several deep bentwood vessels (left), another vessel full of fish (right), bundles of cloth and furs (left and right), and snowshoes (right). Floorboards appear to be of milled lumber.

Lomen Family Collection, Accession #72-71-713N, Archives, Alaska and Polar Regions Dept., Rasmuson Library, University of Alaska, Fairbanks.

SEWARD PENINSULA WOODEN HOUSES

At Ublasaun, a reindeer-herding village of the 1920s, the local style of sod-covered semisubterranean house resembled that from the North Alaska coast in many features. Design similarities include a step-up from the tunnel onto a rectangular housefloor, a wooden sleeping platform raised on posts at the rear of the house, upright wall timbers, a storage nook or bedroom, or both, recessed into at least one side wall, and a gable roof—with a skylight in the roof-pitch nearer the tunnel (Fair et al. 1996:90–93; Gerlach 1996:102–103). The Ublasaun house differed from those of the North Alaska coast in four ways, however. First, it had a large entrance alcove with a rectangular door in its front wall and a skylight overhead. Second, the tunnel rose toward the house itself and led to a rectangular inner doorway instead of a katak (floor hole). Third, the floor's long axis was perpendicular to the tunnel. Last, heavy posts supported the ridgeple. This is not aboriginal construction (e.g. it had Western-style doors) but is consistent with regional architecture. Earlier houses probably differed little from these.

Houses at Cape Prince of Wales (westernmost Seward Peninsula) outwardly seem to have incorporated two sets of timbers. The inner set probably stood upright, forming the walls of the main chamber, tunnel or passage, and anteroom(s), while the outer set was stacked horizontally and held in position using upright posts (figs. 93–94). Commodious anterooms (fig. 95) were linked by a tunnel or passage to the main chamber(s). Outdoors, a large wooden storage scaffold stood over the house itself (figs. 93–94). This may be essentially the same construction as that of a *qargi*[12] from St. Michael (Nelson 1899:fig. 76) and houses from the lower Yukon (Nelson 1899:pl. 82). In all these cases, turf is in little evidence as an exterior building or insulating material.

On the south side of Seward Peninsula, Eskimos around Cape Nome built houses with large, high-walled anterooms at the tunnel entrance, which the occupants entered by a ladder or notched log (fig. 96, top). The plan of the house was unusual and consisted of two discrete sleeping quarters and a sizeable kitchen. Piercing three walls of the antechamber were tunnels leading to each room (fig. 96, bottom). Access to the sleeping quarters was by means of a hole set low in the front (near) wall. Evidently, people had to climb up onto the floor after crawling through the tunnel. Inside, on the back wall, was a raised sleeping bench. There was no hearth in the wooden floor. Overhead, the roof, which was gabled with two unequal pitches, held a skylight. These roof features compare with the roofing of Taġiuġmiut houses (see above).

BERING STRAIT ISLANDS STONE PIT-HOUSES

Inhabitants of the Bering Strait islands (King Island and Big and Little Diomede Islands) exploited an abundant supply of walruses for meat, as well as skin and ivory for raw materials, but otherwise, island life was far from ideal there. "King Island is a rugged mass of granite rising sheer from the water for hundreds of feet on three sides, and on the fourth side, where the village is located, it is very difficult to make a landing" (Nelson 1899:255). On King Island and the Diomede Islands, where sod was extremely scarce, inhabitants made their

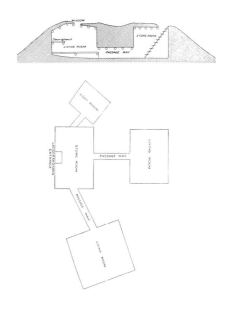

FIGURE 96

Ground plan [and] "section" (facing page) of house at Cape Nome" indicates a large anteroom, two sleeping chambers, and a kitchen—all discrete rooms.

From Nelson 1899:figs. 82–83.

FIGURE 97

View of Diomede village, Little Diomede Island. Old stone houses, with carefully set stone walls and almost flat gabled roofs, remain amid 1930s-era houses and the ubiquitous scaffolds. The large foreground stone house is a *qargi* (cf. fig. 98).

Charles Menadelook Collection, Accession #82-1-12A, Archives, Alaska and Polar Regions Dept., Rasmuson Library, University of Alaska Fairbanks. Published with permission of Eileen Norbert.

winter dwellings in pits excavated from the hillside rocks. At a distance, the fifty or so winter houses on King Island seemed to "rise like heaps of stones among heaps of stones" and were "entered by tunnels" (Muir 1917:120).

The islanders maintained separate winter and summer villages. The King and Little Diomede Islanders shored up their winter housepits with a wood frame, but despite the plenitude of driftwood here, they made exterior walls of stone, insulated (if that is the most accurate term) with granite fragments and earth. Little Diomede Island residents selected uniform-sized beach cobbles for their outside walls (fig. 97), laying them in horizontal courses, whereas King Islanders built more rugged-faced walls and tunnels (fig. 98; Muir 1917:218; Nelson 1899:255; Sczawinski 1981).

The interior and the sleeping platform of the Bering Strait island winter house were walled and floored with driftwood planks. Inhabitants filled any gaps between the upright wall planks with earth. One entered by passing through a square-framed doorway, ascending a long, arched stone tunnel that often had an anteroom for storage, and coming into the residential chamber through a floor hole. Roofs were flat (and at least sometimes pitched downhill, too) to reduce snow buildup (fig. 98). A narrow, whale-liver membrane skylight brightened the interior. Leaving little medial space, platforms perhaps bordered three of the four walls. Interior dimensions of the always-square Little Diomede dwellings ranged from six to twelve feet. Sczawinski's detailed plans of a Little Diomede *qagri* (*qargi*) probably give the best surviving approximation of the old pit-houses (Sczawinski 1981).

The negligible historical record suggests that Big Diomede Islanders also had stone-walled houses, very likely excavated. However, they built these houses amid their summer dwellings, roofing them with skin and covering the whole with gravel, a seemingly poor insulator. King Islanders arched their tunnels but made them shorter than those found on the other islands; they also built whale-bone scaffolds on which to store umiaks away from their

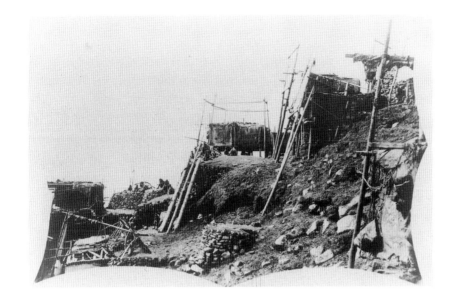

FIGURE 98

Stone-walled winter houses contrast with summertime stilt houses on King Island. The dry masonry of winter-house walls is less artful than that of Little Diomede houses (cf. fig. 97).

USRC Bear Collection, Accession #95-264-20N, Archives, Alaska and Polar Regions Dept., Rasmuson Library, University of Alaska Fairbanks.

dogs (Bogojavlensky 1969:103; Hawkes 1913a:379–382; Muir 1917:36, 120, 218; Nelson 1899:255–256; Sczawinski 1981).

ALTERNATIVE WINTER DWELLINGS

This part of the Arctic is extremely rich in architectural diversity. In other chapters, we discuss the most common forms first, and then return to less significant types. However, the northwest region includes so many alternative dwelling types that it is easier to address them according to the groups that constructed them.

MACKENZIE DELTA

Snow Houses—Mackenzie Eskimos were the westernmost regular builders of domed snowblock houses, the iglo-riyoark (Stefánsson 1914:61). The Mackenzie snow house, except for its curving, flat-roofed tunnel (possibly shorter than that leading into the wooden winter house) resembles those of Central Eskimos: it was built mainly on sea ice and in relation to seal hunting (see Petitot 1970:167; Richardson 1852:207–208). At other times Mackenzie Delta snow houses were built on river ice (Petitot 1876:11, caption A) but in either instance people might stay in them for days to months away from their mainland villages. That shift from wooden house to snow house took place in January or February,[13] when stored foods began to dwindle, the sun had barely returned, and river and lake fishing was again feasible (McGhee 1974:24).

These snow houses were unremarkably basic, with single or multiple sleeping domes, antechambers, short entrance tunnels or entryway windbreaks, and ice windows. Those used for brief sojourns might call for shortening or completely dispensing with a tunnel. Although peeking above the floor by only one foot, the sleeping platform spilled across three-quarters of a dome's interior. It consisted of either packed snow or long snow slabs (Petitot 1876:10–11).

On the right side of the dome near the entrance sat a snowblock lamp platform, and on the left a chamber pot.

Certainly among the most intriguing-sounding aspects of Mackenzie-style snow houses involved water. Drawn from beneath the ice, water was essential to house construction in several ways. First, water came in handy to cement snowblocks together; this was brought about by the builders' squirting it by mouth into the joints between snowblocks. Second, water was flung onto the snowy envelope of the structure as an instant coating. Then the builders tossed chunks of soft snow upon the building's surface, which, on impact, burst over the dome (Petitot 1981:16). The end result was a little "crystal palace" (see Petitot 1876:9, 10), "which by melting on the inner surface [would] become milky like an opal" (Petitot 1981:23). Finally, water was judiciously poured over the snow to form an ice barrier against winds from without and heat leaks from within. Once insulated, a Mackenzie Eskimo house purportedly maintained temperatures around 41 to 59°F even before the lamps were lit (Petitot 1876:15, cf. 1981:38).

While the Mackenzie Eskimos were on sea ice, if they ran out of powdered moss, the normal Eskimo lamp wick material, they would substitute wicks of skin (Petitot 1876:11). Heat from these lamps could make household air stuffy, in which case the inhabitants might pierce their dome with extra vent holes. Even this airing could not rid a house of its pervasive smells, however. Petitot, like other Western visitors, had difficulty acclimating to the air inside Eskimo winter houses: "These offensive odours are a plague which attaches itself to the snow walls, is incrusted on them by melting and is resistant to the most intense cold. Only the melting away of the whole fragile edifice purifies this filth, as the fires of purgatory purify the sinful soul" (Petitot 1981:23).

Mackenzie Delta travelers' houses consisted of either a circular snowblock wall or a true vaulting dome.[14] For the wall-only design, a fur roof came into play; rafters may have prevented the furs from sagging. It could be that these flat-roofed dwellings used snowblocks (in place of furs), like Taġiuġmiut snow houses, which would need rafters even more. Other salient features were a snowblock door and windscreen wall that replaced the passage. The door then became vital protection against cold and wind. To enhance its efficacy builders used the same arched piece they had cut out from their portal. Once everyone had entered, someone reinserted this door and sealed its seam with water.[15]

Other Houses—Three winter dwellings do not fit comfortably with other Mackenzie Eskimo types, and it may be that they have north Alaskan Eskimo origins.[16] The first of these dwelling types strongly approximates a Nunamiut or Kuuvaŋmiut turf-covered house. Its log skeleton and pole walls are very similar, although the one Stefánsson describes (1914:178) was rectangular and "stretched" lengthwise. The second is a hemispherical, framed, willow-withe structure covered with moss and brush (Stefánsson 1922:93, 173). Third is a dome-shaped tent; its fabrication recalls the moss-covered willow shelter (described below) that was the Mackenzie Eskimos' second-choice dwelling. Coincidentally, these putative tents housed those without relatives, that is, "orphans, though mostly old people," much like the similarly small-sized dwellings of northern Greenland (Stefánsson 1922:92, 166). A fourth dwelling does not suit our terminology in that it was a natural cave—and probably one-of-a-kind. This small hollow in a cliff face measured seven by ten by five feet, wherein planks apparently leveled its floor (Ostermann 1942:20).

NORTH ALASKA COAST SNOW HOUSES

Another snow house design, the *apuyyaq*, safeguarded north Alaska coast Eskimo—Taġiuġmiut—village visitors, winter travelers, and hunters stationed near game grounds (Murdoch 1892:82). Snow houses throughout Alaska were not erected as spiraled vaults, although Russian explorer A. F. Kashevarov vaguely refers to domed ones. However, Kashevarov simultaneously confuses this context with the idea and function of hunters' snowpits, dug to trap caribou (VanStone 1977:86, 94n13).

Modeling snow houses after their wooden homes, the Tagiugmiut raised vertical walls around an excavated rectangular room some six feet by twelve. Finding deep snowdrifts, such as those along riverbanks, meant less work in shoveling snow and cutting blocks. Wood rafters upheld the main chamber's flat ceiling (presumably made of tent furs before canvas became standard), and people buried this roof under loose snow. For extra lighting indoors, builders brought their distinctive arched skylight assembly, or at least the gut portion, from their wooden *iglu* to install above the doorway (Murdoch 1892:81).

Whether for one or two families, Taġiuġmiut floor plans differed between *iglu* and *apuyyaq*. For example, the sleeping quarters boasted broad platforms of snow, situated to the side as one entered. These platforms stood roughly eighteen inches high and were overlain by boards and undercut for storage niches. As another deviation from wooden houses, a low lamp platform ran across the back wall. Pegs stuck into the snow walls permitted objects to be hung indoors, one of which would have been a drying rack over the lamp. Canvas door flaps no doubt replaced more traditional skins or furs (Murdoch 1892:81).

A straight tunnel ten feet long communicated with this room and also, via short passages, with a kitchen and a storeroom. Faithful to the wooden house layout, a tiny snow-house kitchen opened off to the tunnel's right side. Women hooked cooking pots on a stick pushed into a kitchen wall. This entire arrangement was walled and roofed in snowblocks. In smaller snow houses, though, kitchens apparently did not couple with the main chamber and consequently carried roofs that doubled as hatches to the outside (Simpson 1855:932). The Taġiuġmiut also built up a little snowblock wall around the tunnel entrance, probably to reduce drafts. A dogsled, set on its end and braced with spears, substituted for the wooden *iglu*'s huge storage scaffold.

A teacher assigned to government schools on Alaska's North Slope during the early 1900s describes a rectangular snow house resourcefully adapted to modern cloth wall tents:

> In the deep snow a space sixteen feet square was excavated by removing the packed snow in blocks about three feet thick. The blocks were stacked up around the excavation, making the total wall height eight or nine feet. Inside,

a tent twelve by fourteen [feet] was put up, and then a drill covering was stretched over the top of the snow walls, thus sheltering the tent beneath" (Van Valin 1941:118–119).

Steps descended to this tent's floor and, following traditional practices, a snowblock tunnel (attached to the chamber's front wall) housed built-in storage recesses.

Should a full-blown snow house be too much to construct while traveling, the Taġiuġmiut would hunker down in smaller shelters burrowed into snowdrifts. Once excavated, walls and a roof of snowblocks probably completed the chamber. Some kind of door would have been expedient, too.

NORTH ALASKA INTERIOR SNOW HOUSES

The Nunamiut apparently had two kinds of snow house. Confusion regarding names for the two dwellings (cf. Gubser 1965:29, Ingstad 1954:39, and Larsen 1958:576) probably extends to their structural features as well. The *aniguyyaq* truly had walls of snow and a fur roof and was an emergency and overnight shelter (Gubser 1965:72, 236; Ingstad 1954:39). It could even augment one's own full-size tent in camp. The other Nunamiut snow house (*apuyyaq* or *aputyaq*) was a tiny, temporary domed tent blanketed with snow instead of furs. People would weave willow boughs or spruce branches closely together, a reinterpretation of the wide-gapped, willow-pole frame typifying their dome tents. Using snowshoes as shovels, they would next apply snow to the exterior. Afterward, heated stones would be brought in to glaze the snow (Campbell 1998:pls. 22–23). A fur or parka became a door flap and freshwater ice served occasionally as a window. Larsen (1958:576) considers this dwelling "more simple" than the snow-walled house. Its name and use of windows recalls the more complex Taremiut snow house.[17]

KOBUK RIVER DWELLINGS

The Kuuvaŋmiut had several dwellings other than their primary winter and summer ones. Chief among winter forms was the "moss house" or *ivrulik*, a short-term shelter (Giddings 1961:126–127). Quite basic, it employed a simple A-frame of two forked uprights and a ridgepole, with many willow poles inclining against the ridge and ends. People also covered one end with a skin or fur door flap and cooked over a hearth built beneath some sort of smokehole. Turf and reindeer moss acted as both sealant and insulator, thus giving this shelter a name akin to the Nunamiut pole-and-turf house. In the Brooks Range mountains "several families" could live in this kind of structure, or something similar, which they covered with snow. Its floor shape was "irregular, generally long, low and narrow" (Stoney 1900:46).[18] There were evidently hearths inside for each family and ice windows at the ends.

While hunting, a Kuuvaŋmiut man by himself might erect "a small, circular shelter, with a frame of willow hoops, the whole covered with moss" (Curtis 1907–1930:209). It was obviously a traveler's dwelling and its description suitably coincides with another that Giddings recorded. This version incorporated willows still rooted in the ground. Men bent the boughs toward a midpoint, tied or wove their tips together, and tossed a sewn cover of caribou furs on top (Giddings 1956:43). Its overnight or short-term nature, tiny capacity, and (exclusively?) moss sheathing are reasons why we classify this dwelling separately rather than merely as a simplified version of their adaptable, domed *echellek* (see next section).

TRANSITIONAL DWELLINGS

NORTHWEST ARCTIC AND BERING STRAIT ESKIMOS HAD FEWER TRANsitional housing types than the Central Eskimo groups, but more than those living in Greenland. The autumn *qarmaq* as it was known farther east evidently existed in the Mackenzie Delta (Ostermann 1942:22–23), but not west of there. Of all Alaskan Eskimos, the Kuuvanmiut built the most innovative transitional house. In spring, summer, and fall they opted for a highly adaptable, domed, willow-framed structure (*echellek*), which was smaller than their main summer dwelling. Builders would drive home six or so willow poles into a circular outline and weave them together, basket-fashion, to supply the framework. However, the coverings changed from season to season, as did the presence of hearths (Cantwell 1889a:62–63, 60 ff, 1889b:80; Curtis 1907–1930:208–209; Giddings 1952:11; 1956:5, 7, 23, 43; 1961:48; Stoney 1900:46).

In fall, the Kuuvaŋmiut willow frame supported a water-resistant skin cover, made from a dozen or so dehaired caribou pelts. This structure had a smokehole (hence a hearth), whereas about half as many caribou furs made up the springtime cover. For extra warmth in colder circumstances, people piled snow on the outside of the house. Because interior hearths would have been unnecessary in summer, the covering consisted of lashed-down spruce bark overlaid by moss, an ideal protection during the rainy season. On the other hand, Cantwell (1889a) depicts a "summer fishing village" of hemispherical houses, but their covers look more like skins or furs than bark, and they lack a mossy sheathing (fig. 99).

FIGURE 99

"Summer fishing village, Kowak [Kobuk] River." Tents with skin-like covers house summer fishers, whose catches hang from drying racks. These Kuuvaŋmiut boats (not the steam-powered vessel) were, as depicted, more like American Indian canoes than Eskimo kayaks.
From Cantwell 1889a:61 ff.

With spring at its warmest, the Kuuvaŋmiut might build a *miluq*. To do so, one looked for a large live spruce and then chopped down a series of spruce saplings to place upright in a circle about this big tree (Giddings 1956:48, 1961:46). People assembled the *miluq* in spring time as a short-term dwelling before settling into their fish camps for the summer. In late fall to early winter, Kuuvaŋmiut families lived in "a simple lean-to" of unspecified design, instead of "a temporary *itchalik*," while they prepared their wooden winter house (Giddings 1956:28).

At the border with Yup'ik (Southwestern) Eskimo territory, probably in the Kauwerak Eskimo area, people erected a simple cone-shaped wooden shelter during spring and summer to accommodate fishers and marmot hunters in season (Nelson 1899:253). This structure began as a lashed-pole tripod. Logs were leaned against this tripod to round out a roughly conical wall. The interior included a sleeping platform raised on short posts, and an entrance much like that of a conical tent (that is, a triangular gap from which wall material was absent). The presence of sleeping platforms would have allowed for storage beneath.

SUMMER DWELLINGS

PRIMARILY TWO NORTHWEST ARCTIC-BERING STRAIT ESKIMO TENT TYPES, either conical or dome-shaped, were in use during summer. Most coastal populations from the Mackenzie River to the Seward Peninsula lived in conical tents, a type that may have originated in Asia (Birket-Smith 1936:130). Northeast of Cape Nome, people used short-pole conical tents in summer, although a few groups (probably the former riverine populations) preferred dome varieties (Nelson 1899:260; Ray 1885:106, 130, 173; Thornton 1931:225–226). Going to another seasonal extreme were the Nunamiut, who lived in the mountains of Alaska's Brooks Range and, in the contact phase of the early historic period, relied on dome tents all year long.

SHORT-POLE CONICAL TENTS

A short-pole conical tent (figs. 100–101) is sealed at its peak instead of having tepee-style poles extending above it. As cooking was done outdoors in the summer, such tents lacked a hearth, thus needing no smokehole. Variability in short-pole conical tent designs depends mostly on the layout of their interiors.

Following the usual habit of Eskimo settlement, conical tent openings faced south or away from the water (fig. 101). In 1826, Thomas Elson, a member of English explorer Frederick W. Beechey's expedition, cruised northeastward along the Arctic Ocean coast and made contact with Point Barrow Eskimos. Documenting the people and this tent type for the first time, he wrote that "they resided in tents, the frames of which were made of poles, and covered with sealskins: the bottom or floor was merely a few logs laid sidewise on the ground: inside there was a second lining of reindeer skin, which did not reach quite to the top: this constituted the whole of their dwelling" (Elson in Beechey 1831:1:432).

FIGURE 100
Idealized North Alaska Coast short-pole conical tent: cutaway view (top); Mackenzie Delta floor plan, with pole-covered sleeping area (bottom).
After Murdoch 1892:fig. 15.

Eskimos could erect and dismantle their tents with astonishing speed, as an early twentieth-century writer observed: "[Eskimos from Point Hope] arrived last evening at a camping ground. . . . They had eight tents and all the food, canoes, arms, dogs, babies, and rubbish [of] the village. The encampment looked like a settled village that had grown by enchantment. Only one [tent] was left in the morning " (Muir 1917:147).

MACKENZIE DELTA

Petitot portrays a camp of at least six tents (tupiqs) on a Mackenzie Delta riverbank, with large European-made iron cauldrons suspended from tripods over hearths set between some of them (Petitot 1970:170, fig. 19). As usual, women put up the tents (fig. 100). Four or five twelve-foot poles were cinched together about six inches from the top, the point at which each pole had been drilled to receive a thong. Women spread them out to begin shaping a cone twelve to fifteen feet in diameter.[19] At a height of four to six feet, the women braced these main poles by lashing on a horizontal wooden hoop that they had dropped over the apex to stabilize the tent (fig. 100, top). Shorter poles leaned against this hoop, which served the additional purpose of interior storage rack.

Requiring some six seal or caribou skins apiece, each of two tent-cover halves had a sewn-in pocket that fit over the top of the poles. After women set the poles into these pockets, they draped the two halves one over the other so that the covers overlapped, and then either secured them to the frame with long thongs wound around the exterior, or laced them shut (Murdoch 1892:84; Nelson 1899:261; Simpson 1855:933). Before canvas and drill became available from Yankee whalers and traders, Mackenzie people made tents of sealskins with the hair left on and turned outwards (Hooper 1853:228). More recently they used caribou skins and faced the covers hair-side-in.

A doorflap separated inside and outside domains of Mackenzie Delta tents (Petitot 1981:fig. 19). Given the opacity of fur-on tent covers, when the door was shut, lamps would have been necessary for undertaking tasks that

FIGURE 101

"Scene from Uglaamie [Barrow]. Tent with natives at work. Summer camp." The conical tent has a translucent material around the doorway to admit more light. Someone works on a kayak's cockpit while children sit near its stern. Bentwood vessels and other artifacts lie about, and tools and weapons lean against the tent.

From Ray 1885:38 ff.

required strong light. The sleeping area apparently was not raised like the platforms or benches in winter houses. Nevertheless, a layering of sticks in that area separated it symbolically and practically (fig. 100, bottom) from the remaining interior space (Petitot 1970:170).

NORTH ALASKA COAST

Point Barrow people moved out of their wooden houses in early July and stayed in tents, sometimes erected in the same villages (fig. 89), until late September (Murdoch 1892:76). The Taġiuġmiut conical tent, or tupiq, was quite similar to that of Mackenzie Eskimos. A photograph from the International Polar Expedition (fig. 101; Murdoch 1892:cover of 1988 reprint) was the template for Murdoch's (1892:fig. 15) line drawing of a tent, which shows a rounded peak (fig. 100, top). Taġiuġmiut tents sometimes used two hoops, instead of one, doubly ensuring the stability of the conical framework. Another possible distinction is that the Taġiuġmiut lined the inside, probably from hoop to ground, with caribou skins (see Elson's quote above). Also, either the Taġiuġmiut tent cover or door flap had a panel missing higher up, which was replaced by a window-like swatch of processed seal gut to improve lighting within. During the low-sunlight night hours and on cold days, occupants sometimes tossed a fur over this window. Again, no one lit a lamp indoors for light or heat (Murdoch 1892:85); perhaps enough summer sunlight beamed through on its own. In any event, women cooked outdoors the way Mackenzie Eskimo women did.

Boards and poles floored the Taġiuġmiut tent's posterior sleeping area, further demarcated by a floor-dividing log (Murdoch 1892:85). Under proper conditions, the doorway led outside by way of a snowblock tunnel that could have an appended snowblock kitchen. Sometimes a short snow wall also anchored the cover and long objects (spears, paddles, etc.), resting against the sides, could serve as further anchoring devices (fig. 101).

As a final comment on Taġiuġmiut tents, an old ivory *ulu* handle from the Pingasugruk site (fig. 102) has a motif on both sides that looks like a *long-pole* conical tent (Reinhardt 1997). The same element occurs on both sides of the handle and differs from north Alaskan whale-fluke motifs on other artifacts from Pingasugruk and elsewhere. Assuming this element is a tent, and that the handle originated from Pingasugruk, it indicates that prehistoric conical tents in the area were not short-poled.

NORTH ALASKA INTERIOR

The Nunamiut sometimes traveled with a short-pole conical tent (nappaqtaq). Like Mackenzie Eskimo and Taġiuġmiut versions, those of the Nunamiut were indeed aboriginal (Campbell 1998:pls. 20–21). Still, given their location inland, they undoubtedly favored caribou fur over sealskin tent covers. Moreover, the short-pole conical tent was certainly secondary to the better known Nunamiut summer dwellings, and for the most part its use was limited to summer trading jaunts to the coast (fig. 103; Ingstad 1954:39; Larsen 1958:577). Another distinction was the possibility of extremely large frame heights and diameters, and the use of four horizontal, concentric hoops to stabilize the tent poles (Campbell 1998:pl. 21).

FIGURE 102

Detail of prehistoric ivory *ulu* handle from Pingasugruk, showing an incised long-pole conical tent motif—the same image appears on both sides.

Photograph by Carlos Zambrano; cf. Reinhardt 1997:slide 40.

FIGURE 103

"Noyatog [Noatak] River Innuits, met at Hotham Inlet [near Kotzebue Sound]." Tall, narrow conical tents, apparently cloth-covered, the nearest having a fur door flap, are probably part of an annual Eskimo trading festival on the coast.

From Hooper 1881:40 ff.

In addition to their other dwellings,[20] the Kuuvaŋmiut pitched conical tents when they met downriver at Kotzebue Sound for midsummer trade fairs, at which they bartered with Yankee sailors, neighboring Eskimos, and Siberians alike. Kuuvaŋmiut tent peaks stood ten feet high, and about half a dozen sewn caribou furs, hair-side-out, covered the poles. By the late nineteeth century, these tents were covered by an additional layer of imported canvas or calico (fig. 103). To keep the multiple-layer Kuuvaŋmiut tent cover from flapping open, thongs were wound around the canvas (fig. 103; Cantwell 1889b:86 ff; Nelson 1899:261–262, pl. 83b, figs. 88, 89). Willow withes possibly floored these tents, the general Kuuvaŋmiut practice. Along the coast in this region Eskimos pitched tents in dry places on hilltops or beaches and sometimes among the semisubterranean winter houses in a settlement (Hooper 1853:227).

NORTH ALASKA INTERIOR DOME TENTS

At some point in Nunamiut prehistory, the people became too mobile for their earlier pole-and-turf houses. As a result, the Nunamiut, unlike other Western Eskimo groups, adopted a willow-frame skin tent (*itchalik*) in which they could live all year long. Of all the Eskimo tent types, this one is perhaps most distinctive (fig. 104). As if its year-round usage were not unusual enough, the domed tent had two terms associated with it, both having numerous orthographic renderings throughout the historic period. Native words reproduced as *itjerlik, itsalik, iccellik,* and *itchelik* refer to the tent itself while *qalorwik, qalurwigaq,* and *kalukvik*—correctly spelled *qaluugvik* (Lawrence Kaplan, personal communication to Lee 1999)—indicate the frame (Ingstad 1954:159; Larsen 1958:575; Petitot 1970:169; Rausch 1951:159; Spencer 1959:44).

In inclement weather the Nunamiut domed skin tent[21] has several advantages over a conical tent. First, dome tents could be either stationary or transportable. Second, because heat loss is minimal in this kind of structure, space is maximized. Third, unless winds are severe, the domed skin tent needs no anchoring (Stefánsson 1944:197). These advantages were not lost on surrounding groups. Toward the end of the nineteenth century, possibly because of demographic shifts among the Nunamiut, as well as the observed efficiency of their dwellings by other Eskimos, the dome shape appeared as far east as the Mackenzie River (Stefánsson 1914:173). In at least one instance the Taġiuġmiut established a village of dome tents on the sea ice near the Chukchi Sea coast between Wainwright and Point Barrow (fig. 105; Van Valin 1941:75),[22] and other Eskimo dome tents were spotted around the coast at Kivalina, on Kotzebue Sound (Brower 1950:32), and even at Cape Nome, on Norton Sound (Ray 1975:149).

Men and women worked together to set up the Nunamiut tent. First they had to level the ground and stamp it flat, and then they laid down two to three dozen hefty willow poles in parallel rows. The men drove these poles, each twelve to fifteen feet long, into the hard-frozen soil (or snow at midwinter) in a circular to elliptical plan. Afterward, the people bent opposing pairs of poles (and as many as eighteen additional ones) toward the middle and tied them

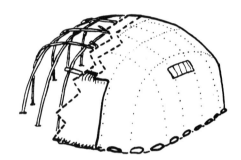

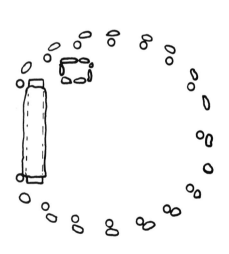

FIGURE 104

Idealized North Alaska Interior year-round domed tent (Reinhardt and Lee 1997:1798; courtesy of Cambridge University Press). *After Larsen 1958:fig. 1; Rausch 1951:fig. 10).*

together. The result was a cross-arching, near-rigid framework, essentially hemispherical to semi-ellipsoidal and around five to six feet high at its center (fig. 104). The closest thing to lateral bracing was a lone pole lashed over the doorway, centered in one long wall whenever the floor was long rather than round (Campbell 1998:pls. 14–16; Gubser 1965:69–70; Rausch 1951:159–160, fig. 10).

Sheathing the Nunamiut tent dome were hair-on caribou-skin panels, swathed in turn by a sheet of ten to twenty dehaired, water resistant skins (Larsen 1958:576; Rausch 1951:159). Rausch specifies a named series of inner-cover panels: six skins as a roof, two three-skin sets closing off the back, two more twin-hide leaves around the front, and a single hide next to the door (and hearth or stove) (Rausch 1951:159). A ring of turf, moss, or snow held the exterior cover's edges in place. Sewn into this outer layer was a window of bear-gut strips or caribou (or caribou calf skin) (fig. 104, top). Overhead, the dome tent had a smokehole but no skylight. Next came a door flap of prime grizzly bear or caribou fur. "The [bear] hide extended well beyond the opening on either side so no cold air seeped in when it was dropped into place" (Oliver 1989:2). A recent overview suggests that a log attached to the door flap kept it from blowing open (Faegre 1979:134). To seal the entrance further, a turf threshold set just inside the doorway, prevented its erosion from foot traffic by wrapping it with a caribou skin (fig. 104, bottom). Last, thin willow poles or spruce boughs floored the whole interior (Gubser 1965:69–70; Ingstad 1954:38–39; Rausch 1951:159–160; Spencer 1959:44–46).

People evidently shovelled moss or soft snow over the skin-covered structure for added insulation, although Rausch refutes this (1951:160) and a knowledgeable Nunamiut informant also fails to mention it (Campbell 1998:pl. 16). At the back, caribou blankets indicated the sleeping area. Sources differ as to how the Nunamiut warmed their tents: they most likely had indoor hearths (Campbell 1998:pl. 16; Gubser 1965:70, 74; Rausch 1951:159), but

FIGURE 105

"Summer village—Point Belcher." A mixture of (cloth-covered?) conical and dome tents at or near Nunagiak, once the largest village in the area. The large scaffold (right) is accessed by a ladder from the roof of a house. In the distance is another scaffold (center left), plus a whale-oil barrel (far left) probably from a Yankee whaling ship.

Thetis Album, Accession #58-1026-1877, Archives, Alaska and Polar Regions Dept., Rasmuson Library, University of Alaska Fairbanks.

another source states that they heated the tent with stones fired outside and then carried indoors (Ingstad 1954:39).[23]

In any event, the Nunamiut used sandstone, soapstone, or pottery lamps for light, if not heat. Building a fire or using a lamp within caused ice to form on the outer surface of the tent skin. Eventually, when the tent dried, there was a dead-air space between the skin and the ice, which further insulated the structure. Sometimes the tent was removed later, from the inside, and the ice dome could then stand on its own (Gubser 1965:70; Ingstad 1954:38–39; Stefánsson 1914:205–206).

Most likely cooking took place indoors in winter and outdoors during summer (Campbell 1998:pl. 16). The Nunamiut compare with most Eskimos in that they cooked meat by boiling. However, even though they made unfired ceramic cooking pots,[24] they apparently preferred to stew foods by dropping heated stones into bentwood containers. Summer allowed women to build bigger outdoor fires, over which they roasted meat by dangling it (Gubser 1965:74, 233).

In the 1950s and later, canvas came to replace caribou hides as the preferred outer tent covering, although caribou still lined the insides. Similarly, framed glass windows and metal stoves displaced their aboriginal counterparts. Ethel Ross Oliver provides a personal glimpse of recent Nunamiut tents in winter. The interior features probably differed little from earlier examples:

> Little willow twigs laid close together floored the tent. Placed on them, at the rear half of the tent, were caribou skins and bedrolls. Dim light filtered through a plastic window, once belonging to an airplane, sewed into the tent at one side of the doorway. On the other side, just inside the doorway, stood a tiny sheet-iron stove which warmed the tent. The heap of broken, dead willows lay in front of it.
>
> The back half of the stove was covered by a huge round kettle in which chunks of clean, white snow melted. From the front half, a big blue enameled roaster gave off savory odors. Between the stove and the tent wall, marrow bones and a hind-quarter of caribou thawed. Near the stove, toward the back of the tent, two wooden gasoline cases piled together made a cupboard. An assortment of enameled cups and plates and [a] meager stock of staples was kept here. Atop the cupboard sat a battered old battery-operated blue table model radio, a Zenith. Over it, tied to the tent frame, hung a single burner Coleman gasoline lantern. Hanging against the wall nearby was a square of cloth covered by a series of pockets. Other than the human occupants, this was all the tent contained. (Oliver 1989:3)

Nunamiut dome tents ultimately gave way to walled canvas tents, sod-covered houses, and today's Western-style houses.

KOBUK RIVER BARK HOUSES

Two kinds of summer dwelling are reported for the Kuuvaŋmiut. A small number of people, probably those who lived along the lower Kobuk, pitched dome tents (fig. 99), but the majority seem to have chosen the aurivik, an entirely different dwelling (fig. 106). Perhaps more durable than a dome tent, this gable-roofed summer house was raised on "two end posts and four corner posts" (cf. Giddings 1952:11, 1956:19). Women and children were the

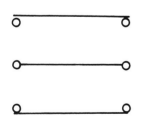

FIGURE 106

Idealized Kobuk River summer bark house.
After Giddings 1956:19.

principle residents. While the men hunted inland or traded downstream at the annual fair on Kotzebue Sound, the women and children lived in aurivit erected at prime fishing sites along the river (Giddings 1952:11).

The willow walls of the *aurivik* were woven into an untidy wattle. The roofing and siding material consisted of spruce bark cut into large slabs. Once flattened, fifteen of these slabs sufficed for both house and associated fish cache (Giddings 1961:35). Anchoring the overlapping roof shingles were poles that had been lashed to the roof ridge with thongs or spruce-root cords. One important feature of the *aurivik* was that it was designed to be mosquito resistant. Curtis says the roof was sealed with pitch (1907–1930:209). There was a door flap of some kind at the front of the dwelling (fig. 106) and the rear wall was also sealed off, presumably with pitch (Giddings 1956:7; 1961:127). Little smudge fires indoors further helped repel mosquitoes, although the women cooked outside over open hearths.

BERING STRAIT ISLAND STILT HOUSES

After snow houses from the Central Arctic, the cube-like envelopes of walrus hide that dotted the shoreline cliffs of King Island and the Diomede Islands are arguably the most memorable of all Eskimo structures (fig. 107). Anchored to the islands' steep and rocky escarpments with driftwood pilings as long as twenty feet (fig. 108), the structures themselves (*inipiaq* or *tuviq*) consisted of depilated walrus hides lashed to a driftwood frame, which in

FIGURE 107

"Walrus skin summer house on King Island." Note the pole framework and pilings, the walkway around the house, and the door hole facing seaward.
From Nelson 1899:fig. 84.

FIGURE 108

Details of a summer stilt house, King Island, circa 1899–1900. Many pilings and crossbeams support the house, which lacks walrus hide on one side, while other struts run almost horizontally and no doubt strike deeply into the hillside.
USRC Bear Collection, Accession #95-264-22N, Archives, Alaska and Polar Regions Dept., Rasmuson Library, University of Alaska Fairbanks.

turn was elevated on a pole platform. Materials for the pilings either drifted toward the island seasonally or were towed there from the mainland by means of umiaks, or skin boats. The need for lumber was a serious concern, for "the islanders are constantly on the lookout for the drifting timber, and put out to sea in the stormiest weather for a distant piece, be it large or small. They also patrol the coast after a high tide for stray bits of wood" (Hawkes 1914:13).

Bering Strait island stilt houses terraced upward a good 150 feet above the sea (figs. 109–110), and, according to ethnologist Edward W. Nelson, resembled "a cluster of cliff-swallows' nests" (Nelson 1899:255) or, in the words of another visitor, "daddy longlegs crawling up a wall" (Borden 1928:138). One approached the dwelling from a plank walkway, which extended out from the cliff and encircled the house (fig. 111). For safety, the back ends of the poles that supported this walkway had been anchored well into the boulders of the forty-degree hillslope behind the house (fig. 108). Around on the seaward side was an oval or circular doorway.

Oiling the skins increased a stilt house's light transmission and, undoubtedly, its resistance to rain and sea spray. According to naturalist John Muir, who visited King Island in 1917, the sun's rays shining through the oiled skin created an eerie, dreamlike effect:

> The skin is of a yellow color, and quite translucent, so that when in[doors] one feels as if one were inside a huge blown bladder, the light sifting through the skin at the top and all around, yellow as sunset. The entire establishment is a window, one pane for the roof, which is also the ceiling, and one for each of the four sides, without cross sash-bars to mar the brave simplicity of it all. (Muir 1917:218)

When severe storms blew up, however, the romantic illusion ended. According to Father Louis Renner, who spent many years on King Island, "At times [the house] shakes so violently that [the inhabitants] cannot sleep at all" (Renner 1979:71). Still, it may well be that placing walrus-hide drying racks immediately before most stilt houses (figs. 98, 110, 112) would deflect the wind's ferocity from the houses themselves. Even without skins in place (figs. 107–109), it seems likely that the drying-rack poles (and the stilts themselves) further mitigated that ferocity much as "special windpoles, which stood in front of the house and broke the force of the wind" once did for houses in Switzerland (Rapoport 1969:101).

Measuring eighteen by twenty-four feet, space inside a walrus skin house was divided into a long storage anteroom and, behind it, two sleeping rooms partitioned off for separate families. Wood framed the rectilinear walls and ceiling and was used for the flooring. The two-layer skin cover, insulated with dry moss or grass in between the two layers (Renner 1979:71), required about thirteen walrus hides. Hides were lashed in place when newly flensed, and shrank as they dried (Van Valin 1941:23), thereby tightening their fit to the frame. No doubt the last hide attached was for the roof (figs. 108, 112). Both kayaks and skin boats were hung directly beneath the house for easy access to the water and safekeeping from hungry dogs (Muir 1917:36; Nelson 1899:255).

FIGURE 109

"Native village, King's Island." Early view of summer stilt and winter stone houses, showing walrus-hide drying frames before most stilt houses (cf. fig. 110) and the steep hillside.

From Cantwell 1889b:82 ff.

FIGURE 110

Stilt houses on King Island, circa 1899–1900. Same view as in figure 109, but some fifteen years later. Summer and winter houses commingle on the much-trodden semiterraced slope; large panels facing the sea (before most stilt houses) are walrus hides being stretched on drying frames.

USRC Bear Collection, Accession #95-264-23N, Archives, Alaska and Polar Regions Dept., Rasmuson Library, University of Alaska Fairbanks.

FIGURE 111

"Natives of King Islands [*sic*]." Note the weight capacity of the dual-level gangway to this summer stilt house, and the stone walls of winter houses (background).

From Healy 1887:10 ff.

As was true for their transition-season dwellings, Northwest Arctic and Bering Strait Eskimos' summer options were sparse in most places except the Kobuk River. Mentioned above is the Kuuvaŋmiut domical bark-and-moss hut (ivrulik), a versatile shield against summer rains when indoor hearths were unnecessary. The Kuuvaŋmiut and Nunamiut frequently stayed in short-pole conical tents while trading at the coast (Ingstad 1954:39; Larsen 1958:577; Nelson 1899:261–262), where dome tents also appeared among the more common cone-shaped type. Lone Kuuvaŋmiut hunters sometimes set up a small, circular moss-covered structure shaped from willow hoops (Curtis 1907–1930:209).

According to Murdoch, Eskimos living south of Kotzebue Sound[25] spent their summers in above-ground houses (Murdoch 1892:84). The most southerly of the Northwest Arctic Eskimos had no tents, and relied instead on "driftwood tipi structures" (Staley 1985). Centering on Seward Peninsula, they occurred mainly around the bights of Kotzebue Sound and particularly Norton Sound, which was the Iñupiaq/Yup'ik borderland (Staley 1985:map). A wood tripod allowed people to add on driftwood until they had roughed out a tall cone (Nelson 1899:253); with enough overlapped wood poles, they would have been fairly waterproof (Staley 1985:5). An opening in the side became the entrance and at the back was an elevated sleeping platform. One large historic example measured seventeen feet (in outside diameter) by about ten feet high (Staley 1985:6). Apparently these short-term dwellings mainly housed seasonal fishers and marmot hunters (Ray 1984:289).

One Northwest Arctic (and probably Bering Strait) shelter might be regarded as a lean-to variant but not as a true dwelling type. During summertime, the Kuuvaŋmiut would sometimes prop up a bark canoe—not a true Eskimo kayak (fig. 99)—while other Eskimos would set an umiak on edge (figs. 113–114).[26] In either case, they leaned the boat on one or two oars, paddles, or on forked, standing willows about three to six feet long, with the keel facing into the wind (fig. 113). Then, people either covered the inboard (leeward) side with birch-bark slabs (Cantwell 1889a:opp 69; Giddings 1961:39) or with skins or tarps attached to the gunwales (fig. 113; Healey 1887:14 ff), or they left this windbreak otherwise unprotected (fig. 114; Nelson 1899:261; Stoney 1900:93).

SPECIAL-USE STRUCTURES

LESSER STRUCTURES

Mackenzie Eskimos built semicircular snowblock walls five feet tall as windbreaks at ice-fishing holes. Even without its erosive effect, the wind shifted enough so that fresh windbreaks had to be started daily. Returning to the same fishing hole, as long as it was productive, still made more sense than digging a new one through some thickness of solid ice (Stefánsson 1922:144). Mackenzie conical tents sometimes performed as springtime kitchens and enclosures for cleaning fish and beluga whales (McGhee 1974:22; Stefánsson

FIGURE 112

Walrus hides on drying rack lean against a hide-covered summer house, with winter houses nearby, on either King or Little Diomede Island, circa 1899–1900.

USRC Bear Collection, Accession #95-264-17N, Archives, Alaska and Polar Regions Dept., Rasmuson Library, University of Alaska Fairbanks.

FIGURE 113

"Esquimo camp at Port Clarence." Part of this umiak lean-to is open (left), while cloth drapes down over the midsection and fans out to the right. A kayak dries on the gravel beside a sealskin float (far left).

From Healy 1887:14 ff.

FIGURE 114

"Family of King Island Eskimos living under skin boat. Nome, Alaska [1904]." A long horizontal pole attached to uprights (top) upholds an awning framework made from modern-style oars. Trade goods abound (e.g., three rifles, an umiak model, a large tea kettle, a basketed bottle, enameled basin, and furs) and the people are clothed in a mix of traditional and imported materials.

Edith G. Fish Collection, Accession #73-202-20, Archives, Alaska and Polar Regions Dept., Rasmuson Library, University of Alaska Fairbanks.

1914:fig. 9). Reports from across the Arctic mention miniature tents set up for various purposes. Most come from the Northwest Arctic, where Eskimos used them for sewing, summer kitchens, housing orphans and old people, and for childbirth (Murdoch 1892:83, 86; Ray 1885:39, 46; Steensby 1910:fig. 18; Stefánsson 1914:328, 166).

North Alaska Coast Eskimos made snowblock structures for use as workshops. Some were either mere holes that women dug into snow for preparing sealskins or "small rude tents" for sewing caribou skins in autumn. Others included windows and were big enough to enclose women while they refitted umaiks with new skins (Murdoch 1892:83, 86). Seal hunters and fishers used snowblocks, and whale hunters iceblocks, as windbreaks (Murdoch 1892:270; Rainey 1947:259; Van Valin 1941:103).

Among the Kuuvaŋmiut another snowblock structure was used for ice fishing. In order to net fish through a river-ice hole, which lay over the bottleneck to a prebuilt spruce-bough fish weir, Kuuvaŋmiut men had to see the fish approach. Accordingly, they erected an enclosure that provided enough shadow to let them look into the river below and so drop their nets effectively over a good catch (Giddings 1956:31–32). These tents (Giddings 1961:133–134), or possibly another structure in earlier times, also made practical windbreaks during ice-fishing vigils.

Special-use structures are less diverse in the Northwest Arctic and Bering Strait region. One worth mentioning is the ever-present storage rack, usually positioned immediately behind every dwelling on the north or seaward side on the North Alaska coast (figs. 84–85, 88–89, 93–94, 97, 105). This outdoor scaffold consisted of four to eight vertical posts, generally eight to ten feet high. Walrus jaws, lashed high up, sometimes formed the crotches that held one or two levels of crossbeams (fig. 85). Umiaks, kayaks, sleds, and other gear would be stored here well above ground level to outwit the hungry dogs eager to make a meal of thongs and boat skins (Murdoch 1892:75; Simpson 1855:931).

At a spot near the scaffold, each Taġiuġmiut family could usually claim a supernumerary ice cache. This was an underground storeroom, framed and roofed with whale bones, in which permafrost kept meat and blubber freezer cold (Murdoch 1892:76). The Kuuvaŋmiut kept dried fish in "a store-house made of heavy pieces of timber stood on end and a flat roof made of small poles ... [and] a rude door ... " (Cantwell 1889b:81). Sources differ as to whether the Big Diomede Island Eskimos erected a scaffolding of whale bone posts and crosspieces (to support their watercraft) or built elevated, walrus-hide covered storehouses, which approximated their winter houses on stilts (Bogojavlensky 1969:103; Hawkes 1913a:379–382; Muir 1917:36, 121, 218; Nelson 1899:255–256; Sczawinski 1981).

BIRTH, MENSTRUAL, AND DEATH HUTS

The Western Arctic, subject of this chapter and the next, is where birth huts and menstrual huts achieved the greatest cultural prominence. As death huts were more widespread in the Central Arctic (chapter 2), we summarize these structures only briefly here, focusing more attention on birth and menstrual huts.[27]

FIGURE 115

(Opposite, top) "Eskimo grave, Hotham Inlet." At least ten feet high, this cone-shaped cluster of logs houses at least four skulls. Large horizontal logs (left) suggest a rudimentary platform within the structure.
From Cantwell 1889a:66 ff.

FIGURE 116

(Opposite, middle) "Point Hope. Esquimo graves." Taller timbers create a near-conical effect to the center burial; coffin platforms rest on whale mandible frames of others.
From Healy 1887:12 ff.

FIGURE 117

(Opposite, right) "Eskimo grave at Point Hope." Above-ground burial with mortise-and-tenon wooden coffin on a wood and whale mandible frame.
From Call 1899:126 ff.

Just before bearing a child, expectant Taġiuġmiut women would be isolated in a sudliwin. The period of childbirth included a ten-day postpartum seclusion in one of two cramped structures, depending on the season. In winter the hut was of snow but in summer it was tented (Murdoch 1892:86, 415; Van Valin 1941:212). While both structures differ, we treat them as one type because their design is dictated by their function.

Nunamiut women bore children within a "small willow frame covered with moss and snow." Informants knew of death huts, too, although these were definitely uncommon by the 1960s: "On rare occasions an old person, who knew he was going to die, built or had built a small hut so that his death would not affect the family house" (Gubser 1965:72). Thus, the Nunamiuts shared with most other Eskimos the inconvenient taboo against dying at home.

Remembering the Kuuvaŋmiut *miḷuq* as a short–term or travelers' shelter, it is disorienting to find the same word applied to their birth huts (Giddings 1956:16). Women moved to these structures for this purpose and they stayed there for a ritualized four-day postpartum seclusion. Winter birth huts were either small snow creations (Giddings 1961:21) or some other structure cloaked in snow. Again, the number of forms, one or two, does not outweigh the birth hut's ritual "decontamination" function. Pubescent Kuuvaŋmiut girls also confined themselves to these huts during menstruation and for the year following the onset of their menstrual periods (Giddings 1961:20–21). The Kuuvaŋmiut isolated a woman when menstruating, a state that made her *quhuq* (taboo) then; it was "something to be avoided at all cost," because she was in a state "as though she were dying or giving birth to a child" (Giddings 1956:16, 48).

BURIAL STRUCTURES

In different sections of the Northwest Arctic, various Eskimo groups had diverse options for housing and remembering the dead (e.g., Garber 1934). For example, people sometimes entombed their dead in conical structures made of logs (fig. 115). These burial cones, or nuiqsaq, occurred around Seward Peninsula, between the bights of Kotzebue and Norton Sounds. They are so similar to the local summertime "driftwood tipis" (Staley 1985:1) that it is tempting to interpret those used for the dead as symbolic reminders of the relatively carefree summer life of the living. Before placement in the wooden tepee, the deceased was removed from his or her house through a special exit, a round hole punched in the dwelling's rear wall (cf. Petitot 1970:169, 207 on the Mackenzie Delta custom). Once inside this tepee, the body was placed on a raised platform (fig. 115). From the poles, people hung personal effects of the dead person (Beechey 1831:457; Staley 1985). Similarly, Point Hope villagers erected for the dead a tall cone or parallel rows of timbers or whale half-mandibles (figs. 116–117). Near the top, in either configuration of uprights, they constructed platforms upon which rested the rough-hewn coffin.

A century ago, Father Edward Devine witnessed events preceding and following the death and burial, on a wooden scaffold, of an old Eskimo man from Kotzebue Sound (fig. 118).

FIGURE 118

FIGURE 118

"Eskimo graves on the Arctic coast." Probably the same elevated grave Devine refers to, which would be near Keewalik, on Kotzebue Sound. Cloth covers a presumed wooden coffin on the platform (right); grave goods include a tapered pole (harpoon shaft?) leaning against the coffin, a possible box or satchel (near right post), and a rifle hanging from the platform's back edge.

From DeVine 1905:266 ff.

An Eskimo was dying of pneumonia at Keewalik; I found him on a bearskin in his igloo and burning with fever. His wife and four children were sitting beside him, silent and immoveable (*sic*), and unable to help him.... [He] died a few hours later, and the family abandoned the igloo [forever], leaving everything behind them. The grief of his little children, who appeared to realize vividly all they had lost, was one of the saddest sights I ever witnessed. Great tears rolled down their cheeks, and they sobbed as though their little hearts could break.

The [men] constructed a rude coffin of boards and canvas.... The coffin was raised to its four posts, six feet above the ground, and the dead man's hunting-knife and rifle were hung alongside. But it was a sad commentary on our white civilization to see the friends of the Eskimo breaking the trigger of the rifle before they hung it up on the post. They knew by experience that the weapon would soon be stolen by white men, if it were worth having. (Devine 1905:255–257)

CEREMONIAL HOUSES

The Western Arctic is also the region in which the men's ceremonial house reached its zenith. At one time the ceremonial house (qargi)[28] was common to most Eskimos (see Taylor 1990:52–53 for a summary of its distribution), yet the qargi/qasgiq assumed its most elaborated form in the Alaskan Arctic, where it housed males and served as "the church, the townhouse, workshop, and entertainment center, all in one" (Senungetuk 1971:51). According to Murdoch, the literal meaning of the word is "circle of hills around a deep valley," used in this case to signify a "circle of people who sit close together" (Murdoch 1892:79). There could be several men's houses simultaneously in any sizable community, and at least one on King Island survived into the early 1900s (Renner 1979:127).

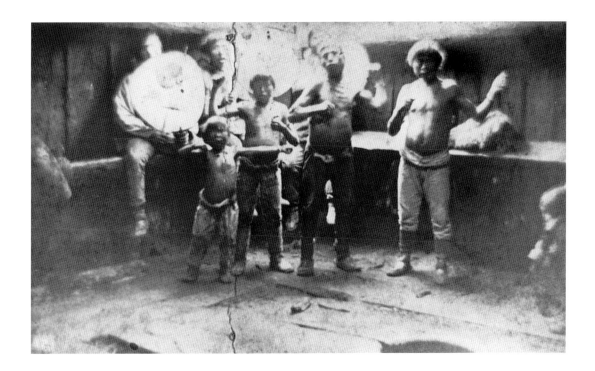

FIGURE 119

Four boys practice dance moves in unison (note similar positions of right arms) in a well-lit *qargi* around Cape Prince of Wales, circa 1892–1902, as three men demonstrate the size and handling of the large Eskimo tambourine drum. Note the floor entry, or *katak* (lower right).

Ellen Kittredge Lopp Collection; courtesy of Kathleen Lopp Smith.

Owned by males of an extended kin group, *qargi*s were the focal point of village life. The community (or a kin group, if there were more than one in a village) built and maintained the structures, which could be large enough to accommodate the entire village and any visitors. The roof of a *qargi* usually was higher than that of dwellings and, in most places, the square smoke-hole could function as a second door, especially during ceremonies. Instead of sleeping platforms, benches stretched around two to all four walls of the structure.

Qargi sizes varied, but some could be huge compared to houses (figs. 120–121). One *qargi* at Cape Prince of Wales was square, about twenty-four feet on a side, and reached by a covered entrance forty feet long (Wickersham 1902:223). On relatively unpopulated Little Diomede Island, *qargi*s reportedly measured a mere thirteen feet square (fig. 97; Sczawinski 1981:19). However, "when one considers the toil and pain with which [wood] is gathered, the building of a *kásgi* becomes an important matter" (Hawkes 1914:13), even if the finished structure was small. The King Island *qargi* was made like the stone winter house, although people used it year round (Bogojavlensky 1969). Even the Nunamiut constructed *qargi*s: more recently they pitched a large tent but formerly they had structures akin to their old-time pole-and-turf houses (Gubser 1965:168; Larsen 1958:577; Stoney 1900:72).

Kuuvaŋmiut men might spend most waking hours in *qargi*s, but they established them only if their village was going to host a trade festival (Giddings 1961:24–25). Still, Northwest Arctic and Bering Strait Eskimo men and older boys used *qargi*s as ceremonial "assembly halls" for the community and as male-only "club houses" for more routine activities. The men and boys generally remained therein all day long, except in winter (Murdoch 1892:80),

"Indian [actually, Eskimo] *keshagem* (Dance-house)." Probably an impromptu structure, this North Alaska coast *qargi* consists mostly of unmodified driftwood; the roof might be cloth. Three people inside provide scale (cf. fig. 121).

From Cantwell 1889a:84 ff.

usually returning to their homes only to sleep. In the *qargi* they chatted, lounged, taught the younger males, made and repaired tools, weapons, and so forth; they even took their meals there (fig. 119). The *qargi's* socializing benefit to boys (i.e., learning customs and crafts from their elders) has not been forgotten by today's descendants in Barrow, where a move is afoot to re-establish *qargi*s as a conceptual tool for teaching male—and female—children about traditional culture.

Southwest arctic groups, the subject of the next chapter, went a step further, virtually living in the *qasgiq*. Not surprisingly, then, the presence of a *qargi/qasgiq* was so intrinsic to the Western Eskimo conception of cultural space that Eskimos frequently resorted to improvised substitutes. As a case in point, Cantwell shows a large makeshift *qargi* seen around 1884 at Icy Cape (figs. 120–121). Its span was at least seven by thirty feet and its pitched roof was about seven feet high in the middle. Skins or cloth covered both end walls and the rafters but left the side walls were mostly exposed. At about the same time, a temporary *qargi* near Icy Cape (the same structure?) was said to have eighty caribou skins invested in its "tent cover" (Lantis 1947:105n134).

MACKENZIE DELTA

Mackenzie Eskimos used their *qargi* in the warmer months only, and the structures were probably less durable than the Taġiuġmiut type (McGhee 1974:22). Richardson (1852:155) describes Mackenzie Eskimo qargis as having an outer wall of beluga whale skulls and a beluga-skin doorflap. These construction materials attest to how economically pivotal whales were to this society. While Mackenzie houses were heated by lamp, their *qargi* contained a hearth for this purpose, along with a big smokehole above. *Qargi* abandon-

FIGURE 121

"Natives at rendezvous near Icy Cape, Alaska." The same *qargi* as in fig. 120, with its presumed celebrants.
From Cantwell 1889a:64 ff.

ment in deepest winter coincides with the time when this heat source and the structure's seeming openness made it too cold to use (Stefánsson 1914:136). Considering its implied size (fifty to sixty feet on a side, a good ten to eleven feet high in the middle, and at least six feet high behind its wall-skirting benches), the amount of fuel consumed—even with driftwood available—must have been astronomical as winter approached.

In 1829, Sir John Franklin saw a *qargi* tent—large enough to hold forty people—west of the Mackenzie Delta (King 1836:vol. 2, 122). It may be, too, that Mackenzie Eskimos more recently started putting together a snowblock *qargi* for certain occasions. This would explain Rasmussen's journal reference to a similar structure[29] in a sea-ice village: "Farewell feast for us. Large dance-house, built on our arrival" (Ostermann 1942:17).

NORTH ALASKA COAST

Few specifics have been recorded about the Taġiuġmiut *qargi* (also transcribed in the literature as *karigi, kudrigi, kudyigi, qalegi*). Its gable roof sloped uniformly in both directions but lacked a turf covering. The interior consisted of upright plank walls bordered by three or four benches. Two large examples around Point Barrow averaged fifteen feet wide by nineteen feet long, the bigger of which was seven feet high in its center and held sixty celebrants (Murdoch 1892:80; Simpson 1855:933). The one known archaeological *qargi* from Barrow used mainly bowhead whale bones as structural members (another allusion to the centrality of whaling). It showed no signs of a tunnel (cf. Simpson 1855:933) or even a passage of any length, but it was turf-covered [Sheehan (1990)]. Unlike the Mackenzie Eskimo qargis, Taġiuġmiut examples were used in winter—at least during ceremonies (Murdoch 1892).

Taġiuġmiut communities often consisted of several extended families and/or whaling crews. These larger Taġiuġmiut villages often had several ceremonial houses. For example, the village of Point Hope had at least seven open at one time in the nineteenth century (Rainey 1947:244). During the whaling season, while men were camped on the ice, an improvised substitute for the *qargi* appeared in the open area at the center of their on-shore whaling camp. This extemporized *qargi* consisted of a square hole dug in the ground, as well as four timbers (for benches) lining its sides (Murdoch 1892:80; Simpson 1855:933). As late as 1900, another men's house at Barrow had walls of upright logs that were five feet high and roof supports that were seven to eight feet long (Stefánsson 1914:189).

NORTH ALASKA INTERIOR

Gubser (1965:168) treats the Nunamiut qargi as "merely an enlarged caribou skin tent, a temporary edifice" and Ingstad (1954:38) points out that, merely by spreading willow poles farther between their ground insertion points, domed tents could be enlarged sufficiently to house "sixty people at a pinch." More consistent with Stoney's (1900:72) record, Larsen (1958:577) reports the Nunamiut structure somewhat differently. In this second version a qargi consisted of tripods at four corners, connected by stringers against which people leaned willow pole studs at intervals. Sometimes a centerpost replaced horizontal rafters, but in either case this quadrangular skeleton was fur covered.

FIGURE 122

Man sitting on the floor of a probable *qargi*, with broad floor boards and at least one tier of raised bench behind him (upper right); he wears a fancy split-glass-bead-on-white-stone labret (cheek plug) below his mouth and holds a Siberian-style tobacco pipe.

Lomen Family Collection, Accession #72-71-2917, Archives, Alaska and Polar Regions Dept., Rasmuson Library, University of Alaska Fairbanks.

112

The men's house was a cooperative effort shared by several related families, and each household provided a few furs. A Nunamiut *qargi* was occupied daily from dawn (Gubser 1965:168), housing men while they ate and worked during the day, and the general community during dances at night (Larsen 1958:577; Stoney 1900:72), but in the 1960s its utility lessened to the carrying out of public events held "four or five times a year" (Gubser 1965:172).

KOBUK RIVER

The Kuuvaŋmiut seem to have lacked "any very elaborate festal or ceremonial rites" (Cantwell (1889b:89). They did, however, erect a qargi if the community was hosting a trade fair, as occasionally happened. If so, throughout the preceding winter the men and older boys not out hunting would spend their waking hours working and socializing in this building (Giddings 1961:24)

Oddly, Kuuvaŋmiut men constructed their *qargi* away from the village. Its basic design, a bridged pair of high central posts as well as four corner uprights and a moss-coated (then earth-layered) roof of poles, resembled summer houses more than winter ones. The doorway, which had no tunnel, was covered by a bear skin.[30] Inside, a centralized smokehole penetrated the roof above a wood- or stone-framed hearth. Poles paved only the middle, while drummers' and guests' benches lined all four walls. Giddings presents conflicting data on whether lamps or fireplaces heated the Kuuvaŋmiut *qargi* (Giddings 1956:45; 1961:24).

ASSOCIATED RITUALS AND BELIEFS

THERE ARE CONTRADICTORY REPORTS ABOUT OTHER DEATH-RELATED BELIEFS associated with houses. Mackenzie Eskimos, for instance, abandoned their houses when an occupant died. Similarly, the Kuuvaŋmiut considered it "unlucky to return to the same house, even though one might set up another in the same neighborhood" (Giddings 1952:11). Furthermore,

> the house must be rebuilt each year. This is not because the old one is uninhabitable, but . . . [because of] the well being of people and the animals they hunt. A former house is like an old shell of one's self. . . . The house itself is evacuated with care. Each member of the family searches closely for personal items that may have been dropped inside—hair clippings, bits of torn clothing, even willow beds must be removed and thrown out upon the ice of the river to be carried away in the spring flood. If any personal thing is left behind in the winter house it will be sure to bring bad luck. (Giddings 1956:28, 47)

Nevertheless, the Kuuvaŋmiut were not averse to robbing last year's house for this year's lumber. "No particular harm can come from using old material . . . [as long as] the old house is avoided as a unit" (Giddings 1956:28).

Another set of house-linked beliefs concerns the Taġiuġmiut:

> When returning to his winter hut after the summer season, the [Point Barrow] native goes about cutting a small chip off every piece of timber and

board that can be reached easily.[31] The significance of this is probably to break whatever spell the devil may have cast over the abode during the absence of its occupants. When deserted in the spring, the window is broken in, the entrance-way blocked up, and rubbish thrown in, to give it the appearance of having been abandoned, probably to throw the devil off the scent. (Aldrich 1889:154)

Although Aldrich's notion of "the devil" might be imprecise (perhaps "malevolent spirits" would be more accurate), some sort of customary, formalized abandonment-and-reoccupation rituals—no doubt taboo-related—was in effect in northern Alaska, at least in the later 1880s.

The literature records many other house-associated beliefs, rituals, and stories. Among Point Barrow Eskimos, for example, part of the celestial constellation Cassiopeia "is called the 'house-building' and represents a few people engaged in constructing an iglu, or winter hut" (Simpson 1855:940) or "'the house builder' from some fancied resemblance to a man in a working attitude" (Bockstoce 1988:351). However, MacDonald agrees with a more recent analysis that the Native name for the same star grouping "might refer to the instrument [a triangular-bladed tool used to cut sod blocks] for making houses . . . [rather] than to a person building a house" (MacDonald 1998:63). The Taġiuġmiut also spoke of "a land named *Ig'-lu*, far away to the north or north-east of Point Barrow. The story is, that several men, who were carried away in the olden time by the ice breaking under the influences of a southerly wind, after many sleeps arrived in a hilly country inhabited by a people like themselves who spoke the same language" (Simpson 1855:939). A Nunamiut story "tells of the two old women who dragged their turf house and some of the frozen ground under it across the tundra" (Ingstad 1954:183). Residents of Diomede Island "produced a string-game figure described as 'Siberian House = *kochlinee*'" that is vaguely reminiscent of the new-style Siberian winter dwellings discussed in chapter 4 (Gordon 1906:fig. 22).

Ritual associations between people, the animals they depended on, and the houses they lived in were also important in the cosmology of the Mackenzie Delta and northern Alaska. Thus, in an area where whales provided more than half a winter's food supply (Bockstoce 1980; Sheehan 1985), it is not surprising to find that whale imagery was incorporated into many domains of culture, including the architectural context. To illustrate, one MacKenzie Eskimo *qargi* was "supported by whale-skulls built round its outside wall" (Richardson 1852:155). Around Barrow, moreover, *qargis* were placed on the highest ground, securing the best vantage point from which to scan the ocean for bowhead whales (Simpson 1855:933). Taġiuġmiut men reportedly entered at least one *qargi* through a roof-hole rather than the tunnel (Simpson 1855:933). It is possible that this unusual entrace symbolically reiterated the all-important spout of water that indicated, to the whale-hunting Taġiuġmiut, the presence and location of bowhead whales. In addition, an archaeological structure at Barrow, interpreted by archaeologists as a *qargi*, included far more bowhead bones than were found in nearby wooden houses. These included a skull, scapulae apparently used as backrests, as well as both an atlas (first neck vertebra) and some fluke-end vertebrae, bones that symbolically span the whale's length (Sheehan 1990:240–286). Near the tip of Seward Peninsula, one turn-of-the-last-century *qargi* incorporated walrus skulls into its walls, acknowledging that species' local economic value (fig. 123).

Finally, *qargis* were the focus of community life in winter (Hawkes 1913b). Here the social status of community members could be discerned by the places they occupied on the benches that bordered the inside walls. The end opposite the doorway was warmest and reserved for the most powerful members of the community (Hawkes 1914:14). At the southeastern limit of northwestern Eskimo territory, Jacobsen points out that status differences in the community were replicated in the seating order in a *qargi*, which had three tiers of benches: "On the bottom row against the walls the Eskimo women were seated; the second row was for the adult men and guests of honor, where we were taken. On the top row above us were the chattering children and young boys and girls" (Jacobsen 1977:134).

At Cape Prince of Wales the door frames of the *qargi* sometimes were decorated with flat pieces of ivory (Wickersham 1902:223). Thornton describes an "annual housewarming" in autumn (*awahpahlazieruktuk*), which seems much like the Greenlandic tent-to-house transition ceremony noted in chapter 1 (Kaalund 1983:54). The more elaborate Alaska ceremony involved masked boys who assembled outside and growled in imitation of "invisible spirits" of animals that the occupants wanted to propitiate during the coming winter. They entered the house and devoured food, only to be dismissed by the head of the household (Thornton 1931:226).

FIGURE 123

A boy and girl look down from the wall of a presumed flat-roofed *qargi*, built of stone and turf and integrated with walrus skulls, circa 1892 to 1902. Note scaffolds, left, and use of roof timber (left foreground) to suspend nets and lines for repair and/or drying.

Ellen Kittredge Lopp collection; courtesy of Kathleen Lopp Smith.

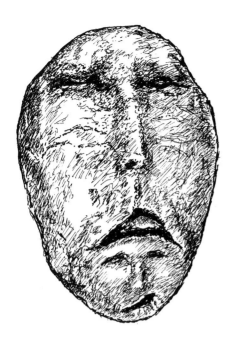

FIGURE 124

Top of a wooden mallet from a *qargi* entrance, Little Diomede Island, collected by Diamond Jenness circa 1926. Note a second face below the open mouth and tongue of the larger face.

Catalog no. IX-F-9658, courtesy of Museum of Civilization, Ottawa; 4.5 in. (11 cm) long; drawn by Stoney Harby.

During autumn whaling ceremonies, the walls and ceilings of Point Hope men's houses were hung with carvings (Rainey 1947:247). On Little Diomede Island, Diamond Jenness collected a broken wooden mallet with two faces (one in the chin of the other) carved on its top; it was "attached to wall of medicine man's house and food offered to it" (fig. 124; Morrison 1991:71, fig. 27e). Another piece he acquired was a wooden mask of a man, done in typical Northwest Alaskan Eskimo style, that was said to have been "hung in dancehouse as the guardian of house" (Morrison 1991:93, fig. 33).

CHAPTER 3 NOTES

1   The sparsely populated coastline between the Mackenzie River drainage and the vicinity of Point Barrow is atypical of mainland Eskimo settlement patterns.

2   These rectangular houseplan variants also carry over into areas described in chapter 4.

3   Smith (1984:349) disagrees, stating that one family occupied each sleeping platform. Six families per house does seem large.

4   These doorway options recall Taġiuġmiut floor holes (see North Alaska Coast Houses) and may have originated from that source.

5   Having this trapdoor in position would explain why Richardson (1852:206–207) regarded the houses as windowless.

6   In summer, tunnels (the only way in and out of the house) filled with water as the permafrost thawed and the snow melted.

7   Murdoch (1892:fig. 9) suggests that houses were greater in width than length, but this seems incorrect more often than not. An archaeologically excavated house from Barrow measures seventeen feet wide by twelve feet front to back and another, seven by twelve feet (Ford 1959:67–73). However, five other archaeological examples from the same site averaged closer to six by nine feet (Reinhardt and Dekin 1990:table 4-1). Three from the Pingasagruk site are of similar size (six by nine feet) and, like most Barrow ones, are longer than they are wide (Reinhardt, unpublished field notes). Spencer's deceptively *round* house floor (1959:fig. 1), which he subsequently describes in terms of "diameter" (Spencer 1984b:327, cf. 1984a:fig. 3), continues to mislead others (e.g., Hunter-Anderson 1977:313; Murdock 1967:60).

8   Copper Eskimos were the main suppliers of these lamps. Pottery lamps were also made of locally available clay in the Point Barrow region. For a full discussion see Spencer (1959:470–474).

9   Simpson (1855:931) mentions even warmer conditions, "seldom below 70 [degrees F]."

10 Our reconstructions of the Nunamiut winter dwelling disregard Spencer's description, which include window(s) fixed in the passage walls. These seem otherwise unverified, as is his suggestion that lamps alone provided heat for the turf dwelling (Spencer 1959:47).

11 These movements intimate some settlement pattern shift during the last few centuries, possibly in response to transportation mode. Archaeological evidence (Corbin 1976) points to more annual mobility, and a transition from foot travel to using dogsleds. Apparently, the same shift affected the Nunamiut, as well.

12 See note 13, chapter 1, for an explanation of the varied Eskimo spellings of the ceremonial house.

13 According to Richardson, the move was in March to coincide with seal hunting (Richardson 1852:207).

14 The basic form seems to have been aboriginal, although we have found no mention of it in the literature before Stefánsson described a canvas-covered version (Stefánsson 1922:112–113).

15 Oviously these short-term dwellings were not so well sealed outside or heat-glazed inside that they prevented fresh air from entering. Otherwise, the inhabitants would have suffocated.

16 All three dwellings were also used by the Nunamiut, the "caribou-hunting Eskimos" (Stefánsson 1922:95, 152, 173). By the 1920s, "a number of natives from Alaska" were trapping foxes and living in the Mackenzie Delta (Ostermann 1942:18).

17 To further complicate Alaskan snowhouse taxonomy, one of George Stoney's officers (Howard) describes finding houses with snowblock walls and roofs reminiscent of the Taġiuġmiut type somewhere in the mountains in neighboring Kuuvaŋmiut (Kobuk River) or Noatagmiut (Noatak River) Eskimo territory, immediately south and west of the Nunamiut. This type was dome-like, its "roof formed by overlapping the higher layers" (Stoney 1900:67).

18 The people here began their winter dwellings by "plaiting mountain willow to form a frame." Thus, it might be that Stoney (1900:46) is describing the Kuuvaŋmiut domed tent (or even a Nunamiut version).

19 In a large settlement upriver from the Delta, Petitot recorded "big tents" that averaged twelve inhabitants each (1970:136). Possibly, these were larger than normal.

20 For the Kuuvaŋmiut, Giddings (1961:127) also mentions a "quick tent" involving skin-covered "tipi of poles," known as an *auwayyuk*.

21 Coverings were variously of skin, moss and snow, or bark, as noted for in the section Kuuvaŋmiut Transitional Dwellings above, but we focus here on the Nunamiut skin variety.

22 By the early twentieth century, after diseases decimated the north Alaska coast population, north Alaska interior Eskimos emigrated to the coast. Thus, it would not be surprising that they took their dome tent design with them.

23 According to Corbin (1976:151–153) indoor hearths were absent from Nunamiut tents, but archaeological evidence points unquestionably to the presence of hearths in two tent rings from the ethnographic era (Hall 1976:118–120, 128–129).

24 Spencer (1958:473) says these vessels were made on the coast and imported.

25 Alternatively, Ray cites Cape Nome (on the southern, or Norton Sound side, of this peninsula) as the terminus (Ray 1975:130).

26 Farther south Alutiiq travelers almost identically propped up their umiaks for use as windbreaks and traveling shelters (see chapter 4).

27 Among the Western Eskimos the only people for whom we found no reports of birth huts are the Mackenzie Delta groups or those immediately to the east of them. Some Central and Eastern Eskimos, such as Copper Eskimos (Jenness 1922:164n2) and the Ammassalik (Holm 1914:62), specifically denied that they ever segregated full-term pregnant women. Perhaps the birth hut was more widely distributed in earlier times, however.

28 See note 13, chapter 1, for an explanation of the varied Eskimo spellings of the ceremonial house.

29 These particular snowblock *qargi* builders were immigrants from Victoria Island, which is well within Copper Eskimo territory. That would mark the design as a Central Arctic creation.

30 A 300-year-old *qargi*-like structure unearthed near the mouth of the Kobuk River did have a tunnel (Giddings 1952:20, 22–23).

31 Similarly, the Taġiuġmiut refreshed their existing sea mammal hunting equipment each year by shaving a thin layer from all wooden parts.

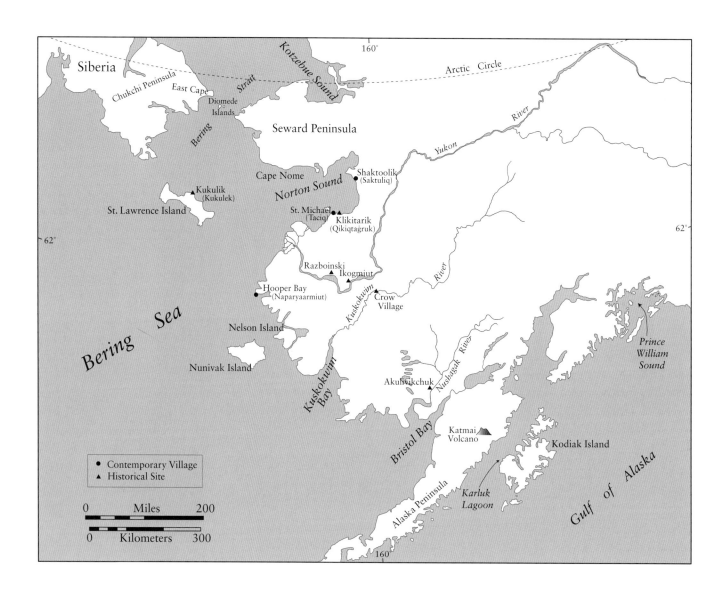

Map of southwest Alaska, Bering Sea,
Siberia, and Gulf of Alaska.

Produced by Robert Drozda.

4

SOUTHWEST ALASKA, BERING SEA, SIBERIA, AND GULF OF ALASKA

The [Alutiiq] barabara answers

the purpose of a court-yard, kitchen,

and, when requisite, a theatre.

(Lisiansky 1814:213)

STRETCHING FROM BERING STRAIT TO THE GULF OF ALASKA, THIS architecturally diverse zone includes Yup'ik-speaking groups on the Alaska and Siberia mainlands and across the major Eskimo-occupied islands, including Saint Lawrence, Nunivak, and Kodiak. Eskimos here had the highest regional population, exceeding 20,000 (Oswalt 1979:314ff), and were the most ecologically and culturally diverse.

On the North American side of the Bering Sea, driftwood was more available and the climate less extreme than farther north and east in the Arctic; many Central Yup'ik groups (plural Yupiit) from Norton Sound to Bristol Bay lived in more or less permanent settlements all year long. The Alutiiq-speaking Pacific Yupiit, southernmost of all Eskimos, lived around the Alaska Peninsula, Kodiak Island, and Prince William Sound in foggier climes. However, warmer seas and weather in the Gulf of Alaska, abundant trees for building materials, and more reliably plentiful food resources compensated for the weather. Toward the northern end of Bering Strait, homeland of the Siberian Yupik,[1] Saint Lawrence Island and the eastern fringes of Siberia's Chukchi Peninsula offered comparatively harsher environments.

WINTER HOUSES

THE CENTRAL YUPIIT (SOUTHWEST ALASKA) CHALLENGE THE GENERAL NOTION of Eskimo dwellings because these groups divided their housing virtually along gender lines. In this area, the *qasgiq* was a community ceremonial building at certain times of the year, but men and older boys also stayed in the *qasgiq* virtually all the time. That is, they normally lived there rather than in smaller family houses, which were inhabited by women, girls, and younger boys. At least among the Nelson Island Eskimos, where boys as young as five moved into the *qasgiq*, the female-focused dwellings (*ena*) were called "sod houses" or even "women's houses" (Ann Fienup-Riordan, personal communication 1999). For these reasons we break from the format of previous chapters by describing men's houses in this section (rather than in Special-Use Structures).

MAINLAND AND INSULAR ALASKA MEN'S AND WOMEN'S HOUSES

East of Bering Strait, Cape Nome is at the southern edge of the range of Iñupiaq-speaking Eskimos and of summer tents used during historic times. Yup'ik-speaking Eskimos south of there lived in their semisubterranean sod-covered winter houses all year long (Ray 1975:130). The southwestern winter house found along the mainland coast and inland was essentially a variant of north Alaska coast houses.

NORTON SOUND YEAR ROUND WOODEN HOUSE

Figure 126 depicts a composite of design variants that typify the northern Central Yup'ik area. It represents the Unaligmiut, or Unaleet, dwelling found around Saint Michael (Nelson 1899:fig. 74; Ray 1966:32, 47–51, 53), as well as another type from the opposite (north) shore of Norton Sound.[2] One design had neither antechamber nor second platform, but both a tunnel and a passage (fig. 126; Nelson 1899:fig. 74). Its occurrence toward the northwest edge of Unaligmiut territory insinuates some transitional form drawing partly on the Kauwerak (Northwest Arctic) Eskimo type (cf. Nelson 1899:253–255). Another Unaligmiut design had an antechamber, near-surface passage or tunnel, and two tiers of sleeping platform (fig. 127). The Unaligmiut lived in their tunnel-and-passage house (*ini*) throughout the year (Nelson 1899:243), and inhabited their alternative dwellings at times, at the least from October to June (Ray 1984:287, 289).

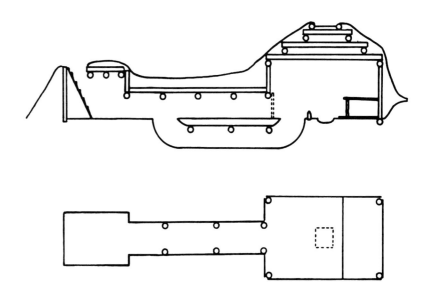

FIGURE 126

Composite of idealized Norton Sound year-round wooden house, showing both forms of entry.

After Dall 1870:fig. on p. 13; Nelson 1899:figs. 74, 80–81.

Unaligmiut house construction differed from that of many Eskimos. For instance, ends of wall planks might be dovetailed to fit snugly into mortised corner uprights (about ten to fourteen feet long). This technique ssuggest historic-era Russian influence (Wendell H. Oswalt, personal communication with Gregory Reinhardt, 1985), or at least reflects more labor and technical detail than ocurs in most Eskimo house construction. In another deviation from more northern Eskimo building methods, the walls consisted of logs or planks laid horizontally, not set on end.[3]

Unaligmiut men dug the housepit some two to four feet deep, then built the whole house themselves. By 1900, floors were usually planked (Ray 1966:47), but some three decades earlier, evidently before planked floors, houses lacked sleeping platforms. In this case, people covered the bare earth with grass or spruce, then carpeted it with twined grass mats, dividing the floor lengthwise into thirds by laying down two presumably parallel logs (Dall 1870:14). Most floors were rectangular but some had oblong or hexagonal outlines (Ray 1966:47). Typically, houses at Saint Michael rose eight to nine feet in the center and stood five feet at the walls (Nelson 1899:243). Floor dimensions ranged from seven feet to between twelve and fifteen feet square (Dall 1870:13; Jacobsen 1977:125; Michael 1967:115).

In some Norton Sound houses people came up onto the floor by means of a subterranean tunnel, whereas others members of the group entered through a higher, ground-level covered passageway that breached the front wall (figs. 126–127). Tunnel crawlways emerged either at the middle or in the anterior section of a house floor. Still other builders chose to incorporate both sorts of entryway (fig. 126). In such cases, surface passages would be sealed in winter, obliging occupants to rely solely on the cramped tunnel and to emerge from it face-first before the fireplace. To block the inevitable breezes caused by daily traffic through the door, residents hung bear or caribou pelts or grass mats from the tops of doorways. They also placed stone slabs on end before the hearth (figs. 126–127), which further deflected drafts that would otherwise make sparks and cinders blow about the room. People often dug small sleeping chambers or storerooms into the tunnel's sides. Along the coast, where invasions of Siberian and insular Eskimos posed severe threats, villagers might

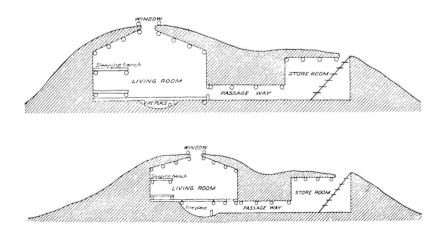

FIGURE 127

"Section of house[s] at Ignituk." Top contains a surface passage (leading to a doorway in the front wall), two levels of sleeping platform, and a hearth in the central floor. Bottom encloses a submerged tunnel (leading to a hole in the floor), two levels of sleeping platform, and a hearth under removable floorboards. *From Nelson 1899:figs. 80–81.*

FIGURE 128

A superbly carved wooden *qasgiq* model (lower Yukon River) illustrates the use of two black saucer-shaped lamps, which rest on tapering posts set into floorboards near the left and right centers of the bench. The small wooden "slat" rising from each lamp represents a flame to light the room. All but one man on the benches is nude, indicating great warmth indoors, while the central floor-hole boards cover a now-extinguished hearth beneath. Four shirtless men and a fully clothed woman present the "ritually correct configuration—four corners and a center" (Fienup-Riordan 1996:200) of five dancers, who move to the rhythm of four drummers.

Courtesy of Sheldon Jackson Museum, Sitka, catalog # II-H-46.

stockade their winter houses and fortify the outside entrances to passage or tunnel by adding a wood-lined shed (Murdoch 1892:78). A notched log served as a ladder, allowing access to the outside via a hatch in the ceiling of the small main room.[4]

For heating and cooking, Norton Sound houses always included a central fireplace, from which residents could remove floor planks (if any were there to begin with) when they wanted to stoke a bigger fire (fig. 127). Shallow, saucer-shaped pottery lamps, about eight inches in diameter, contributed light from flat-topped posts whose opposite, pointed ends people embedded into or through the floor near the corners of their sleeping platforms (figs. 128, 135, endpages).

The most impressive of the north-shore Norton Sound houses were those with two-tiered sleeping platforms, with the lower one barely clearing the floor and neither evidently allowing much headroom (fig. 127). Platforms either stretched across the back wall or skirted both lateral walls; some lower platforms were about eighteen inches off the floor. Grass mats partitioned platforms into family cubicles, even though the room was not particularly large. Inhabitants stored their possessions underneath platforms and along the front main-chamber wall. Occasionally, extra storage or sleeping cham-

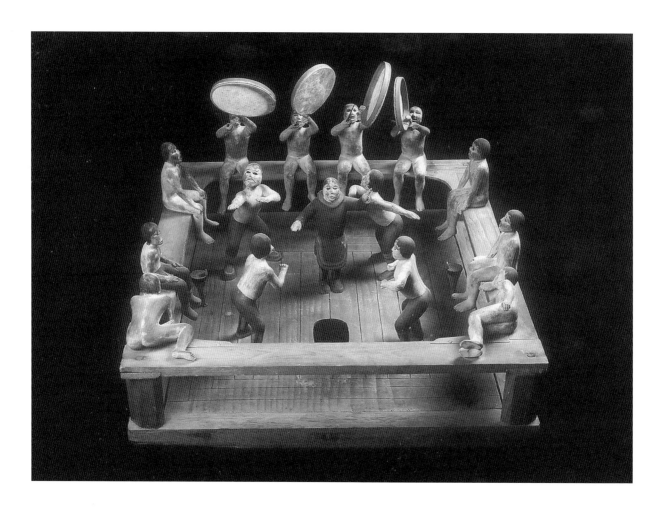

bers were installed midway along house passages (cf. fig. 96). Some houses lacked platforms per se although people slept on a wood floor (Dall 1870:14; Jacobsen 1977:126).

Overhead, a flat crib roof of logs narrowed to a square smokehole in its center. This opening acted as another doorway to and from the house. An unmounted seal-gut or sea mammal or fish-skin skylight (generally weighted down) closed off the opening, except when smoke accumulated inside, in which case someone would push it ajar. To keep the roof's earthen envelope from dropping into the house, planks or poles filled any gaping spaces between the cribwork timbers. Sea captain Adrian Jacobsen tells of watching as one family tried to reduce the smoke level after a meal: They tossed out the burning firebrands through the smokehole (sensible only in winter), where the embers should have fizzled out in the snow. This time, however, they surprisingly set the roof sods on fire (Jacobsen 1977:124).

In his turn-of-the-century description of Unaligmiut culture, Edmonds reacted to household conditions in less than glowing terms:

> The houses of the Eskimos being provided with such small entrances and apertures in the roof for light, are easily kept warm by a small fire. Often, however, the occupants stay inside when the skin covering is removed from the roof hole, and the air inside, unwarmed by any fire, is damp, raw and extremely chilly. If the opening is closed and a fire started, the houses soon become close and evil smelling, the eyes suffer from the smoke from the fireplace, and the tobacco used by everyone; everything is black and sticky and there is a general creepy sensation. (Ray 1966:53)

Despite these seeming discomforts, people used the same houses for years or even generations, and, in Eskimo fashion, typically moved out either to build a new one or because someone had died within. Abandoned houses, except in the case of death, were a handy source of village firewood and undoubtedly supplied lumber for other constructions (Ray 1966:49, 52).

NUNIVAK ISLAND YEAR-ROUND WOODEN HOUSES

Connected Houses—It may be that this house form (VanStone 1989:21–22, figs. 59–65) was the principal type on Nunivak Island (a Cup'ik-speaking area); in any case, it differs notably from another model described below. Some Nunivaarmiut villages had layouts apparently unique among Eskimos. Each house had its own tunnel doorway. However, what makes Nunivaarmiut communities so noteworthy is the individual tunnels that fed into a shared underground channel (fig. 129), which connected all the houses to each other and to the *qasgiq* (Fienup-Riordan 2000:108, top; Himmelheber 1980:6). For an entire community, then, there might be only one entryway into this complex. Pratt refers to archaeological examples of these communities as "depression complexes" (U.S. Bureau of Indian Affairs ANCSA 1995:1:41–42). Type A complexes have a linear tunnel to which housepits are attached; in Type B complexes, housepits connect spokelike, via individual tunnels, to a central point or pit. A surface doorway led to the main *qasgiq* tunnel, while lesser conduits fed off toward individual houses. A large whale scapula acted as a door cover—not doorway frame—to this entryway (James W. VanStone, personal communication with Gregory Reinhardt, 1991).

Once dug, Nunivaarmiut housefloors were as much as four to five feet deep, depending on the height of the walls. Rectangular in shape, the floor led to a tunnel cut into one of the narrow end-walls. A short pair of standing logs upheld another log lintel, which framed the doorway. A different source (Fienup-Riordan 2000:109) indicates that houses could have two entrances, one through the front wall (for summer), the other through a floor hole toward the front of the main room (for winter), and both originating from a single tunnel to the outside (cf. figs. 126–127). Sleeping platforms consisted of split logs placed on earth banks, about fifteen inches high, around two or three sides of the room. In some houses there were no platforms. Instead, the builders opted for a log to delimit each sleeping area and they filled the space between log and wall with dried beach grass.

The Nunivaarmiut house framework began with four center posts, arranged in a rectangle. Onto these the builders placed a pair of rafters that paralleled the room's long axis. A crib roof followed: First a pair of crossbeams to span the rafters (but set inward from the rafters' ends), then shorter rafters atop the crossbeams (again placed nearer to the center), and finally another set of still shorter crossbeams (fig. 129, top). Around the perimeter of the housepit, the vertical lower walls were simply the soil sides to the original housepit. On top of these walls, four horizontal logs became sills on which rested the in-sloping split logs of the upper walls and the ceiling (James W. VanStone, personal communication with Gregory Reinhardt, 1991). Their split surfaces always faced inward.

At their upper ends, the split logs of the ceiling leaned against the lower level of rafter-and-crossbeam pairs (fig. 129, top). Another, more horizontal, course of split logs started higher and reached farther inward toward the roof center, which the Nunivaarmiut completed by adding a row of short split logs to all but a remaining square central hole. A frame over this hole held the skylight, a gut-strip square bordered with fish skin and weighted in place with stones (Fienup-Riordan 2000:7, top). Then "a thin, bent stick was arched between opposite sides of the frame . . . to keep the gut window from sagging. It could be pushed back and forth to knock water and snow from the skylight" (VanStone 1989:22). Grass covered the roof, followed by packed-down earth and, finally, sod blocks. Most turfed-over Eskimo houses had dome-like roofs, although flat at the top, but Nunivaarmiut examples were comparatively more hipped in appearance (fig. 129, bottom).

A hanging grass mat or, less often, "a low plank door" (VanStone 1989:21) greeted the Nunivaarmiut at their house entrances. It seems the tunnel and house floors were on the same level sometimes, but in other houses the threshold was higher than the tunnel (James W. VanStone, personal communication 1991). Upon entering, people stepped across either a few coarse-sand-covered planks, on which to wipe their feet (fig. 129, top), or onto a fully planked floor.

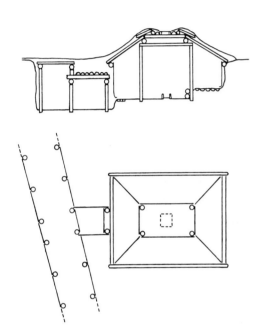

FIGURE 129

Idealized Nunivak Island winter house (cf. Fienup-Riordan 2000:109). Note the underground channel is on the left side of the drawing on top.

After Collins 1937:fig. 25, VanStone 1989:figs. 59–64; cf. fig. 111.

A slightly raised hearth, bordered with stone slabs resting edgewise, usually lay in the floor's center. The alternative hearth arrangement was a firepit in the center of the room, with an air vent opening into its end nearer the summer-and-winter entrances; presumably (as shown in Fienup-Riordan 2000:109) it would have been boarded over when not in use. When people opted not to add split-log lower walls (probably a later trend), they could line these earthen sides of the housepit by draping coarse grass mats in front of them (Fienup-Riordan 2000:7). The mats (e.g., fig. 130) likely hung from the pit-rimming logs, where the ceiling pieces rested (as shown in fig. 129, top right). However, tunnel walls were normally faced with upright split logs (not shown in fig. 129).

Himmelheber intimates that these houses had heating problems:

> The sod house is heated only by the warmth of human bodies. Once a fire is lit, the entrance tunnel and the upper window [skylight] must be opened to provide the draft needed to funnel the icy wind through the dwelling. Therefore, the sod house gets really cold when a fire is started. The structure has to be kept very small to retain a comfortable temperature solely through body heat. (Fienup-Riordan 2000:7)

FIGURE 130

"Pair of masked dancers performing in Qissunaq, photographed by Alfred Milotte during filming of Alaskan Eskimo, 1946" (Fienup-Riordan 1996:110). Although photographed on the mainland some 70 miles north of Nunivak Island, the image shows grass mats probably like those found in Nunivaarmiut houses and *qasgiqs*. Their suspension (upper right, woven grass cord-age?) is also no doubt similar. Behind the two male dancers wearing walrus masks and wielding feathered dance fans stands a woman who wares a fancy fur parka and a beaded and fur-ruffed dance headdress (*nasqurrun*, Fienup-Riordan 1996:135), and and waves caribou-fur-trimmed dance fans ("finger masks"), next to a man manipulating a dance stick (*eniraraun*, Fienup-Riordan 1996:137) and another beating on a typical tambourine drum. Note the horizontal wall boards (upper right) and their articulations with a crossbeam and the high-pitched ceiling planks.

Negative no. 109. Courtesy of Alaska State Museum, Juneau.

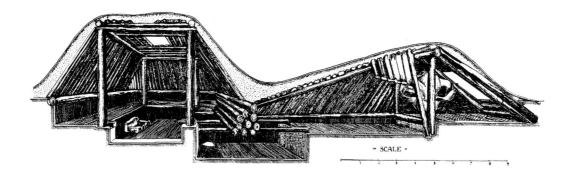

- SCALE -

FIGURE 131

"Cross-section of an Eskimo house on Nunivak Island."
From Collins 1937:fig. 25; cf. fig. 129.

Isolated houses—One of the more recognizable Eskimo dwelling illustrations is the "typical unmodified example" of a Nunivak Island house (fig. 131; Collins 1937:258). This second house type occurred on an unspecified part of the island, and we describe it as *isolated* because it was apparently not connected either to other dwellings or to the *qasgiq* in a settlement. It was generally similar to the preceding (connected) house-type, but differences in construction details are many (cf. fig. 129). It had: (1) a square-floored main chamber; (2) less height to the vertical lower walls, with a higher, more steeply pitched diagonal course of timbers above them (the "upper walls"); (3) a very low tunnel, especially near the main chamber; (4) a down-sloping roof at the outer end of the tunnel, which consisted of a diagonal ridgepole (resting on a square, vertical log frame, near the outer hatch, and on the lintel timbers above the house entryway); (5) split timbers leaned against the ridgepole from its left and right sides, forming a tunnel triangular in cross section; and (6) a small, square-floored antechamber with a whale skull that might have been used structurally. It may be that the diagonally slanted tunnel hatchway, with its square framing, was the same entrance found in the other Nunivak house type.

OTHER CENTRAL YUP'IK WOODEN HOUSES

At Hooper Bay (a partly Cup'ik-speaking area), up the coast from Nunivak Island and near the Yukon River outflow, houses resembled the Nunivak isolated house on the outside (VanStone 1984:fig. 4, top). Their roofs were noticeably hipped but flat in the center. The external doorways had square frames, although they led directly into the houses via a tunnel. These tunnels seem to be less deeply excavated—more like a near-surface passage—and consisted of almost vertical walls made from logs leaned against the roof supports, with some turf covering (Curtis 1907–1930:88 ff).

At one village (seventeen miles east of St. Michael in the Yukon-Kuskokwim Delta), Dall recorded a few settlement observations (fig. 132): "On the right side is the casine [*qasgiq*]. There are several ordinary winter houses, which are on the brow of a high bank. Caches are scattered about, and stages, on which the kyaks [*sic*] are elevated out of reach of the dogs" (Dall 1870:128). This architecture is externally much like the construction of a St. Michael *qasgiq* (fig. 133): The exterior walls are horizontal logs probably held in place, at intervals, with standing posts (the *qasgiq* posts are tall and connected well above the house with crossbeams). Also, the passages seem rather short and their outside entrances were probably cut as an above-ground hole between two vertical planks (rather than notched across the base of several upright planks). It may be that the crawlways descend behind the entrance (see fig. 132, left house), making them tunnels rather than surface-level passages.

Five archaeological examples of historic-period houses at Crow Village on the Kuskokwim River show greater connections with Nunivak Island architecture than with Norton Sound styles. For example, four of the five give at least some indication of four center-post roof construction. For another, none shows any trace of a passage that overlies the excavated tunnel in each, and four houses clearly had two or three sleeping areas against the back and lateral walls. These houses differ from the Nunivak style, nevertheless, insofar as their walls consisted of horizontal rather than vertical pieces of wood (Oswalt and VanStone 1967:13–23).

Horizontal logs also constituted dwelling walls as far south as the Nushagak River. At Akulivikchuk were semisubterranean, four-center-post, central-hearthed houses similar to both Nunivak and Crow Village designs. Nevertheless, some Nushagak houses differed in notable ways, and might have had some of the following characteristics: (1) a forechamber leading into the tunnel; (2) a lack of a cold trap at the house end; (3) square floors; and (4) one sleeping platform at the rear of the dwelling (VanStone 1970:20–38).

SOUTHWEST ALASKA MEN'S HOUSES

The men's house (*qasgiq*, alternatively *kashgee* or, from Russian derivation, *kashim* or *casine*), so widely distributed in the Western Arctic, reached its architectural apogee on the American mainland; yet it was lacking on Saint Lawrence Island and in Siberia. It is important to note again that the Central Yup'ik *qasgiq* was the normal residence for all men and boys. This is why we deviate from the organization of previous chapters and include it in the section Winter Houses instead of Special-Use Structures.

FIGURE 132

"Kegiktowruk in the fall." Sod-covered winter houses are on the left, a *qasgiq* on the right; note the scaffold (far right), kayak racks (left and center foreground), and a raised storage cache (center background).
From Dall 1870:128 ff.

FIGURE 133

"Kashim at St. Michael." Generally like some Central Yup'ik houses, the construction differs in its double-walled make-up. A man stands beside the passage/tunnel entrance. *From Nelson 1899:fig. 76.*

FIGURE 134

"Khashgii (community house) in use among Eskimos on western coast of Alaska, south of St. Michael." Note the near-surface entry way above an abandoned tunnel.

Anderson and Eells 1935:fig. 7; courtesy of the Board of Trustees of the Leland Stanford Junior University.

VIEW SHOWING INTERIOR AND MEANS OF ENTRANCE – OLD TUNNEL NO LONGER IN USE

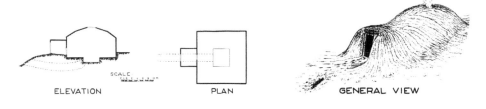

ELEVATION   PLAN   GENERAL VIEW

FIGURE 135

"Section of kashim at St Michael." Next to the sleeping bench (right) is a saucer-shaped lamp on a post (cf. fig. 128). The hearth's location is unclear, but there are separate entrances for winter and summer. *From Nelson 1899:fig. 77.*

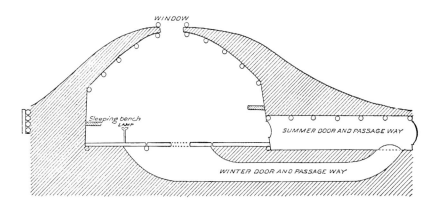

128

In this area, the *qasgiq* used greater-than-normal-sized timbers. When Unaligmiut builders started a *qasgiq* (figs. 133–135), they set the logs upright, side by side in a broad trench. Then they reinforced and insulated this seven-to eight-foot high inner wall by adding an outer one of horizontal logs, packing the interstice with earth, and stabilizing the whole with an external skeleton of tall struts and crossbeams (figs. 132–133). Logs for the roof slanted inward and upward, usually being cribbed. Across the tops of interior walls, it was common to span the corners by laying down horizontal beams diagonally to the corners (fig. 134). Doing this eased the addition of subsequent beams that went into forming crib roofs (Curtis 1907–1930:9; Fienup-Riordan 2000:109, bottom; Himmelheber 1980:7; VanStone 1989:fig. 65) and ensured that a *qasgiq's* roof rise was dramatically greater than that of women's houses (e.g., Fienup-Riordan 1996:123, 128). Some nine to twelve feet above the floor, the topmost cribbed level left a two-foot-square or larger smokehole, to be shut at times by a gut skylight (Michael 1967:115; Nelson 1899:245). On ceremonial occasions (e.g., the "inviting-in" ceremony) guest villagers would paint these skylights with designs reflecting deeds of the painters' ancestors and give the skylights as gifts to the host village (Fienup-Riordan 1996:124–125).

During Southwest Alaska Eskimo ceremonies, if someone wanted to demonstrate a trick, or when men wished to take a sweat bath, they would take up floor boards from the middle (figs. 135, 138). Without doing this, a fire could not be stoked. Men (and, after them, the women[5]) took sweat baths every week to ten days in winter (Maressa 1986; Nelson 1899:245, 287). In the course of bathing, temperatures rose to nearly intolerable levels, so searing that bathers needed respirators (mouthpieces woven from spruce or willow shavings; fig. 139) in order to breathe without burning their lungs; loon-skin caps protected their heads. Bathers kept cool by ladling urine—kept in a tub beside each person—over themselves (Nelson 1899:288, fig. 96).

Unaligmiut *qasgiq*s were almost as technologically complex as their winter houses and differed from them in some respects. For one thing, they were larger, averaging twenty to thirty feet across (Ray 1966:50).[6] Apparently, more parts went into its roof, which people assembled with "some ingenuity" and finished with saddle-jointed timbers (Ray 1966:50).

Qasgiq bench-style platforms (figs. 134–138) could employ enormous planks, sometimes only one to a wall, measuring thirty feet long, two feet wide, and four inches thick (Dall 1870:127). Benches skirted the interior walls (figs. 135–138), sometimes forming two or more tiers (except along the front wall; see fig. 114) in Kuskokwim and Yukon River *qasgiq*s:

> The back of the qasgiq... would have benches all the way around... called *ingleret*... high enough so that a person could sit underneath. People would be sitting up there.... And the space under the bench would be filled with people all the way around. And those down there would have a wooden bench in the back too. (Fienup-Riordan 1996:124)

A shared, structured hierarchy within and between villages dictated individual seating arrangements in the qasgiq (cf. Special-Use Structures, Ceremonial Houses, chapter 2):

FIGURE 136

Model of *qasgiq* from St. Michael, Norton Sound, Alaska. The two-tiered seating in this men's house is characteristic of Central Yup'ik communities on the lower Yukon River. Fourteen ivory dancers populate the inner bench, waiting for one more to emerge from the floor-hole and complete a third five-performer trio (five constituting a "ritually significant group"—Fienup-Riordan 1996:122); one holds a tambourine drum, which obscures two of the figures (upper right of inner bench). Note the mostly-shirtless wooden viewers seated on the outer bench.

Courtesy of Sheldon Jackson Museum, Sitka, catalog # II-H-31).

Inside the qasgiq each man had his accustomed place. The rear of the qasgiq, the warmest and driest spot, was reserved as the place of honor, while older men and inactive hunters occupied the corners to the sides of the door: "The elders, especially, would stay closer to the entrance hole. An elder was called *uaqsigilria* [one who is nearing the exit].... And the others stayed further inside.... (Fienup-Riordan 1996:122).

Although a *qasgiq*'s covered surface passage might have been short (figs. 133–134), it still seemed more substantial than the passages of women's houses. At the inner end of this access, a summer alternative, was a hole in the main room's front wall (figs. 133–135, 138). For winter service, a hole in or near the middle of the *qasgiq* floor (figs. 128, 135–136) led downward to a short, deep tunnel that descended below the surface-level passage and reemerged somewhere along the passage floor (figs. 134–135).

FIGURE 137

"Inside a men's house in Napaskiak, facing the entrance covered by a bear's skin" (Fienup-Riordan 2000:7), this photograph shows how the skylight beams brightly into a lower Kuskokwim River *qasgiq*. Note the bench (a bit higher than the seated boy's legs, left), an angled doorway in the front wall, a threshold "ramp" that ends in a worn-down log bordering the central (dirt?) floor or hearth, wood flooring elsewhere, and struts (both sides of the doorway) that might be bench supports. Two boys peek from behind the bear skin doorflap, while a girl (right) faces the camera as well. Behind her is a magazine on the bench, and near the boys are a pole and metal pail (left), plus a walrus-tusk pick (behind the seated boy) for heavy-duty digging.

From Fienup-Riordan 2000:7; courtesy of Hans Himmelheber.

FIGURE 138

"Interior of kashime [*qasgiq*]—Shageluk [upper Yukon River]/ Illumination from skylight/ Entrance under the shelf, at the left. The object in front of the entrance is the stuffed skin of a diver, that figured in some feast." Note the square herringbone fitting of boards immediately around the hearth (lower center) in contrast to the uniform orientation of floor boards farther right (cf. fig. 128, lower right). Over the entrance, two men recline on a fairly high bench.

John Brooks Collection, Accession #68-32-138, Archives, Alaska and Polar Regions Dept., Rasmuson Library, University of Alaska Fairbanks.

ESKIMO ARCHITECTURE

People sometimes pulled themselves up through the hole in the *qasgiq* chamber's floor-hold by handles of ivory—on the lower Yukon Delta, at least (Nelson 1899:250, fig. 78). Other Yup'ik people report handles of wood and a step built into the subfloor:

> [There was a] step inside the *qasgiq* by the firepit under the floorboards. They stepped on that and went up. Short people would lean on the side, swing their legs up and, lying down, they would go up.... But when children put their hands on the side of the entrance, [adults] would go down to them and hoist them up.... We call [the handles] *ayaperyarak* [dual, from *ayaper-*, "to lean on one's hands"]. The entrance to the *qasgiq* was traditionally a hole. When you came up through the hole you would find *pall'itak* [two handrails] here on the sides. You would place your hands on them and come up into the *qasgiq*. (Fienup-Riordan 1996:122)

Another overlooked function of floor-hold handles was to avoid "placing the hands on the wet planks at the side of the hole" (Nelson 1899:250). Slippery boards would not have been a problem after sweat baths, but entering and leaving through this hole was probably a bit more precarious when the hearth was cold and people entered wearing boots with wet soles.

When the sun shone, skylights lit the interior (fig. 137), but at other times indoors light glowed from saucer-shaped lamps as much as from the hearth.[7] They rested on two series of broad-topped posts sunk into wood planks. One set of posts perforated the floorboards just inside in the wall benches (e.g., figs. 128, 135), while the second set pierced the bench edges themselves (Ray 1966:51).

SIBERIAN YUPIK HOUSES

Before 1850 both the Siberian Eskimos and their close relatives on Saint Lawrence Island, fifty miles offshore in the Bering Sea, built semisubterranean sod houses in winter. In summer they stayed in bone-framed walrus-hide tents (Geist and Rainey 1936:12; Hughes 1984:251). By the 1870s, however, they had replaced their traditional winter house with a modified version of the Chukchi *yuranga* (Bogoras 1913; Murdoch 1892:78; Nelson 1899:259).

OLD-STYLE WOODEN HOUSES

The more traditional Saint Lawrence Island and Chukchi Peninsula dwelling (nenglu) ranged from sixteen to twenty-five feet in its greater dimension (fig. 140).[8] Although normally square, floors could be oblong; one from Kukulik was twenty-four by thirteen feet (Geist and Rainey 1936:61). People framed their houses with driftwood, stone, or whale bone, using generous thicknesses of turf to insulate the entirety. Reminiscent of Bering Strait houses, these needed four (or sometimes six) wood or bone uprights to sustain their flat-topped, hip roofs. Notching the posts would have allowed residents to climb up to reach objects hung above them (Geist and Rainey 1936:62) and could have provided an escape route in times of conflict.

In old-style Siberian houses, a pair of wood or whale-jaw rafters straddling the center posts were mortised on their medial faces to receive lighter tenoned

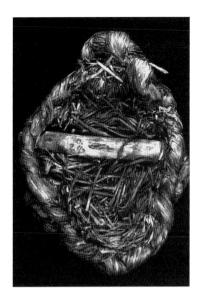

FIGURE 139

Woven respirator of wood shavings and grass from King Island (see chapter 3). Used to protect the throat and nasal passages from searing heat in the sweat bath, its wearer would bite the wooden bar (top) to hold it in place against the mouth and nose.

Photographs by Gregory A. Reinhardt; object #0/24, courtesy of Department of Anthropology, American Museum of Natural History.

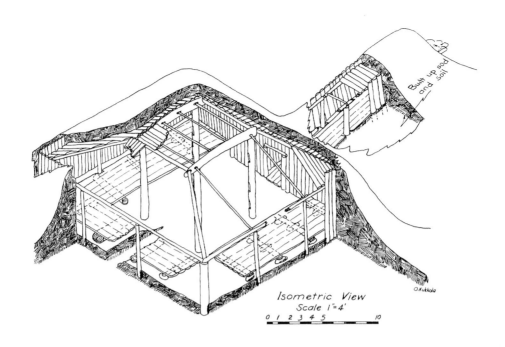

Isometric View
Scale 1"=4'

FIGURE 140

St. Lawrence Island and Chukchi Peninsula old-style wooden house.

From Geist and Rainey 1936:fig. 2; courtesy of University of Alaska, Fairbanks.

crossbeams over the horizontal central roof (fig. 140). On the rafters' lateral faces, additional mortises allowed beams with longer tenons to extend from the rafters' ends downward to the four short corner posts of the house (figs. 140–142). Other lateral-face mortises held beams (probably for sideways stability) that sloped transversely down to stringers along the room's outer edges. At intervals around the room were additional short posts, cut to the height of the corner posts, positioned to hold up the stringers (fig. 140). For the ceiling, timbers (probably split logs) bridged the diagonal gap between lower stringers and the upper central framework, and more timbers spread across the flat medial roof (figs. 140–142). A hollowed-out whale vertebra (covered by a vertebral disk) acted as a vent hole in the roof. Upright split logs leaned inward against the lower stringers to form the house walls (figs. 140–142). Bone pegs, which could include sharpened walrus bacula (penis bones), tacked down the floor boards; these pegs sometimes helped to secure the structural members of the house (Geist and Rainey 1936:58–64).

From seventeen to seventy-five feet long and less than three feet high, the tunnel of this old-style Siberian Yupik winter house was built entirely underground and lined with split logs. Like tunnels in many mainland houses from the Central Yup'ik area, Siberian Eskimo ones had a stockaded entry and were sometimes curved to impede incoming drafts. Stone and/or wood normally walled and paved the entryway's exterior; paving within the tunnel, however, was optional. Unlike most Eskimo tunnels, these did not end in a trap door or heat-conserving cold trap but simply slanted downward, ramplike, to the house floor (Geist and Rainey 1936:59, fig. 14; Nelson 1899:259–260, fig. 87; Carius 1979:3).

FIGURE 141

"Ruined house on Punuk Island, abandoned about 50 years ago." A wood and whalebone framework stands at the floor's center. Two diagonal roof supports stretch from the central cross beams to the lateral wall stringers (cf. fig. 142).

From Collins 1935:pl. 10, top.

FIGURE 142

"Interior view of same [ruined house on Punuk Island]." Note the four center posts (front left post notched) holding up two cross beams (left one wood, right one whale mandible), the roof pitching diagonally from one cross beam (left), standing wall timbers (left background), collapsing wall timbers (left foreground), and heavy wood floor planks; a man crouches on the floor amid the four posts. The bone with a hole through it, sitting on the roof, might be the house's whale-vertebra vent hole—perhaps out of place (cf. fig. 141).

From Collins 1935:pl. 10, bottom.

Inside the old-style Siberian Eskimo house sleeping benches lay on three sides (fig. 140). The benches appear to have been fairly low, consisting of dressed planks that sat on perpendicular joists, in turn sitting on stones to raise them off the floor. However, some houses had a second row of sleeping platforms, accessible via a notched-log ladder. Vertical split-log walls were about five feet high and ceilings rose another two feet or so. The moss-wick lamps were "almost two feet long, shallow, with elevated 'rim' along two sides.... Three lamps to a platform ... were kept burning day and night [and] two others for light at the ends of the room" (Collins n.d.). Household goods were stored on overhead wall racks around the house perimeter, or in the entryway when not in use (Carius 1979:12–13).

In at least one site from East Cape, Siberia, Nelson saw previously abandoned houses spread among then-occupied ones. Older structures were "similar in character to those seen on the Diomede Islands—partly underground, with external stone walls" (Nelson 1899:258). Thus, this dwelling form is obviously distinct from other Siberian Eskimo houses.

FIGURE 143

"Village at East Cape, Siberia." Some houses (center) lack complete walls, while others (right) may be occupied (note objects leaning against the walls).

From Healy 1887:16 ff.

FIGURE 144

"Houses and natives of East Cape, Siberia." Meat dries from a rack (left house), thongs are being stretched and air-tanned between houses, and wood panels (a door?) frame a doorway (right house). Items leaned against the sides presumably help to keep the skin roof-cover in place.

From Healy 1887:16 ff.

FIGURE 145

"Koara's home and friends" (cf. fig. 126), circa 1899–1900. New-style hide-roofed house, giving a sense of capacity and the number of walrus hides needed to cover the structure, peak to base. A thick horizontal thong, about five feet up, anchors the lighter roof-hide thongs by being counter-anchored (via twisted vertical lines at regular intervals around the circumference) to the weights on the ground. A toy boat sits on the roof (left); behind two boys (center) is an inflated sealskin float for sea-mammal hunting; and in the foreground (right) is a wooden vessel (steam-bent rim with a concave base).

USRC Bear Collection, Accession #89-193-106N, Archives, Alaska and Polar Regions Dept., Rasmuson Library, University of Alaska Fairbanks.

The newer "Chukchi style" winter house (*maŋtaŋa.aq*) was situated on a level spot on a high sand bar (figs. 143–148). People entered these oval or octagonal dwellings, about twenty feet in diameter, through a wooden door sometimes placed about two feet above the ground. Builders started the whalebone or driftwood frame by predetermining a floor size, placing uprights either side by side or periodically around the circumference, then driving them into the ground (fig. 149).[9] When positioned side by side, these posts were bound together with walrus-hide thongs; when apart, the interstices would be packed with turf to the posts' full height. In both cases, the result was a round wall about four to six feet high (figs. 143–148).

Wood or whale mandible rafters either rested on the wall or, when wall posts were periodic, on the posts (or on post-top stringers—see fig. 149). They rose inward, supported by a few uprights within the house, to focus on an apex well above wall height. Differing in length, the slender wooden rafters intersected the uprights from various directions to become a starburst of poles at the peak, which was off-center toward the door (e.g., figs. 145, 147). This domed or conical roof could be upheld by two to four uprights, each pair spanned by a crosspiece (Hughes 1984:fig. 9). Once completed, people roofed the house with overlapping sheets of walrus hides that had been sewn together and, at times, banked the structure with sod as much as a foot thick. Old parkas of feather and fur provided further wall insulation (Cremeans 1931:129–130; Moore 1923:348).

Each new-style Siberian Eskimo house had a double wall of walrus hide. Another Chukchi innovation was the split-walrus-hide inner room (*agra*) enclosed in the winter house (fig. 150). The *agra* or *polog* measured about four to five feet tall, twelve to twenty-five feet deep, and about eight to twelve feet broad. Forming a kind of "covered square or rectangular box without a bottom" (Nelson 1899:258) suspended over a slightly raised floor, these hide chambers were anchored by inch-wide thongs that passed through the walls and toggled outside to boulders, driftwood, whalebones, etc. A network of these and other lines held down the roofing (figs. 145–148). Occupants insulated the floor by layering it with grass and walrus hides. Two vents pierced the *agra*, and its curtain-like front could be opened. Inside the rooms were raised sleeping platforms of earth and/or driftwood (fig. 151). Each family member had a designated sleeping place and slept with his or her head toward the house door. Chief among the household furnishings were low stools of whale vertebrae (Cremeans 1931:130; Kennan 1870; Nelson 1899:258). Heating was confined to the inner room, whereas the larger remaining space consisted of an enclosed, protected storage area (Carius 1979:21).

In one Eskimo village at East Cape, Siberia, the houses had "a stone wall laid up two or three feet from the ground, in oval form, and continued in the shape of an arched or open-top entrance passage three or four yards long" (Nelson 1899:257, fig. 85) instead of the usual bone-and-turf or wooden walls (fig. 152). The hide roofs were similar in lashing and general appearance, except that they seem not to have generated the starburst effect of

FIGURE 146

New-style hide-roofed house that is more modern-looking (insofar as its walls are of milled lumber), circa 1899–1900. Meat (perhaps seal ribs) dries from racks, the posts of which allow storage for a sled (right). Note the hinged window shutter (left).

USRC Bear Collection, Accession #95-264-28N, Archives, Alaska and Polar Regions Dept., Rasmuson Library, University of Alaska Fairbanks.

FIGURE 147

"Eskimo winter hut, Plover Bay, Siberia" (Grinnell 1910:172 ff). Smaller example of new-style hide-roofed house, circa 1899. Walls consist of whalebone uprights with sod blocks in between. Part of the roof cover is skin (right), the rest cloth (left), and some of the cover extends to the ground. A whale scapula blocks half the doorway; a wooden serving dish rests behind the woman (center), and an unfinished wall stands in the background (right).

Edward H. Harriman Expedition Collection, Accession #RBD 0201-163, Archives, Alaska and Polar Regions Dept., Rasmuson Library, University of Alaska Fairbanks.

FIGURE 148

Still smaller new-style hide-roofed house. Several sleds lie about (right), and three caribou or reindeer hides (weighted with rocks) dry in the sun (foreground). The child on the woman's shoulder is a boy, with the crown of his head shaved (see Nelson 1899:fig. 120).

Thetis Album, Accession #81-163-59N, Archives, Alaska and Polar Regions Dept., Rasmuson Library, University of Alaska Fairbanks.

FIGURE 149

"Unfinished winter house, showing framework of whalebones." Circular wall of new-style hide-roofed house (probably abandoned), Plover Bay, Siberia, with some stacked sods in position, circa 1899. Stringers (evidently nailed or pegged to the whalebone posts) would make the structure more sturdy. Long roof poles lie in the foreground, the left one more curved and probably made from a whale mandible; a (seal?) skin dries on the ground nearby (right).

From Grinnell 1910:173. Edward H. Harriman Expedition Collection, Accession #RBD0201-162, Archives, Alaska and Polar Regions Dept., Rasmuson Library, University of Alaska Fairbanks.

FIGURE 150

"Ko-ara's extra wives" (cf. fig. 145), circa 1899–1900. View of an *agra* (hide-walled inner room), showing large roof braces and smaller horizontal poles to which fur-and-cloth walls are tied. Doubled-up partitions suggest these are the fronts to two separate sleeping areas (left and right); daylight shining through roof creates glare (above).

USRC Bear Collection, Accession #89-193-108N, Archives, Alaska and Polar Regions Dept., Rasmuson Library, University of Alaska Fairbanks.

FIGURE 151

"Two Eskimos inside dwelling," or interior of new-style hide-roofed house. Light streams through the translucent roof hides, supported by an extensive network of arching roof poles, tied-on crossbars, and heavy, diagonal floor-to-ceiling braces. The woman sits by an evidently small *agra* (inner room), lined with reindeer furs and raised slightly above the house floor. Walls are of horizontally-set milled wooden boards, and footwear hangs near the wooden door (right), with a seal-skin before it on the floor. Fish or meat appears to be drying (top, center) from a roof brace.

C. W. Scarborough Collection, Accession #88-130-35N, Archives, Alaska and Polar Regions Dept., Rasmuson Library, University of Alaska Fairbanks.

FIGURE 152

New-style hide-roofed house, probably from East Cape, Siberia. Roundish stone walls distinguish these houses from those at other locations. Note the convergence of poles, erupting through the front ends of these houses, from which meat hangs to dry. Whalebones lie against some walls, as people sit below the front walls.

Barrett Willoughby Collection, Accession #72-116-40, Archives, Alaska and Polar Regions Dept., Rasmuson Library, University of Alaska Fairbanks.

poles overhead. Rather, they project farther forward toward the entrance, and it may be that only one prominent pole (a sawed length of whale mandible?) emerged from the cover (fig. 152). Internally, the people here engaged the same *agra* design for sleeping, the remainder of the interior again being used for storage (Nelson 1899:257–258, fig. 85).

A recollection from childhood on Saint Lawrence Island, circa 1930, illustrates aspects of life in the new-style Siberian house:

> [Linda Womkon Badten's] earliest memory was of watching her mother scrubbing down the interior walls of this house. By the time she began to "be aware," to use the Yupik phrase, the walrus hide walls had already been replaced by lumber walls [cf. fig. 146]. Still, the house in which she spent her youth had one main room and an outer room (unheated) which was used for storing family belongings.... She spoke with nostalgia of the times when, as a young child, she was invited to listen to the stories of her grandparents, to move from her own nuclear family section of the family home to her grandparents' section. Each segment of the family group had its own assigned place in the room. Her oldest sister, because she was approaching adulthood, also had a special place. No one, according to Linda, entered another person's space without some kind of implicit permission. This gave each space its own sanctity while reinforcing respect among those who shared the home together. (Jolles n.d.:8, 9)

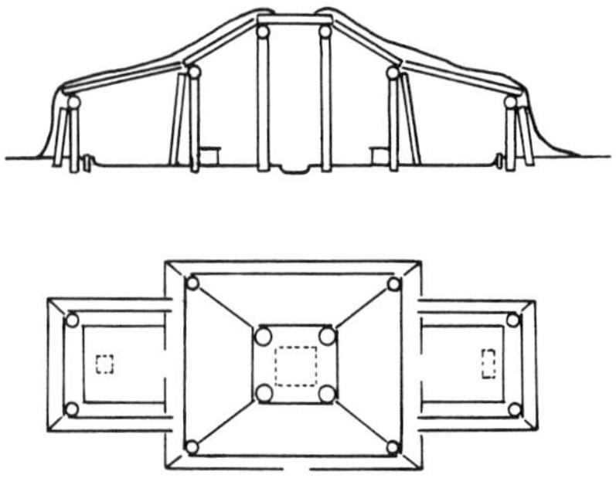

ALUTIIQ HOUSES

FIGURE 153

Idealized Kodiak Island year-round house, with two lateral sleeping chambers.

From Reinhardt and Lee 1997:1797; after Cook and King 1784:Pl. 58; Griggs 1917:25; 1920:321; 1922:18, 24, 26; Knecht and Jordan 1985:fig. 6; Martin 1913:144–146. Courtesy of Cambridge University Press.

Housing of the Alutiiqs (i.e., the Koniag Eskimos of Kodiak Island, Cook Inlet, and the adjacent mainland, and the Chugach Eskimos of Prince William Sound) is one of the most challenging types to reconstruct from the Eskimo literature (fig. 153). Its common name, barabara, comes from the Russians,

who borrowed the word from Siberia. However, the Alutiiqs called it *ciqlluaq* (also written *chikliuak*, *checkhliok*, and *tsikluak*) or *naa* (Black 1977:90; Knecht 1995:746; Lisiansky 1814:332; Merck 1980:100). The Koniag occupied these houses from late October to the end of March, situating them "behind a headland, in the lee of a small island, or in a small embayment" (Clark 1984:191; Sauer 1802:178).

There is an almost total absence of suitably detailed illustrations of Alutiiq houses, but even more frustrating is the disagreement among sources, which also tend to be vague or ambiguous about their appearance. We know for certain that the *ciqlluaq* consisted of a rectilinear, mat- or board-lined communal room adjoining one or more smaller sleeping chambers that, in historic times, doubled as sweatbaths. Reinhardt (1986:162) argues that the Alutiiq house is structurally related to Aleut houses (fig. 154). However, even the hypothesized similarity to Aleut houses is uncertain, given the divergence of primary sources on this point. For example, one observer says that "[their habitations] resemble those of the Aleutians" (Sarychev 1806:18), whereas another states that "the dwellings of the [Alutiiqs] differ from those of Oonalashka" [or Unalaska, one of the eastern Aleutian Islands] (Sauer 1802:175).

KODIAK ISLAND YEAR-ROUND WOODEN HOUSES

The first well-documented archaeological example of a Koniag *ciqlluaq* is from Karluk Lagoon, Kodiak Island, and dates to the mid-1800s (Knecht and Jordan 1985). However, this example was built well into the Russian period, thus representing two to three generations of colonial influence.[10]

Unlike other Eskimo winter houses, the Koniag *ciqlluaq* had neither tunnel nor passage, but simply a wood-framed doorway in one wall (figs. 155–156).

FIGURE 154

Interior of a house from Unalaska, Aleutian Islands of Aleut—*not Eskimo*—cultural affiliation, showing features *similar to* those in Koniag houses.
From Cook and King 1784:Pl. 58; courtesy of the Lilly Library, Indiana University, Bloomington, Indiana.

FIGURE 155

"Ash-covered barabaras [*ciqlluaqs*] at Douglas Village, July 14, 1912." Mainland Alutiiq house (left; ash came from the Katmai volcano). Note the hip or crib roof (its earthen coating likely intact) and the doorway. Next to it may be a short passage to another house or to a side room (cf fig. 156).

From Griggs 1922:24

FIGURE 156

"A 'barabara' [*ciqlluaq*] buried by the pumice brought down by the great flood: Katmai Village." Mainland Alutiiq house (left) photographed three to four years after the Katmai eruption. More of the crib roofing is visible (cf. fig. 155), as is the framed doorway to the house (left) and another structure (right; a sleeping chamber?).

From Griggs 1917:25, bottom.

Koniag men dug their floors about two to three feet below the surface. Four tall center posts probably surrounded a hearth in the rectangular or apsidal, board- or mat-lined great room. Father Gedeon claimed a typical room size was about nineteen by twenty-eight feet (Black 1977:90), consistent with an archaeological example about eighteen feet on a side (Knecht and Jordan 1985:fig. 6). Rising above the posts was a cribbed central roof (figs. 155–156), but sleeping chambers could have a crib, flat, or shed roof (Oswalt 1967:fig. 7), depending on construction materials. Figures 153 and 157 show a shed roof, the most complex style.[11] As a guess, some rafters were notched so that lighter horizontal crossbeams could overlay them without requiring any lashings (fig. 157).

It may be that four four- to six-foot-high posts (or six if the floor was apsidal) supported sizable horizontal stringers, which bordered the communal area and mainly functioned as roof supports (fig. 158). From these stringers, sloping timbers probably rose up to the central roof, while walls might have taken form from planks leaned against the stringers from floor level (fig. 158). Roofing grass was "harvested by bare hands" (Black 1977:93) and, in all likelihood, laid in clumps without being tied to the roof. Koniag builders covered the whole exterior with grass, then plastered or coated it with earth, mud, or clay (fig. 155).

Most sources describe a square opening, about twenty-eight inches on a side, at the peak of the roof (fig. 153), but no source that we consulted mentions any smokehole cover or skylight membrane. However, Koniag *qasgiqs* did employ at least a gut sheet or board to close this hole, and these no doubt occurred in houses as well (Crowell et al. 2001:36). Side rooms could have their own wood-framed otter-gut or beaver-bladder skylights or windows. It is reasonable to assume that the distinctive, beautifully pecked Alutiiq stone lamps provided supplemental lighting (see rear endpage). Separating the main area from each family's quarters was either a board or a fishskin curtain.

The main chamber in Koniag houses was floored with grass mats or loose grass and warmed by a hearth lined with stones. To come and go people used a ground-level doorway, three feet on a side, which they closed with a framed or unframed sealskin. Families spent their waking hours indoors either in the middle of this room or near one wall, where it seems each group maintained a partitioned area "like we have stalls in stables for the horses" (Merck 1980:205). These spaces were meant for storing family property and for eating. Viewed conservatively, upright boards possibly marked the sides of such partitions while hanging mats separated and "closeted off" their fronts (Lisiansky 1814:213, in Hrdlička 1975:28; Pierce 1978:120). Again, this configuration has Aleut counterparts (fig. 154, spaces at edges of main room).

Other authors also refer vaguely (given varying translations) to storage spots, which bordered the walls at floor level, within the main chamber: "closeted off places" (Lisiansky in Hrdlička 1975:28), "cupboards" (Davydov 1977:154), "benches" (Davydov in Hrdlička 1975:27), "storage pits" (Lantis 1938:128), and "storerooms" (Sauer 1802:213). Whether partitioned or not, these were indeed raised areas (see Knecht and Jordan 1985:fig. 6) and probably were associated with specific families.

Iurii Lisiansky (1814:213) condemns the main chamber as a "filthy hall" but still emphasizes its general utility: "[the Koniag] barabara answers the purpose of a court-yard, a kitchen, and, when requisite, a theatre. In this room the natives dance, build their bidarkas [kayaks], clean and dry their fish, and perform every other domestic office." Around its walls, anywhere from two to six sleeping chambers, containing two or three families apiece, typified a complete household (Davydov 1977:154; Hrdlička 1975:28; Merck 1980:100).

Narrow doorways admitted families to smaller side rooms, called *qawarwik*s (Knecht 1995:746) or *nglok*s (*zhupan*s, to the Russians). These were the normal Koniag sleeping quarters. Corner posts stood just over two feet high, but ethnographic and archaeological data indicate that sleeping chamber floors were lower than those of main chambers. Giving us an indirect impression of one house's overall size, Lisiansky (1814:213) notes its *qawarwik* was thirteen feet, ten inches, by fourteen feet, seven inches. Two nineteenth-century bedrooms in one house measured eight to thirteen feet wide by nine to eleven feet front to back (Knecht and Jordan 1985:fig. 6). This means the Koniag *qawarwik* was larger than most other Eskimos' *entire* house interiors!

Raised sleeping platforms bordered *qawarwik* walls but were less than forty inches wide. Therefore, typically reclining with their heads toward the middle, Koniag adults probably slept in the fetal position. To bolster the inner (earthen) borders of these sleeping spaces or platforms, residents laid down logs or planks (some decoratively inset with sea otter teeth), which also served as headrests. They padded the sleeping surfaces with a bedding of grass mats and sealskins. When more than one family slept in the same room, a "slab" or "blanket" allegedly divided them (Davydov 1977:154; Davydov in Hrdlička 1975:27). During winter, sleeping chambers undoubtedly required lamps to

FIGURE 157

Top: "The desolation of Katmai Village after the eruption." A mainland Koniag community covered with volcanic ash. The shed roofs are partly exposed, with timbers showing through the grass of roof sods.

From Griggs 1922:18.

Bottom: "A portion of Katmai village four years after the eruption." Virtually the same view as above; note how erosion has exposed more of the roof superstructure.

From Griggs 1920:321.

FIGURE 158

"Interior of a barabara [*ciqlluaq*] showing the construction of the native huts." This corner of a mainland Alutiiq house's main chamber reveals a corner post (left), supporting stringers for two walls (made from split logs leaned against the stringers), and a lower set of stringers (or wall reinforcing crossbeams?). A low opening (center, between men) probably leads to a sleeping chamber (*qawarwik*) off the main room.

From Griggs 1922:26.

augment the skylight or window lighting. Auxiliary heat within the *qawarwik* came from stones warmed outdoors or in the great room's hearth, and gravel or grass formed a base for receiving them.

Because Koniag architectural details come almost exclusively from nonpictorial sources, their dwellings are singularly hard to consider. One exception to this visual lacuna came about as a result of the 1912 eruption of Katmai volcano in southwest Alaska. To underscore the depths and subsequent dissipation of volcanic ash, geologists took two diachronic sets of photographs (figs. 155–157) of half-buried, mainland Koniag houses (Clark 1984:191). They provide the best exterior visual image of the *ciqlluaq*.

PRINCE WILLIAM SOUND WOODEN HOUSES

Mainland Chugach dwellings from Prince William Sound probably resembled the Kodiak Island Koniag design insofar as they housed several families. Still, they differed in noteworthy ways, resembling Tlingit Indian plank houses (to the east and south) more than they did the Koniag structures (Crowell and Mann 1998:129–131; Aron Crowell, personal communication with Molly Lee, 2001). The Chugach apparently built houses more weather proof than those of some Northwest Coast Indians (de Laguna 1956:58–59), yet they followed the general Eskimo (i.e., non-Northwest Coast) tradition of semisubterranean construction (Petroff 1884:28). Another obvious difference is that Chugach houses combined bark with the grass used for roofs and walls, securing this with tied-down poles. A further distinction is that their dove-tailed horizontal log walls might postdate Russian contact (Birket-Smith 1953:53–54, 56).

The more aboriginal Chugach winter houses had two-foot deep floors, anywhere from twelve to eighteen feet long by five to twelve feet wide, marked by smoothed split-log or plank walls about four to six feet high and held together by posts at intervals. Bent poles or withes formed the arching roof, which received a covering of turf, soil, and spruce- or cedar-bark slabs, while stones kept the bark in position. Inside walls were lined with another course of finished planks, and moss chinked any wall cracks. A door stood at either side of the house (cf. fig. 128), with a "thatched passage" linking them to adjacent summer houses (Crowell and Mann 1998:130–131).

ALTERNATIVE WINTER DWELLINGS

In eastern Norton Sound the Unaligmiut fabricated a "so-called snowhouse" (Ray 1966:53) that is more accurately described as a snow-blanketed tent. Nelson (1899:242) implies these dwellings were contemplated solely for traveling and supposedly carried the name aniguyuk. Curiously, this is essentially the same name as the extraordinarily similar snow-walled Nunamiut form from Northwest Alaska (aniguyyak), described in chapter 3, even though the respective languages of the Unaligmiut and Nunamiut (i.e., Central Yup'ik and Iñupiaq) differ. In any event, they involved snow heaped over a skin- or fur-sheathed, dome-shaped willow frame.

> Later on, when the place is abandoned, the tent poles are taken out from the inside and then the tent covering separated from its frozen snowy envelope,

and pulled out through the entrance. More or less of the outer snowy wall is thus left, and travelers coming across the remains imagine they have seen snow houses like those made on the Arctic coast [of Canada?]. (Ray 1966:53)

The Kodiak Island Alutiiqs also constructed multiple houses for themselves:

> Almost every family has its own dwelling, and many have more than one dwelling in various places. They settle on the bays and inlets, on the sea shore, and near streams, but change their location and dwellings with the season. In the spring they usually stay in places where the run of fish from the sea toward the streams occurs earliest, and in winter near the shallows where they can find subsistence for themselves. (Black 1977:85)[12]

TRANSITIONAL DWELLINGS

IT IS PROBABLY SAFE TO SAY THAT SEASONALLY TRANSITIONAL DWELLINGS played little, if any, part in the lifeways of Eskimos from Southwest Alaska, the Bering Sea, and Siberia. As expressed in a passage above, however, one Russian source claims otherwise for Eskimos on Kodiak Island (that is, changing sites and housing seasonally). Portlock (1789:253) mentions the one major exception to this region's lack of transitional lodging; a rectangular Chugach house, ten feet long by eight wide, and four to six feet high, which may refer to a family's second-site (and possibly less elaborate) winter home (see Birket-Smith 1953:55). Labeled "smokehouses" by Chugach elders, these buildings

> need not be associated with the smoking of fish at all, as demonstrated by the following: "[they] were quite small, perhaps ten feet by twelve feet, and were used only for overnight sleeping, not for smoking fish." To further confuse the situation, the elders also occasionally used the term 'smokehouse' to refer to smaller, more recent structures that were used prinicpally for smoking fish. For this reason, it is important when working with Chugach oral history to carefully examine the context in which the word 'smokehouse' is used.(Miraglia n.d.:3)

The Chugach smokehouses were impressive, enveloping enough space to shelter several families. Two corner posts and two taller middle posts were sunk at each end of the floor, but no side-wall posts, suggesting that the upright wall planks leaned against lateral stringers connecting the front and back corner posts. Another set of stringers ran between the higher pairs of middle posts, allowing for a flat-topped central roof, which sloped down steeply(?) on both sides (not quite like a mansard roof—Murray Milne personal communication with Gregory Reinhardt, 2002). Planks formed the roofing structure, which the Chugach faced with bark slabs, in turn held down by stone weights. A hole in the roof's middle (at least three feet square) allowed smoke to escape and daylight to enter. Lying next to the smokehole-skylight, a panel of roof boards would cover the hole when the wind picked up.

Centered below that hole, between two logs set lengthwise in the middle of the house floor, was a slightly sunken hearth, and above that hung a fish-drying rack. Within the house were separate sleep chambers, sufficiently high to stand up in, with wood walls and flat, sturdy roofs, on which dried fish and meat could be stored. Each chamber had its own small, square gut window. Snuggled under cormorant-skin blankets, sleepers lay on the floor atop grass and mountain goat or bear skins. A round door stood at each end of the house, next to "a small additional structure used as a bathroom with entrance from the main room" (Birket-Smith 1953:54).

SUMMER DWELLINGS

JUDGING FROM THE SEPARATE WINTER RESIDENCES IN THE CENTRAL YUP'IK region, it can be hypothesized that summer dwellings were also separate, at least on Nelson Island (Ann Fienup-Riordan, personal communication with Gregory Reinhardt, 1999).

NORTON SOUND WOODEN HOUSES

Murdoch implies that none of the Iñupiaq Eskimos of the Seward Peninsula and none of the Central Yup'ik of southwestern Alaska pitched summer tents (Murdoch 1892:84). Petroff (1884), who was Murdoch's source, gives incorrect information for the housing of postcontact times, but is probably correct in stating that summer dwellings were "generally log structures roofed with skins and open in front; no fire is made in these houses, and therefore they have no opening in the roof, all cooking being done in the open air during the summer. They seldom have flooring, but otherwise the interior arrangements resemble those of the winter houses" (Petroff 1884:128). An example of this summer house type appears in an engraving by John Weber from the folio published with the account of explorer James Cook's last voyage (fig. 159). It is probably the first published depiction of a Western Eskimo dwelling. Logs or heavy poles compose the walls of this structure; they are laid horizontally in the fashion of Unaligmiut winter houses. Nevertheless, Cook's written description of this same house indicates that these houses lacked parallel side walls (Cook and King 1784:2:484).

Considered alongside some of Cook's other observations, however, the text and engraving make it possible to reconstruct a description of Norton Sound summer houses. The engraving shows a gable roof of logs meeting roughly along the peak and forming short eaves beyond the lateral walls. This suggests that there was either a ridgepole (and endposts) to support the roof, or that the roof timbers were equal enough in length that their ends formed a more or less straight line. A "solid layer of poles" covered some roofs, which were then finished with earth or mud, and possibly turf. The reference to a small hole near the doorway "to let out the smoke" implies that rooftops were relatively well sealed (Cook and King 1784:2:484). The ends of the dwelling were probably rounded and made of logs leaned against the front and back of the roof, thus shaping an apsidal floorplan (Ray 1984:290, fig. 15). The inhabitants, worried about security in an area where warfare was

FIGURE 159

"Inhabitants and habitations of Norton Sound." The roof is gabled, the walls of stacked horizontal logs.

From the 1785 French edition of Cook and King 1784:Pl. 54.

FIGURE 160

"Winter view of Razbinsky." A snow-covered winter house, with someone looking into its skylight, is just behind the man in foreground. Beyond the people is a line of summer homes, their end-wall bracing highlighted by a dusting of snow.

From Nelson 1899:pl. 82.

FIGURE 161

"Village on the lower Yukon, during the fishing season." Basically the same buildings as in figure 160, these lack apparent structures that would retain the end-wall planks. Low racks (right) are sagging with fish being dried, while caches on stilts (between houses) are the carnivore-protected food repositories.

From Dall 1870:fig. ff. 228.

frequent, sometimes cut little peepholes in the front and sides of the house, covering them with hide or wood as small windows or movable shutters. The house floor was neither excavated nor paved. On it lay a generic sleeping platform, below which may have been a storage space.

Early accounts suggest that the Norton Sound winter and summer houses were alike except for a few features. The floor was bare in the summer house (Michael 1967:115), and, even without exact measurements, it is clear that summer houses were smaller, and probably intended only for a nuclear family. Other minor inferences from these accounts can be drawn as well. Since cooking was undertaken outside, these dwellings probably needed no sizable smokehole. From the notes of Russian explorer Lavrentiy A. Zagoskin is it reasonable to conclude that there must have been some sort of door hatch at the opening in the front wall of the dwelling (Michael 1967:114–115; Ray 1984:290, fig. 15).

NORTON SOUND DOME TENTS

Driftwood houses seem to have dominated the southwestern area during much of the early historic period (Ray 1966:52). Bering Strait Eskimos also erected dome tents for summer travel, although driftwood structures were the preferred type "in many permanent campsites" (Ray 1984:290).[13] Summer tents in this vicinity were "often mere shelters, less than three feet in height," with sealskin covers on a pole frame. They could otherwise contain raised sleeping areas and mat- or fur-lined floors (Ray 1966:52; 1984:290), but they probably lacked hearths, as people cooked outdoors in summer.

YUKON RIVER WOODEN HOUSES

Summer houses around Razboinski (the Razbinsky of fig. 160), elsewhere on the lower Yukon River, and "throughout this part of Alaska" (Nelson 1899:247) deviated from the local winter dwellings in that they incorporated wider planks, set upright. Apparently they were covered only minimally by sod at best (figs. 160–161). The front and back wall planks were stepped, the tallest being at the center of each wall, while the side walls were perhaps six feet high and laid sometimes vertically (Nelson 1899:248) but more often horizontally. Judging from figure 160, the gable roof consisted of planks that ran (from a ridgepole, no doubt) to the lateral walls. Bark slabs lay over the roof planks. Square or elliptical doorways penetrated the center of the front wall (fig. 161), about one foot from the ground outside, the three-foot-high door holes being cut across the seam of two adjacent planks. A long, horizontal crossbeam ran the width of front and back walls just higher than the doorway, and at least two diagonally set struts, or braces, kept these crossbeams in place (fig. 160). The crossbeams pressed both the front and back ends of the house against its side walls and apparently were essential in stabilizing the whole edifice. In some cases, two posts taller than the house were set against the front and back walls, probably in such a way that "hewed sticks" would be wedged horizontally between the posts and the upright wall planks (Nelson 1899:247–248), thus holding the end walls in place.

Inside, the walls were stabilized by being pegged or tied, using withes, possibly connecting interior uprights along the side walls. Across the side walls lay rafters, allowing overhead storage between them and the double-pitched roof. Accommodating up to three families were wide sleeping platforms approximately one to three feet above the floor, sometimes with small square to round windows above them. People made little effort to seal wall cracks, making these houses rather airy (Nelson 1899:248).

SIBERIAN ESKIMO DOUBLE-ARCH TENTS

Descriptions of Siberian summer tents (figs. 162–164) are so meager or inaccessible that the following details rely mainly on visual images of these dwellings, which are plentiful. According to Hughes, "The typical summer house was also basically a walrus-hide (or later, tarpaulin) tent stretched over a wooden framework, rectangular in shape with the roof sloping to the rear. Inside the house there was a small bed platform often simply suspended on thongs" (1984:251, fig. 8).

Siberian Eskimo tents consisted of two arches, the taller and wider one in front. The difference in arch heights created a shed roof that pitched down and to the rear at an angle less than 15° (figs. 162–164). Each arch evidently consisted of two sturdy uprights and used a log lashed on as a crossbar. The two arches had to be linked to stabilize the whole frame and prevent bowing of the lateral roof edges. For this purpose, builders added two poles that connected the front and rear arches at their corners. Moreover, these lateral poles had vertical or diagonal struts lashed to them (fig. 163), which further supported the weighty tent cover. The cover was also secured with thongs weighted down by stones. The print made from a drawing by Louis Choris of a Saint Lawrence Island tent interior shows these details (fig. 163).

In addition, the thicker ends of several long, thin poles—perhaps the same "rafters" used in Siberian new-style hide-roofed winter houses—were tied to the rear-arch crossbar. No doubt these roof-pole ends were set flush with the line of the rear crossbar (fig. 163). Jutting forward in parallel fashion, they rested on the front crossbar, beyond which they protruded as a ragged mix of shorter and longer poles (figs. 162, 164).

Undoubtedly, Siberian Eskimo tent covers, like their new-style winter-house roofs, were made of walrus hide sheets, presumably rubbed with fat to be more water-resistant and translucent (cf. fig. 148). A reasonable guess is that one sheet covered the front, a second the sides (and possibly the rear as well), and a third stretched over the roof. Their boxy shape must have meant that they were severely windblown on blustery days. This would explain the massive boulders, logs, or whalebones leaned against the tent base and rested on the skirt (fig. 164) and thong weights that strapped down the sides (fig. 162).[14]

ALUTIIQ GRASS HUTS

In summer, the Alutiiqs of Kodiak Island erected a type of grass-roofed structure, a shalash (a Russian-language generic for hut, also used to refer to Native houses and qasgiqs). Its first mention, seemingly apocryphal as to

FIGURE 162

Double-arched tent, Plover Bay, Siberia, circa 1899. Boulders hold the tent cover base, a larger stone and a log or bone keep thongs tight across the roof and sides, and two in-flated sealskins hang from roof poles (foreground tent). Meat (and a hide?) dry from other tents' poles, while hides hang from a line between the two right tents. People left of the light-toned tent (with a parka hang-ing from a thong across its back) lend a sense of scale.

Edward H. Harriman Expedition Collection, Accession #RBD 0201-157, Archives, Alaska and Polar Regions Dept., Rasmuson Library, University of Alaska Fairbanks.

FIGURE 163

"Interior of a house on St. Lawrence Island." The sitting man plays an Eskimo drum and, like the other man, wears a waterproof parka made from strips of seal or walrus intestine, uninflated coils of which are hanging to the left. The front and rear arches (left and right, respectively) employ upright poles, but the side (center) is diagonally braced.

Choris 1822:pl. 17, Rare Book B0083, Archives, Alaska and Polar Regions Dept., Rasmuson Library, University of Alaska Fairbanks.

FIGURE 164

"Native summer village, Plover Bay, Sibe-ria." Box-like, double-arched nature of Siberian summer tents are in clear view. The right tent shows a small doorway in the broad front, with a man, woman, and two children standing in front of it (and a small child peek-ing from the mother's parka, right). The middle tent has a large pelt (bearded seal?) being dried and stretched on a hide frame.

From Healy 1889:26 ff.

size, appears in Russian explorer Stephen Glotoff's (Stepan Glotov's) account of 1763: "Glotoff with ten men proceeded to a village on the shore . . . where the natives had begun to reside: it consisted of three summer-huts covered only with long grass; they were from eight to ten yards broad, twelve long, and about four high. There were about a hundred men" (Coxe 1966:110).[15] During Davydov's stay on Kodiak, he once slept in a lean-to made of an upturned umiak (skin boat) (see Alternative Summer Dwellings below) while his comrade spent the night "in a straw lean-to [shalash]" (Davydov 1977:120). On the other hand, it is conceivable that this "lean-to" was really an abandoned summer house "made by some islanders when they had been there" (Davydov 1977:120).

Consistent with the absence of information on summertime Alutiiq dwellings is Clark's (1984:191) synopsis of Alutiiq life, in which he describes only the winter house, and omits any discussion of summer dwellings. Nevertheless, Glottoff records that the grass lean-tos were occupied by nuclear rather than extended families. Possibly this discrepancy and the larger size of Glotoff's "summer huts," which accommodated more people than winter houses, argue for huts being an altogether different class of dwelling.[16]

PRINCE WILLIAM SOUND PLANK HUTS

Early Russian explorers saw small abandoned huts with adz-planed vertical planks and interior hearths. They stood about six feet square and high, with a smokehole in the bark-covered roof. Inside was a central firepit and a sleeping or storage area defined by wide, even planks and a window at each end. Other summer dwellings were described as poorly consructed and less than weather-tight (Crowell and Mann 1998:129–130).

ALTERNATIVE SUMMER DWELLINGS

Short of building a formal structure, the most common summer shelter in southwest Alaska was a tipped-over umiak propped up by oars, forked poles, driftwood, and the like at about a 45° angle (fig. 165). An illustration from 1802 depicts such an arrangement in the Chugach Eskimo (mainland Alutiiq) area, geographically and culturally close to the Kodiak Islanders. This engraving shows three umiak lean-tos, which appear to incorporate bark slabs, skins, and planks as out-thrust overhangs with approximately twenty-degree downslopes (Clark 1984:fig. 5).[17] All three roofs use three- to four-foot uprights to support their lower front edges; their back edges terminate under the umiak's gunwales. The Chugach the Koniags would take planks with them to use as roofing (Birket-Smith 1953:53; Davydov 1977:120). The Kuuvaŋmiut and other Northwest Arctic Eskimos occasionally upended their watercraft for this same purpose (see chapter 3, Alternative Summer Dwellings).

Kuskokwim River people (Kusquqvagmiut) maintained summer homes at hunting camps on the tundra. Six-foot-high turf walls were roofed with split logs (supported by four corner posts), enveloped by turf. Occasionally, these camp houses replicated those in winter villages (VanStone 1984:229).

Saint Lawrence Islanders sometimes built what appears to be a summer version of the old-style Chukchi winter house. Nelson explains how its super-structure was assembled. First, a whale mandible was embedded upright at some spot along the intended circumference of the floor; its distal arc was pointed inward. Once this bone was in place, its top was flattened so that sections of whale mandibles (split or sawn lengthwise) could be added as rafters, which were barely planted around the circle. Their upper ends, which curved inward, were angled so that some were stacked onto the flat-topped mandible and others onto the ribs that had been stacked earlier in the con-struction process. Next, whale ribs were added in between the split jawbones. These arched up and inward. This arrangement was roofed with walrus hides and weighted thongs like the winter dwelling. The result was a roof more rounded than that of the winter house and without any externally evident rafters (Nelson 1899:257–259, figs. 85–86).

Besides upended umiaks, some Chugach summer dwellings were elemen-tary lean-tos, or "small sheds, made of a few sticks covered with a little bark" (Portlock 1789:253). Birket-Smith (1953:54) refers briefly to another Chugach dwelling of sorts: "A temporary shelter might also be made by digging into the ground and covering it with skins."

FIGURE 165

"South Alaskan Eskimo scene." Three men tand between two umiak lean-tos (left), the fore one nearly covered by a tarp, which no doubt adds extra shelter to the other side and might have covered the adjacent umiak as well. People (mostly women and children) occupy themselves (background), while two memorial poles are visible in the foreground: the shorter pole has a person and sea bird mounted on its crosspiece; the taller post has humans on either side of a raised Eskimo drum (the right person possibly holding a harpoon), with canines (seated dogs or wolves?) beside the humans and smaller (land?) birds outside the arch on this cross-piece.

Courtesy of The Field Museum, negative #CSA8038; photographer unknown.

FIGURE 166

"Storehouses at Ikogmut (mission)." Resem-bling miniature summer houses from the Yukon-Kuskowim Delta (see background), these stilt-raised structures have gabled roofs, upright board walls, small doors centered in the front wall, and crossbeams to hold the front and back walls in place (cf figs. 160–161). Apparently, people reached them using notched logs, which dogs cannot climb.

From Nelson 1899:pl. 81.

SPECIAL-USE STRUCTURES

LESSER STRUCTURES

Northern Central Yup'ik houses were distinguished by one ancillary structure, the cache or storage shed, constructed of wood and raised on posts about six feet square and some four to five feet above the ground (figs. 132, 161, 166). Its purpose was to store foodstuffs away from dogs, foxes, wolves, and mice, and it also served to elevate sleds, watercraft, and the like. Caches looked rather like diminutive houses from the region (Fair 1997; Nelson 1899:fig. 75).[18] Around St. Michael, the Unaligmiut stacked logs horizontally to create the cache walls, probably held in place by being fitted into the cutout, inward-facing quarter of each post; its roof appears to have been an assortment of scrap wood. The Ikogmiut of the Yukon River used upright planks to form cache walls and more planks for the gable roofs and a platform on all four sides. Notched logs acted as ladders up to the entrance, which was a square hole in one corner at St. Michael, and a round, centered opening at Ikogmiut (fig. 166; Nelson 1899:fig. 75; Ray 1966:51). At Hooper Bay, on the coast midway between the Yukon and Kuskwim River deltas, caches probably shared features with both Unaligmiut and Ikogmiut examples but had turf added to the roof (Curtis 1907–1930:96 ff). On Nunivak Island, traditional caches "were built like houses." They were either dug into shallower pits, lacked skylights, and had a hatch in one side of the roof (VanStone 1989:23), or they were "sheds built above ground" (Fienup-Riordan 2000:7). Saint Lawrence Island meat caches were deep pits walled with stone, then lined inside with short poles, and roofed with more poles supported by whale mandibles (Geist and Rainey 1936:66–72).

Storage racks appeared alongside houses in southwestern Alaska also. They incorporated either simple crosspieces or platforms built onto wooden or whale mandible uprights or pairs of X-shaped bipods, tripods, or wide-forked poles. Here, as in northwestern Alaska, the racks kept dogs away from dogsleds, with their tempting leather lashings, and from skin-covered umiaks and kayaks (e.g., figs. 132, 157A, 159–160; Curtis 1907–1930:114 ff, 122 ff; Nelson 1899:figs. 85, 88; VanStone 1989:figs. 2, 42–43).

Like Aleut (and to some extent Central Yup'ik) culture, that of the mainland and insular Alutiiqs had been strongly influenced by the eighteenth- and nineteenth-century invasions of Russian fur hunters, who had brought with them the idea of steam baths.[19] Alutiiq steam baths sometimes took place in the winter house, but more often the men built separate structures (*zhupan*s).[20] We cannot be certain that they were anything more than sleeping chambers temporarily employed as baths, but, by ethnographic analogy, the Central Yupiit often erected domed tents and, later, small outlying structures dedicated to this purpose (see Merck 1980:100 and Maressa 1986:154). Later on, under Russian influences, the Alutiiqs (like the Central Yupiit) had bath chambers separated from their houses (Knecht and Jordan 1985:33). Davydov (1977:112) identifies another Alutiiq structure as a shooting blind. It stood about three and a half feet high by two and a third feet square, "was made of grass," and in one case doubled as an overnight shelter (Davydov 1977:112). Pratt assembled an exhaustive list of lesser structures from Nunivak Island: fox traps, wolf pit-traps, sweathouses, storage pits, trail markers, and "temporary" shelters (U.S. Bureau of Indian Affairs ANCSA 1995:1:50–53).

BIRTH, MENSTRUAL, AND MOURNING HUTS

The practice of segregating women in birth and menstrual huts was known in Southwest Alaska from Norton Sound (Ray 1966:30) to Prince William Sound (Birket-Smith 1953:85) on the Alaska mainland, though information about them is sparse. Unaligmiut and Nunivaarmiut mothers delivered in birth huts, regardless of season, with or without assistance from a midwife (Jacobsen 1977:152; Lantis 1946:223). This Unaligmiut information, which comes from a man raised in Northwest Alaska, might be suspect except that Edmonds, who worked in the Central Yup'ik area, is in basic agreement with him. "It is not by any means unheard of, even now, for a woman in a traveling party to be left behind alone in the morning and have her catch up in the evening carrying a new born babe which she alone had attended to—all this in midwinter" (Ray 1966:30).

The Kodiak Island Alutiiqs built birth huts of reeds or branches and sheathed that framework with grass, winter or summer. The entire floor of one birth hut measured only three feet long (Hrdlička 1975:31; Lisiansky 1814:201). After giving birth the women withstood postpartum confinement for five, ten, or twenty days in the same "small low hovels" (Lisiansky 1814:200–201; Pierce 1978:127).[21]

Nunivaarmiut women remained isolated in an unheated hut, summer or winter, for three days during their first menses and twenty days more in the house (Lantis 1946:225). Among the mainland Alutiiqs, menstruation required a ten-day confinement in a hut on the first menses and a shorter stay every month thereafter (Lisiansky 1814:201).[22] Whenever they retreated to these huts, Alutiiq women consumed food and drink from separate vessels (Black 1977:95).[23] Besides birth huts, Lisiansky describes what might be termed an Alutiiq mourning hut:

> In one of the small buildings, or kennels, as they may very properly be called, was a woman who had retired into it in consequence of the death of her son. She had been there several days, and would have remained for the space of twenty, had I not entreated the toyon [village head] to permit her to quit it, representing that the weather was too bad for continuing long in so disagreeable a place. (Lisiansky 1814:184)

BURIAL STRUCTURES

Toward the north, Central Yup'ik groups placed their dead in rectangular wooden boxes. These were either elevated by four corner posts (Dall 1870:146, 227; Himmelheber 1993:figs. 57–58; Nelson 1899:fig. 100, 102,103, pl. 91) or set on the ground and partly covered with short crisscrossing logs (fig. 167). The containers were so small that the dead virtually had to be crammed

FIGURE 167
Detail from "an Eskimo grave on St. Michael Island, Alaska." A tepee-like arrangement of driftwood logs overlies a small wooden coffin.
From Gordon 1906:pl. 12.

inside. Eskimo graveyards up the Yukon River were cluttered with such boxes on posts. Nunivak Islanders placed their dead in wood- or stone-lined "burial chambers" (U.S. Bureau of Indian Affairs ANCSA 1995:45) or shallow pits (Lantis 1946:227).

SOUTHWEST ALASKA AND ALUTIIQ CEREMONIAL HOUSES

Aside from its function as a male-oriented dwelling, the qasgiq (figs. 133–136) operated as "a general workroom, a sort of town hall, a steambath, a caravanserai for travelers, and a meeting place for celebrating their annual dances and festivals" (Dall 1870:16).[24] It has also been labeled a "hotel for visitors" (Murdoch 1892:80). Construction details for the Central Yup'ik qasgiq appear in the Winter Houses section above.

The Alutiiqs sometimes held festivities in their own *ciqlluaq* great rooms, but a few rich men's *qasgiq*s survived into the Russian period. Genuine Alutiiq *qasgiq*s were probably built much like Alutiiq winter houses but slightly bigger, about nineteen by twenty-three feet. The sum of what we have gleaned from ethnographies points to Alutiiq *qasgiq* features such as a large gut window or at least a central skylight, wooden benches (probably against three or all four walls), and perhaps[25] side rooms. As might be expected, only men were permitted to build and repair these structures (Black 1977:91, 93; Davydov 1977:107, 110; Hrdlička 1975:29; Pierce 1978:120–121).

ASSOCIATED RITUALS AND BELIEFS

THE PERVASIVE ESKIMO PRACTICE OF HOUSE ABANDONMENT FOLLOWING THE DEATH OF a family member in the house also was known in Southwest Alaska (Ray 1966:49). In the 1880s, Jacobsen visited Shaktolik in eastern Norton Sound and, pestered by villagers to retrieve things for them, "went to an Eskimo house that had just been abandoned because of the death of a child. Even their longing for tea and pancakes did not overcome their fear of the presence of death" (Jacobsen 1977:165). Much as Central Arctic Eskimos removed the dead by routes other than the house tunnel or passage, Eskimos in this region would extract their deceased through the skylight (e.g., Hawkes 1914:14; Lantis 1946:227; Nelson 1899:311). The Alutiiqs went further, actually burying the deceased in his or her sleeping chamber in the house before abandoning it (Davydov 1977:179; Merck 1980:206). Some Alutiiqs, however, took a more pragmatic approach:

> During my stay in Kad'iak in one village in the winter time one poor old woman who had no relatives became so ill that her death was imminent. The owners of the house in which she was living, in order to save themselves the trouble of having to build a new house at such a stormy time of the year, dug a hole for the woman, placed her in it and covered it with wood. Three days later the unfortunate woman's cries could still be heard. (Davydov 1977:179)

Moreover, important Alutiiq men were mummified and, after death, their bodies secreted in remote caves, where they were posed like mannequins (Pinart

1873). The many skeletons Geist and Rainey unearthed from one Saint Lawrence Island house floor (1936:61) suggest that, at least in earlier times, Siberian Eskimos also felt little dread of death.

Himmelheber catalogs several house-linked practices that involved Nunivak Islanders upon someone's death. These behaviors fall somewhere in between the Alutiiqs' practicality and other Southwest Alaska groups' deeper fear of the dead:

> All villagers . . . must leave their houses and remain in the open until the burial is completed. If it is night, they are roused and are not allowed to continue sleeping. . . . The [seal gut] skin window-covering of the skylight is lifted somewhat so that the lechlgach [unseen spirit] can fly away. If a man dies in the men's house, a great sweat bath is organized in which all men participate. Afterward everyone gets a stick to chase away the lechlgach. All wood must be thrown out of both the family house and storage houes. . . . The corpse is lifted outside through the skylight and carried to the coffin accompanied by relatives. . . . The spouse or parents [of the deceased] must remain in their house for three days . . . [, after which] a man goes to the men's house and a woman washes her hair. . . . From then until the next Bladder Festival . . . relatives [of the deceased] must pull their parka hoods over their heads when they leave the house. . . . A woman may not go in the men's house to bring her husband his meal. . . . Spouses of the recently dead must stand outside during the Bladder Festival. . . . Death is not seen as a reason to abandon the family house [, however]. (Fienup-Riordan 2000:138, 141–142)

Firepits in *qasgiq*s (figs. 134–135, 138) were thought to be the dwelling place of the spirits, and people sometimes poured offerings to them through cracks in the log floors (Hawkes 1914:15; Michael 1967:123). The Alutiiqs apparently felt somewhat differently about *qasgiq*s, razing them "after a festival has taken place" (Davydov 1977:184). This was probably after something akin to a Great Festival to the Dead had taken place (cf. Davydov 1977:180).

Although Alutiiq ceremonialism "was rather weak" (Birket-Smith 1953:108), one *qasgiq*-focused ceremony, the Bladder Festival, was important in Southwest Alaska. It took place in December and its intent was "to insure a continuing supply of sea mammals" (Oswalt 1979:252). A whole village might pack into one *qasgiq*, its ceiling filled with hung-up mechanical effigy animals as well as painted, inflated bladders of animals killed during the year (Fienup-Riordan 1996:126–131). At the crucial point during these activities, everyone paraded from the *qasgiq*—with bladders in hand—to a hole in the ice and immersed the bladders. People then predicted future hunting based on the sights and sounds emitted as the soggy membranes sank (Michael 1967:123).

Men and older boys spent their indoor hours in *qasgiq*s, while women and children stayed in separate family-focused houses. On Nelson Island, then, it seems predictable that the house was symbolically analogous to female reproductive organs:

> The reproductive capacity of the women's house was explicit. In certain contexts, its interior was likened to the womb from which the spirits of the dead would be reborn in human form as they entered the world of the living. Elena remembers the pregnancy taboos that required her to exit quickly and

repeatedly through the doorway so that her unborn child would emerge in a similar manner from her body. One story of an unborn child depicts it as it first becomes aware of itself in a room inhabited only by a toothless old woman. The baby ultimately finds the door and exits.... At puberty [girls were] confined to the house, their social invisibility approximating a fetus' hidden state. (Fienup-Riordan 1990:61–62)

A similar analogy connected houses of women on Saint Lawrence Island: "[A pregnant woman] has rules to follow like when she enters the door, she has to let her head out first before her feet so the baby can come out head first" (Carius 1979:8).

Among the Yup'ik, personifications of *qasgiq*s extended to regarding them as sentient beings:

> ...If a village had two *qasgit*, they had independent [given] names.... Men regularly purified their abode by vigorously sweeping the floor and emptying the urine and water buckets, accompanying this action with noise and drumming to drive off evil influences. During ceremonial distributions, the *qasgiq* might receive gifts in its name, such as a new gut window or clay lamp.... In some cases [the men] even carved masks to represent and celebrate this respected "person." (Fienup-Riordan 1996:125)

CHAPTER 4 NOTES

1 The Siberian and Saint Lawrence Island Yupik do not include the apostrophe in the spelling of their name.

2 Oswalt does a fine job of contrasting these two variations (Oswalt 1967:fig. 4).

3 Laying planks horizontally may suggest Russian influence as well, but the same sideways-laid planks are also found in Unaligmiut *qasgiq*s without dovetailed construction (Nelson 1899:fig. 76; Ray 1966:129–130).

4 As a rule, house-roof entrances were used only when snowdrifts blocked other accesses.

5 From ethnographic analogy it is reasonable to suggest that women took steam baths after the men.

6 The "largest [ceremonial house] in the country [Southwest Alaska]" boasted a floor twenty-five by thirty feet) and a skylight looming fifteen feet high (Dall 1870:126). Another *qasgiq* from the Bering Sea region (probably from St. Michael rather than the Diomedes) was thirty feet square with a skylight twenty feet above floor level (Hawkes 1914:13). Himmelheber describes Nunivak Island *qasgiq*s as being "at least five times as large as a single-family dwelling" (Fienup-Riordan 2000:7). Some Yup'ik *qasgiq*s could hold up to 300 people during ceremonies (Fienup-Riordan 1996:122).

7 Later in the historic period candles were sometimes substituted for seal-oil lamps (Fienup-Riordan 1996:122).

8 The following description relies heavily on one superb example, House 7, from Kukulik, Saint Lawrence Island (Geist and Rainey 1936:62–64, 73, figs. 2, 14). Although turf-covered, it was surface-built in the historic era, but it otherwise reflects the aboriginal dwelling style (Aron Crowell, personal communication with Molly Lee, 1991). Other sources important sources are Moore (1923:346) and Nelson (1899:259–260).

9   On the Siberian mainland, the new-style houses appear to have overlain rock foundations and passages. No information on this point is available from Saint Lawrence Island.

10 Our ethnographic knowledge about Alutiiq house types comes almost exclusively from accounts written at least two decades after Russians arrived (e.g. Black 1977; Davydov 1977).

11 Using curved whale ribs or whale mandibles as rafters would lend hip roofs a domed appearance.

12 This implies either that the Kodiak Alutiiqs had houses of a different type at locations other than their main village or that they had two of the same type of house at different sites. Supporting the latter interpretation is evidence from the Alutiiqs' mainland neighbors, the Chugach Eskimos, who had separate dwellings of the same type at summer and winter sites (Birket-Smith 1953:55).

13 In all likelihood, these were variants of the Northwest Arctic dome tents.

14 Structurally, this tent design shows some similarities with the West Greenland Eskimo and Sallirmiut double-arch tents (see chapters 1 and 2), although we do not posit any direct connections.

15 It is conceivable that this community, wary of foreigners, hid the women and children nearby.

16 Alternatively, given the close cultural connections between the Alutiiq and Aleut people it is quite possible that the Kodiak Island summer house was similar to the Aleut *barabara* (see Lantis 1984:167).

17 Portlock (1789:239, 253) seems to describe the same Chugach shelter.

18 Fair (1997) presents an excellent discussion of Alaska Native caches, including oral traditions associated with some in the Eskimo culture areas.

19 It is possible that the sweatbath known throughout North and South America appeared in Alaska also, though probably not in the form known after Russian occupation. For a full discussion of the debate see Maressa 1986.

20 Alutiiq men apparently did not heat their *qasgiq*s for this purpose.

21 Postpartum Chugach Eskimo mothers stayed forty days in their birth huts, although their husbands could visit (Birket-Smith 1953:85).

22 Another taboo associated with menstruation forbade women from touching "wood which is red or painted red," believing that to do so would increase their menstrual flow (Davydov 1977:170, 171). Unaligmiut women also observed menstrual taboos, which restricted their touching things and required their using separate eating and drinking utensils (Jacobsen 1977:127).

23 Females on Kodiak Island and elsewhere occupied birth and menstrual structures without regard to weather or season (Jacobsen 1977:152; Lisiansky 1814:200–201).

24 Edmonds points out that guests or strangers stayed in the *qasgiq* when they were not invited to stay in a house (Ray 1966:49).

25 Alternatively, the presence of side rooms may indicate that the structure was a regular house but also used for celebrations.

5

SUMMARY AND CONCLUSIONS

In between the lines is something special going on

in their minds, and that has got to be brought to

light, so they understand just exactly what is said.

(Chief Peter John, Athabascan Elder, to Dr. William Schneider, 1999)

CONTRIBUTIONS TO THE
STUDY OF ESKIMO ARCHITECTURE

THIS STUDY IS A FIRST ATTEMPT TO SYNTHESIZE THE VOLUMINOUS INFORM-
ation about early Eskimo house types that has accumulated in the literature
over the past two centuries or so, and to pull together a comprehensive bib-
liography on this topic (cf. Jochelson 1906; Steensby 1917:187–203; Thalbitzer
1914:360–364). We hope to lay the groundwork for more theoretical and
interpretive studies in the future. In this concluding chapter we summarize
the house types discussed in preceding chapters, offer a working taxonomy
of them, and consider some related topics arising from this study and deserv-
ing further research. Finally, we return to some of the cultural dimensions
that have emerged in these pages.

SIMILARITIES SHARED BY DWELLINGS ACROSS THE ARCTIC

For the clearest possible comparisons we will limit our considerations to primary winter and summer dwellings even though all groups used more than just
these two main seasonal types (Reinhardt 1986).[1] Despite differences in the
design of dwellings, there is considerable commonality both in the architecture
of the various Eskimo populations and in the ways they used their dwellings.
These are summarized in Table 1. More intriguing is the disparity between the
winter and summer dwellings: Summer dwellings (mostly tents) have fewer
elements in common with each other than do winter dwellings, another indication of how, for Eskimos, the winter and summer seasons diverge.

TABLE 1

Similarities shared by dwellings across the Arctic.

Features shared by **all** primary **winter** dwellings	• physically discrete main sleeping chamber • moderate to marked excavation for main chamber • use of artificial lighting (oil lamps) • sooty walls due to lamps and/or hearths • barely warm to extremely hot temperatures in main chamber • some means of venting stale air and heat from main chamber • use of natural lighting (from outside main chamber) • raised sleeping platforms or benches with insulated bedding • basic binding methods (e.g., lashing, sewing, pegging, pinning), if any, in construction • middens (refuse heaps) near exterior entrance/exit

Additional features shared by **most** primary **winter** dwellings	• delineations of main chamber entrance, floor, and sleeping area
	• sleeping chamber as the main room
	• sleeping space(s) at back and/or sides of main chamber
	• smaller accessory chambers for storage, dog shelters, and family quarters
	• open storage spaces or inset niches beneath sleeping platform(s) or bench(es)
	• women's stations at edge, if not side, of platform(s) or bench(es)
	• sea mammal (usually seal) oil lamps for heating, cooking, and warmth
	• lamp platforms or stands lateral to main platform(s) or bench(es)
	• cooking done by women over lamp and/or hearth in main chamber
	• cooking pot suspended over lamp
	• drying rack(s) above lamp(s) and pot(s)
	• tunnel and passage traits:
	    - narrow and vertically cramped
	    - usually lower than main chamber's floor level
	    - usually domed construction
	    - sometimes vertical walls and flat roofs
	• one or more windows or a skylight (made of gut, skin, or other animal membrane)
	• skillful hand-fitting of construction materials
	• variations in building materials and design details
	• exterior insulation of sod and/or snow

Features shared by **all** primary **summer** dwellings	• permissive of a less confining way of life[2] • overall continuity in construction materials from region to region

Additional features shared by **most** primary **summer** dwellings	• separate flap or curtain at the doorway
	• four regionally representative tent shapes:
	    - arch (Greenland, Canada, and Siberia)
	    - ridge (Canada)
	    - conical (Canada and Alaska)
	    - dome (Alaska)
	• tent covers were:
	    - made from one or two layers of seal or caribou skins
	    - skins sewn together with sinew
	    - laced with thongs made from same animal skins
	    - held down with weights around the base
	• framework poles usually made of wood (sometimes bone, antler, or ivory)
	• guy lines generally absent
	• translucent gut-strip or oiled-skin panel as a window
	• demarcation of the rear floor as a sleeping area
	• cooking-place outside the dwelling
	• smudge fire outside near entrance

PRIMARY SUMMER AND WINTER DWELLING TYPES

There is no simple, elegant way to categorize Eskimo dwellings. Nevertheless, figures 168–169 are attempts at a classification. These summary maps show the distribution of some—but not all—of the fundamental winter and summer dwelling variations, from Greenland to Siberia. Given that the following data collapse such a wide variety of dwelling types, this narrative, the table, and the drawings and photographs taken together should be considered heuristic rather than definitive.

For Eskimo primary winter dwellings (fig. 168), the main typological organizing principle we use is wall material. In Greenland, two stone-walled houses were in use: the multifamily house and the single- or dual-family house. Stone communal houses also existed in the Labrador area, but other than the scantily reported stone structures of Sallirmiut, the snowblock house was dominant in the Central Arctic during historic times. Among domed snowblock houses, the dome-tunneled forms were widespread, although vertical-sided, flat-roofed tunnels and built-in dance-house dome houses were characteristic of the Copper Eskimo in the westernmost area of snow-house construction.

In the Northwest Arctic and Bering Strait areas (from the Mackenzie River territory to the shores of Western Norton Sound), wood-framed winter houses, either rectangular (gable-roofed) or cruciform (four center posts, with hip or crib roofs), were the most common; turf-covered, pole-walled houses were found inland, and stone houses on King Island and the Diomedes. Finally, in the Southwest Alaska, Bering Sea, Siberia, and Gulf of Alaska region (from eastern Norton Sound to the Alaska Peninsula, Kodiak Island, and Prince William Sound, and out to Saint Lawrence Island and easternmost Siberia), most houses were of the four-center-post, crib-roofed design, although in the Bering Sea and Siberia, the new-style roundish (multisided) house prevailed.

Wooden houses from Southwest Alaska typically had walls laid horizontally. More northerly houses, on the other hand, had wall logs or planks set vertically. One reason undoubtedly is the greater abundance of wood and bigger logs farther south, where direct supplies of timber and major rivers (especially the Yukon and Kuskokwim) as driftwood sources were generally closer.

Tents usually served as the Eskimo primary summer dwellings (fig. 169). Here, our basic typological criterion is shape. Greenlandic tents were arched at the front (although one form in West Greenland had a lower rear arch as well). Nearly all Central Arctic tents were ridged, with either a pole connecting the front and rear upright structures (hard-ridged) or a thong linking these ends (flexible-ridged). One exception was the Sallirmiut double-arch tent; another was the Caribou Eskimos' long-pole conical tent, with tepee-like poles erupting from its peak. A third was the vaguely ridged Netsilik tent, which was essentially conical and had a single centerpole holding up the cover.

In the Northwest Arctic and Bering Strait, coastal tents were conical, but made such that all their tent poles met inside at the peak. Among the Interior Eskimos, dome tents occurred exclusively, but around Kotzebue Sound they coexisted with the short-pole conical type. On the Bering Strait islands, however, people spent their summers in radically different dwellings: boxy,

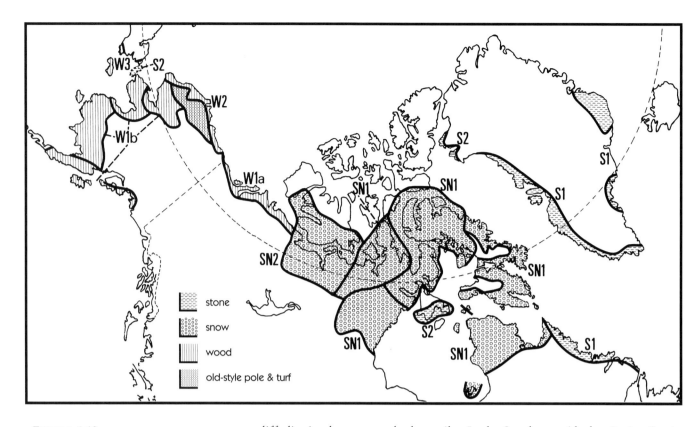

FIGURE 168

Distribution of Eskimo winter and transitional dwelling types: S1, communal house; S2, single/dual-family house; SN1, domed tunnel; SN2, flat-roofed tunnel; W1a, four-center-post winter; W1b, four-center-post year-round; W2, gabled roof; W3, round house.

In the map legend:
- stone
- snow
- wood
- old-style pole & turf

cliff-clinging houses perched on stilts. In the Southwest Alaska, Bering Strait, Siberia, and Gulf of Alaska region most mainland houses doubled as summer residences, but in parts of the Bering Sea and in Siberia a double-arch tent occurred—a great distance across the Arctic from other arched forms. The reason for this morphological similarity is unknown. In Southwest Alaska the main alternative shelter was an umiak tipped on its side, often with some extra covering material for added shelter from wind and rain.

POSSIBILITIES FOR FURTHER RESEARCH

ONE TOPIC WORTH EXAMINING IS THE RELATIONSHIP BETWEEN ENVIRONMENT and culture as reflected in the development of Eskimo architecture. The Eskimo cultural area is wide enough and rich enough in examples to offer a provocative case study of the interaction of environment and culture through variations and similarities in the house types of particular groups. One may observe physical connections between the shape of the house floors and a group's mobility (e.g., Hunter-Anderson 1977:307, 309), for example, or between winter dwelling complexity, floor area per person and mean annual temperature (Appendix; Hayden et al. 1996). It is quite another matter, however, to tease apart the cultural factors in play that lead to these connections. The variability in house types described in these pages should help temper assumptions derived from ecological determinism and archaeology's overriding concern with material things. To what degree do such intangibles as land and sea, kinship patterns, division of labor between the sexes, and world view influence the forms of domestic and nondomestic structures (Alsayyad 1989:528; Douglas 1971)?

Second, indigenous Eskimo architecture exemplifies the tension between homogeneity and local variation characteristic of Eskimo culture in general (Graburn and Lee 1990:25). Pan-Arctic Eskimo studies, probably because the Eskimo cultural area is the largest occupied by a small-scale society, tend to stress culture-wide uniformity at the expense of acknowledging regional variation (e.g., Birket-Smith 1936; Burch and Forman 1988; Weyer 1932), and the study of housing is no exception (e.g., Hunter-Anderson 1977; Nabokov and Easton 1989; Waterman 1924). It is true that winter dwellings were almost always one kind of semisubterranean house with excavated tunnels or roofed surface passageways (Waterman 1924:290) and that tents in one form or other were used for summer living nearly everywhere from Greenland to Siberia. Still, such generalizations minimize regional differences, which in turn were the product of an array of cultural factors including creative imagination, historical happenstance, the wish to be distinct from close neighbors, style, form, aesthetics, and environmental adaptations.

This variability points to the relationships between essentialist and symbolic dimensions of culture. Burch (1983) has investigated architecture as it relates to sociodemographics and settlement patterns, and Reinhardt (1986, 1991) has looked at how settlement patterns and subsistence economies correlate to dwellings. Even so, the quest for common underlying factors that influence homologous patterning (for instance, the layout of dwelling space compared with other cultural realms such as music or folklore) cries out for attention in the Eskimo case. As Glassie has pointed out, "Architecture studies as an expression of personality and culture may provide us with the best means available for comprehending an authentic history" (Glassie 1975:vii). Moreover, a house is not isolated from the community in which it

FIGURE 169

Distribution of Eskimo summer dwelling types: A1, single arch; A2, double arch; R1, pole ridge; R2, thong ridge; C1, single-short-pole cone; C2, multiple-short-pole cone.

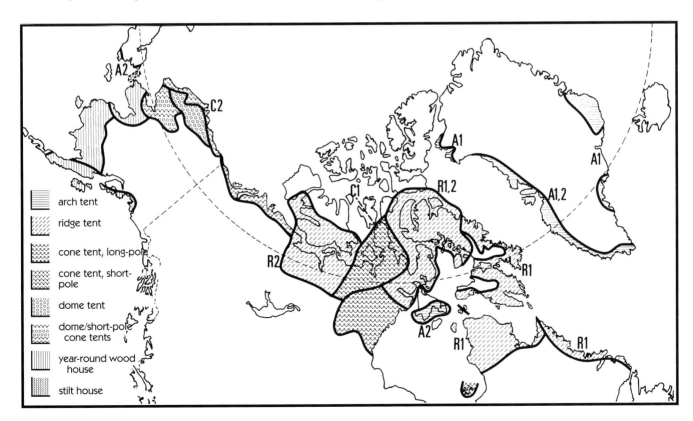

arch tent
ridge tent
cone tent, long-pole
cone tent, short-pole
dome tent
dome/short-pole cone tents
year-round wood house
stilt house

is found, but an integral part of it and used by community members in a variety of ways. After all, a home does not just mirror individual and family choices; it also echoes the wider cultural context in which it was established. One has only to think of the flux in the domed winter dwellings of the Central Arctic to see how rich a field the use of domestic space by the wider community would be to mine.

A third line of investigation is the analysis of indigenous architectural form as a cultural system: what it means as opposed to what it does (cf. Hieb 1990; Oliver 1977; Saladin d'Anglure 1975). From this viewpoint architecture emerges as a metaphorical expression of world order, rich in religious and mythopoetic overtones. Its patterns should be considered according to how they interact with the controlling forces of the universe (in the case of the *qargi/qasgiq*), the orderly and proper arrangements between the sexes, the point of convergence between site and subsistence (Oliver 1977:13–14), and the close and nurturing attitudes toward children for which Eskimos are justly famous. Here, oral history and ethnohistory would be the major sources for data. Specific architectural features such as skylights, as well as the dwellings themselves, figure prominently as backdrops against which narrative is played out [see, for example, the role of architecture in many of the tales recorded by Boas (1901) and Nelson (1899), or the house-as-womb metaphor of some Southwest Alaskan Eskimos (Fienup-Riordan 1990:61–62)]. Most imperative to an understanding of architecture as a cluster of shared symbols and meanings, however, is oral testimony.

This brings us to another line of inquiry, one involving cultural continuity and meaning in the face of radical culture change. Today, in the suburban-type housing imported into Eskimo communities in Greenland, Canada and Alaska, anyone familiar with spatial arrangement in underground winter houses of the past cannot fail to be struck by the similarities in how equipment like hunting gear is stowed in the newer houses. Today, the parkas may come from clothiers Eddie Bauer or L.L. Bean, but the way they are hung in the entryway replicates that of the old fur parkas. Without a doubt Eskimo perceptions of space continue to be influenced by the patterns of earlier times.

FUTURE INQUIRIES

THE NEXT STEPS BEYOND THIS STUDY MIGHT INCLUDE THE CLASSIFICATION of dwelling types, as proposed above; the study of gender in relation to built form; analyses of space, approached from different avenues of investigation; meaning and symbolism related to dwellings, beyond instances cited in this book; further research into subsistence, settlement, and mobility in connection with dwellings; the energy requirements affecting dwelling use; and close attention to specific ethnographic details. We intend our preliminary ruminations below to stimulate additional work on the architecture of Eskimos, as well as that of other societies.

CLASSIFICATION OF TYPES

By concentrating on primary winter and summer dwelling types, we attempt to reduce analytical noise in the wealth of detail that would be a distraction from the pursuit of typological classification. Our approach emphasizes three materials for winter dwellings and four shapes for summer tents, but what can we say about the nonprimary dwellings? There are many transitional-season forms, such as the Central Arctic qarmaq and other alternative dwellings and simple shelters, which add complexity to any typological discussion. Special-use structures—ceremonial houses; birth, menstrual, death, and mourning huts; and nonshelter structures (scaffolds, caches, tepee and raised-coffin burials)—increase the diversity of types and variants.

Other sources of noise are linked to classification. Why are there arch tents at both ends of the Arctic? How can we account for the uniqueness of Sallirmiut dwellings? Where does the Bering Strait stilt house fit into a dwelling typology? How should we deal with umiaks used secondarily as small prefabricated dwellings?

GENDER STUDIES

We know relatively little about the differences between men's and women's relationships to their housing. Certain facts are clear: Women built some houses (e.g., tents), making or helping to maintain others, while men engaged in heavy construction tasks. However, the things we do not know are many: What did women and men think of dwellings—of the structures, the components, the householders' interactions inside and out, of commonalities within a type, or the singularities of individual dwellings? How did their thinking about children, younger or older, gender-focused or not, reflect or influence men's or women's relationships to their architectural traditions? Can architecture reveal those thoughts, with or without recourse to ethnographic analogy? Do patterns of the past continue, or have they been irrevocably transformed?

SPATIAL ANALYSES

Much has been written about the ways Eskimos used their primary dwellings. Judging from our research, however, there is an absence of information about the use of space in other dwelling types. How did Eskimos use space immediately outside their dwellings? How do special-use structures relate to and perhaps affect concepts of domestic space? Are there gender-based differences in spatial use and perception (proxemics)? How do children fit into the spatial picture?

MEANING AND SYMBOLISM

This book presents some specific linkages between dwellings and cultural behavior, and our citations are meant to be illustrative rather than exhaustive. A major question reaching beyond the scope of this book concerns the variations in response to the dwelling across the Arctic. Aron's story of the Greenland Eskimo whose heart burst upon seeing his home again (chapter 1) stands in stark contrast to Giddings' account of the Kobuk River people who reportedly had little sentimental or symbolic attachment to their dwellings (chapter 4). Neither of those shares much with the uterine symbolism of a Nelson Island house in the Central Yup'ik area. Perhaps the only difference is in the observational abilities of the outsiders.[3]

Murray Milne (personal communication with Gregory Reinhardt, 2001) observes that Eskimos spent little or no excess energy on art in their structures. Indeed, the Spartan utilitarianism of Eskimo housing stands in sharp contrast to Northwest Coast Indian houses, which were lavishly resplendent with carved and painted woodwork inside and out. If art is emotive, what does this austerity say about Eskimo sentiments toward their dwellings? Still, Eskimos did create art (often in miniature), and some of its most extravagant expressions took form in Southwest Alaska, where communal houses (*qasgiqs*) and graveyards could mark scenes of abundant and creative artistry.

Surely there is more to understand, too, about the disappearance of the *qasgiq* from Greenland, especially when compared to its elaboration in Alaska. How can we explain the different cultural intensities in the uses of *qargi* and *qasgiq* between the Northwest Arctic and Southwest Alaska? What did these distinctive structures signify to males and females, to adults and children?

Many specimens of Eskimo art, from models and miniatures to drawings and scrimshaw, depict dwellings (fig. 170). Where and how does art illuminate architecture with regard to community, conflict, "typical" culture, or specific events (figs. 171–172)? Some Eskimo art was made for sale and trade to non-Natives, but a significant proportion was made for Eskimo consumption. The East Greenland tents (fig. 25), the mask-like mallet head from Little Diomede Island (fig. 124), and the carved images of tents from the Sallirmiut (fig. 74) and Pingasugruk (fig. 102) are examples of art in association with dwellings. The ivory and bone scrimshaw found in many museums (e.g., Hoffman 1897) and private collections would, by themselves, be worth pursuing in order to learn more about dwellings and their builders. Also warranting symbolic consideration are the human-shaped stone cairns, or *inuksut* (particularly common in the Central Arctic), other cairns and simple stone works (e.g., kayak rests), structures unrelated to villages such as caribou fences and corrals, etc., that we did not address in this book.

FIGURE 170

Detail of a house on an incised ivory tobacco pipe, most likely from the Kuskokwim River, Alaska. This structure is probably a house, not a *qasgiq*. In the structure, someone is next to the central hearth, from which smoke billows up through the open skylight. The entryway appears to be a surface passage with anteroom. Inflated sealskins hang from a rack above it, next to a square-doored food cache on stilts—with ladder access (cf. figs. 131, 161, 166). Off camera, left, are two inverted kayaks, each resting on two pairs of pole bipods (see fig. 132).

Courtesy of The Field Museum, artifact #A13693, photograph by Gregory A. Reinhardt.

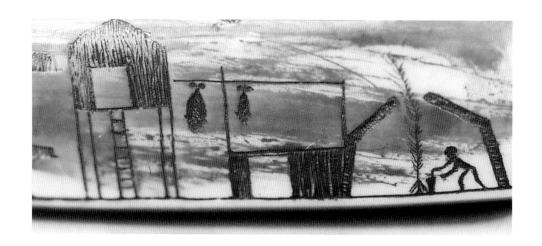

FIGURE 171

"Engraving on bone." Scene at the top shows summer life (left to right): fishnet in water, with floats and weights; drying rack being filled up with split fish; someone near a fire (cooking?); and two people inside or outside a short-pole conical Bering Strait tent. Bottom scene shows dogsledding: left person holds whip (dogs probably in fan-trace array) and right person runs beside another sled (dogs in linear-trace array). *Hoffman 1897:fig. 79.*

SUBSISTENCE, SETTLEMENT, AND MOBILITY

Architecture responds to the physical world as interpreted by people. Much more remains to be discovered about how dwellings are tied to such issues as food-getting, village size and membership, and the seasonal round. These and other material matters appear below in our elaboration of physically limiting factors. Still, there is probably a great deal yet to investigate about those factors relevant to sociocultural concerns, including politics, economics, trade, site selection, and so on (e.g., Dawson 2001).

ENERGY REQUIREMENTS

This topic is what might be called "energistics," the study of energy acquisition and exploitation, in this case as it affects architecture and, specifically, dwellings (e.g., Strub 1996). Energistics relates, in part, to architects' conceptual measurement units abbreviated as clo (referring to layers of clothing, or insulation) and met (referring to human metabolic rates, or body heat). However, energistics moves away from issues of air circulation, comfort levels, and heating efficiency in modern buildings. Instead, its focus should intersect the realms of cultural ecology, cultural geography, and cultural materialism. It should address such issues as technologies used in small-scale societies, the economics of societies' caloric input and output, the extent of societies' choices within natural landscapes, the impacts of those choices on such landscapes, and even the usually slow rates of evolution in vernacular architectural forms.

For example, how much does it cost, in terms of work (measured in standard units of energy) to fabricate and occupy dwellings? How much of what goes into producing a dwelling is due to physical requirements, and what proportion results from culturally determined needs? How do people weigh the energy costs of dwelling construction and maintenance against travel either within or between seasons (McGuire and Schiffer 1983)? How does fuel for heating figure into the socially calculated energy equation? Human bodies generate heat, but, in winter, Eskimos normally supplemented body heat with sea-mammal oil lamps or hearths. What did it take, actually, to survive the cold, and what did people spend (or even choose to waste) on heating (e.g., see Appendix, Alutiiq *ciqlluaq* discussion)? What aspects of energistics restricted or encouraged household size and dwelling dimensions? With or without computer modeling, the answers to such questions are discoverable.[4]

Regrettably, some dwellings discussed in this book were never illustrated (as far as we know) but they were described, and vice versa. In most cases, neither information set is adequate by itself to reconstruct such a dwelling completely. As the myriad questions above indicate, the problem all too often is that we do not know enough about construction specifics, whether our typology would be meaningful to the builders of the dwellings, or how past events affected particular groups and shaped their lives and material world. Although elucidating the past is difficult, a partial solution is to start recording what exists now—contemporary architecture as well as what survives of past forms (e.g., Schaaf 1996).

Indeed, contemporary ethnographers take their responsibility to record house types seriously. There is a vast material culture associated with every human society, but indispensable among the products of technology—almost universally—is a society's architecture. Our proposed solution is basic and straightforward. First, make thorough investigations of extant house types, including interior and exterior photographs and drawings (figs. 173–174). Later analysis is possible only with adequate visual tools. (Indeed, roughly half the information in this book is from pictorial sources.) Second, record everything while it still exists; look for consistency and variability, tradition and innovation, and, whenever feasible, involve the people who live there and who can articulate meaning, symbolism, and other architectural concommitants that are not materially evident.

CULTURAL DIMENSIONS

ONE OF THE MOST WIDELY ACKNOWLEDGED CHARACTERISTICS OF ESKIMO CULTURE IS its astonishing cohesiveness over the 6,000-mile spread of its homeland. The kayak, the fur parka, and the tambourine drum are a few of these unifying elements (Schweitzer and Lee 1997). Despite the limited geographical range of the snowblock igloo, Eskimo architecture shows an equally pronounced homogeneity over this widespread area. From Greenland to Siberia, Eskimo groups excavated turf-walled houses for winter and moved into portable structures—usually skin tents—in summer. To attribute this cohesiveness to environment alone would be to forget one of Franz Boas' most important contributions to our understanding of human groups: the notion that geography

FIGURE 172

"Winter habitation, with wood chopper at work." Architecture scene: one person sits on bench and plays drum, while three others dance, in a house or *qasgiq*; two people look in through large roof hole, and two more wave or dance atop the passage (one perhaps preparing to enter via ladder). Woodworking scene: one person chops or splits wood on a block, using non-indigenous axe (left); two people carry wood (to the chopper?). *Hoffman 1897:fig. 50.*

FIGURE 173

Entrance to the Tooyak family house at Point Hope (cf. fig. 87).

Photograph by Molly Lee, 1997.

FIGURE 174

The last sod-covered house in Barrow, Alaska (later demolished). By then a burned-out shell, some wall sections (this one cut for a window) were intact, and extant sods extended only part way up the exterior. Tarpaper and military-type canvas tent fabric once covered the walls and roofs of transitional houses such as this one.

Photograph by Gregory A. Reinhardt, 1981.

and environment limit, but do not determine, the response of a particular group to the world around it (Lowie 1937:144–145).

Within the broadly shared similarities of Eskimo dwellings there is considerable regional variation, however, and we can legitimately say that certain of these are direct responses to geographical limitations. In the Polar Eskimo area of northern Greenland, for instance, where wood is exceedingly scarce, people made do with narwhal tusks or whalebones as tent uprights. Other limiting factors include: 1) subsistence prospects (e.g., location, season, and known versus potential abundance of food species), which had to be weighed against group size; 2) weather elements such as temperature, wind direction and velocity, ambient light at a given time of year, long- versus short-distance visibility, and precipitation, as well as the local predictability of these elements; changeable exploitation of resources, whether affected by season, site, or long-term climatic shift or by differential access (social, economic, or political) between groups; 3) human mobility across a particular landscape, affected at times by the ease or difficulty of traversing land, sea ice, or bodies of open water, by the kinds and condition of sleds and/or watercraft, by the weight and volume of materials being transported (furs, foodstuffs, clothing, fuel for fires and lamps, dwelling parts such as tent poles and covers or ice windows, etc.); and 4) the number of dogs and the strength of people (healthy or starving) in a given year and season. Any number of these factors, combined with personal and group choices, could affect the location, size, material composition, integrity, durability, and orientation of a dwelling.

In sum, this study has argued that, as a cultural domain, Eskimo architecture of the early historic period should be credited with greater variation over its vast geographic spread than is usually evident from the literature. Nonetheless, this investigation confirms that the winter-summer alternation argued by Mauss and Beauchat to be the organizing principle of Eskimo culture of that time was indeed fundamental to daily life, whether in securing game, perpetuating a cosmology, or constructing a dwelling.

CHAPTER 5 NOTES

1   On the Kobuk River, a rather limited area, there were seven dwelling forms (Reinhardt 1986:143–147), but it is unlikely that every group along the river used all of them.

2   Tents were more cramped, of course, but the season allowed everyone frequent access to the outdoors.

3   In discussing "symbolic mapping of domestic space" for the Malagasy of Madagascar, Kus and Raharijaona (2000:102) refer to the cross-cultural vitality of what dwellings can signify to particular cultures: "In many societies that anthropologists study, house form and organization map social and cosmological principles, allowing them to be appropriated somatically, emotionally, and intellectually by individuals. . . ."

4   Harold Strub (1996) exemplifies a practical school of architecture focused on the vernacular (Rapoport 1969:5) as a source of enlightened contemporary construction in the same region. He posits design recommendations only after systematically discussing Eskimo traditions, design problems, and corrective strategies.

APPENDIX: DATA ON DWELLING AND HOUSEHOLD SIZES AMONG SELECTED ESKIMO GROUPS*

* Adapted from "Crystal Domes, Creepy Homes: Eskimo Dwellings as Mirrors of Cultural Complexity" (Gregory Reinhardt, unpublished manuscript).

INFORMATION BELOW DERIVES FROM REINHARDT'S EFFORTS TO ASSESS averages, by Eskimo group, of dwelling dimensions and occupant number in order to compare them statistically with other cultural traits (e.g., Hayden et al. 1996; Reinhardt 1986, 1991). Assembled for a separate research project, these data are not meant to be complete for other than the thirteen Eskimo groups listed. Even for them the available records are obviously spotty, as information on either dwelling or household size is often sparse at best. This in itself is instructive, reminding us of how little we know and observe about vernacular architecture and the people who produce it. Floor size is the most common trait reported, while occupancy data lag far behind, almost after house interior height references. Where assessments of mean floor area per person appear, the fewer calculable volumetric possibilites are left for others to compute. The information below is mostly quantitative, but worth reading nonetheless, especially for those interested in community and household matters.

GREENLANDIC GROUPS

AMMASSALIK

Itte (multifamily communal house): Houses had a maximum height of about 2 m (6.5 ft) inside. Floor plans for these communal houses were trapezoidal and wider at the rear of the house, measuring 7.3–15.2 m (24–50 ft) long near the chamber's midwidth and 3.7–4.9 m (12–16 ft) wide (Holm 1914:fig. 31). Given this range of house dimensions and extremes per household of two to eleven families (Holm 1914:fig. 31; Mauss 1979:46; Thalbitzer 1914:357, 1941:fig. 167), many partitioned spaces may seem cramped by Western standards. Data from twelve Ammassalik houses (Holm 1914:36; Thalbitzer 1914:356) yield means of 6.7 m long by 5.4 m wide and 25.8 people per household. Putting this household space in a more standardized light, an Ammassalik communal house granted a mean floor area of 1.4 m^2 per person.

Tupeq (arch tent): The floor shape described most of an ellipse or oval, although Holm (1914:42) saw it as a semicircle some 3–4.6 m (10–15 ft) in diameter. Dimensions for two floor widths averaged about 5.5 m (18 ft) wide, 5.5 m (17.9 ft) long, and 2.7 m (8.8 ft) high (Thalbitzer 1914:364). Using the semicircle as a model, and the mean tent width as a diameter, the mean floor area is 11.9 m^2. Of course, the maximum height sharply slants to floor level on all sides, so that a tent's interior volume approximates that of a half cone instead of the communal house's near cubic space. Tent occupancy records from 1884 reveal thirty-seven tents as being used by 413 individuals, or just under 11.2 people per tent (Hansen and Holm 1914:185). Therefore the mean floor area per person, as it were, is about 1.1 m^2. Given its conical volume, however, the tent offered remarkably less space than what each occupant had in the communal house. We should remember, though, that a tent's confinement relative to the communal house's comparative spaciousness is offset by a shift to activities outdoors.

When juxtaposed, what Ammassalik ethnographers assert and what their demographic figures indicate are a bit confusing. We know that in 1884 a total of 413 Ammassalik lived in thirteen winter houses, or about 31.8 people per residence, whereas thirty-seven summer tents translate into 11.2 people apiece (Hansen and Holm 1914:385). Considering the notion that the Ammassalik dispersed in summer (Mauss 1979:47, 48; Thalbitzer 1914:364) and that single families occupied one tent each, does this imply that a family averages 11.2 members? Not according to Holm, who writes, "only nearly related families live together" [in these tents] (Holm 1914:42). Thalbitzer's own numbers contradict his one-family idea, insofar as he refers to "family stalls," or partitioned compartments, in winter communal houses (Thalbitzer 1914:356–357). Here the data (271 people in sixty-seven stalls) reveal families averaging only 4.0 persons. So, although winter households might separate for the summer, each family apparently coalesced, and it seems two to three nuclear families would share a tent. Thalbitzer (1914:fig. 66–68) provides visual evidence for multiple families, showing a tent rigged for two separate lamp set-ups (stand, lamp, and cooking pot, all beneath a drying rack).

WEST GREENLAND ESKIMO

Igdlo (multifamily communal house): Crantz gives the house dimensions as "two fathom in breadth, and from 4 to 12 fathom in length, according as more or fewer live in them, and just so high as a person can stand erect in," hence 3.7 m wide by 7.3–21.9 m long and maybe 1.7 m high (Crantz 1767:1:139). Elsewhere he records the population of a whole community:

there lived at New-Herrnhuth 470 Greenlanders in sixteen houses. Three of them are choir-houses. In one live fifty-five single men and boys; in another seventy-eight single women and girls; and to the third belong sixty-two widows. The chief part of these last live together in this house, but others, who have children, live with families in other houses (Crantz 1767:2:400).

There are sixty-four families, a few widowers included; these have divided themselves into the thirteen other houses; so that a set of families, from two to seven, live together in one house.

These numbers permit an approximated mean household size. To start, the three choir-houses of the sixteen houses should be eliminated from calculations. Next, subtracting the unwed male- and female-house members leaves at least 337 people from the thirteen houses. The only problem remaining is what to do with the sixty-two widows, the majority of whom live in their own dormitory. One solution is to look at the extremes: a simple majority of the widows (thirty-two) versus the total number of widows (sixty-two). The range of people per household therefore falls between 23.5 and 21.2, respectively. Now, extrapolating from the Ammassalik mean family size per stall of 4.0 persons, West Greenland houses would have averaged four to five families apiece. This is also the midpoint of Crantz's stated range of two to seven. Dividing the thirteen houses into sixty-four families produces a slightly higher figure, 4.9 families per house.

Regrettably, this analysis lacks solid data on floor areas, but calculating the extremes above yields four possibilities for a mean floor area per person (table 2).

Significant differences obviously exist between these numbers and those for the Ammassalik communal house. It seems likely that the household population might be low or the floor area exaggerated. Otherwise, one would have to conclude that West Greenland Eskimos could afford to heat *three to nine times* the house-interior volume that the Ammassalik did. Still the tendency toward smaller numbers—at least in terms of household size—continued through time. Well into the Mission era Rink lists a census of people and houses in Moravian settlements: "985 winter houses, of which 880 had less than 16 inmates each, the rest 16 or more, the highest number being 36

	Fewer people (21.2)	More people (23.5)
Smaller area (27.0 m²)	1.3 m²/person	1.1 m²/person
Larger area (81.0 m²)	3.8 m²/person	3.4 m²/person

TABLE 2
Mean floor area per person.

persons in one house" (Rink 1877:183). This suggests that population attrition was a fact of West Greenland Eskimo life after contact.

Tupinaq (arch tent—the more common form): Up to twenty people might share a tent as one large family (Crantz 1767:1:142; Nansen 1894:84).

Spring houses, or "separate huts": These dwellings appear to have substituted for tents and totaled nineteen at one site in 1855. Averaging Rink's (1877:182) dimensions yields a mean floor area of 5.8 m² (63 ft²).

POLAR ESKIMO

Iglu, or *qarmaŋ* or *qaŋma* (one- to two-family stone house): It seems that no more than two families normally lived in the home (Steensby 1910:313) although they might host many guests. Kane writes of eight regular residents plus six guests in a house 4.6 m long by 2.1 m wide (15 by 7 ft) (Kane 1856:2:113). Regrettably little supplementary information deals with house measurements. Peary mentions lengths ranging from 2.7–4.3 m (9–14 ft) and depicts a floor plan 3.0 m (10 ft) long and 2.4 m (8 ft) wide (Peary 1898:2:268, 270). As for demographics, one twentieth-century tally indicates 230 people in fifty-four houses (Holtved 1967:145), or 4.3 people in each. This follows, given an earlier estimate of two children per family (Bessels 1884:873).

One household census mentions six residents: a man, his wife and child, his father and father's wife, as well as another young man (Peary 1898:1:259). These last three were visitors, thus leaving the normal occupancy at three for the sole inhabited dwelling among six at that settlement.

Tupeq (arch tent): Compared to Ammassalik and West Greenland tents, this one's subcircular or elliptical floor shape perhaps allowed more headroom toward its posterior edges. Ekblaw gives the average floor dimensions as 4.6 m long and 3.7 m broad (15 by 12 ft) (Ekblaw 1927–28:162). Based on an apse this big, the floor area would be about 13.9 m². In 1909 one site had five tents used by six families, totaling twenty-eight people (Steensby 1910:324), whereas some fifteen years earlier Peary counted sixty-one in ten tents (1898:2:267–268). This yields a range of 5.5 to 6.1 people to a tent, for a combined mean of 5.9. Dividing this figure into the floor area above produces 2.3 m² per person in a tent.

These data imply two things. First, significantly more people lived in a tent than in a house, on average. This suggests two small nuclear families per *tupeq* instead of one larger single family in the winter house. Second, *if* the floor area is truly an average, then Polar Eskimos erected more commodious tents than those of the Ammassalik (and possibly West Greenlanders, too).

Iglooyak or *igluiya* (snow house): Originally, the house was built up from both sides of the doorway and peaked at around 1.8 m (6 ft) although it still took on a "semi-elliptical" to circular plan (Kroeber 1900:271). At one site "over two-thirds of the entire tribe" of 253 Polar Eskimos assembled in more than forty snow houses because walrus hunting was good there (Peary 1898:2:428–430). Taking these numbers and creating minima by adding one more to each value (i.e., (2/3 x 253) + 1 = 170; and 40 + 1 = 41), snow houses would have averaged 4.1 occupants each. The result, albeit simply a speculation, accords nicely with *iglu* residence. Using an average diameter of 3.7 m, or 12 ft (Kroeber 1900:271), the circular floor area was about 10.5 m². Pressing the data still further, this works out to be 2.5 m² per person.

CENTRAL ESKIMO GROUPS

LABRADOR ESKIMO

Igluqsuaq or *iglu* (communal house): Because of their generality, occupancy figures are at first glance conflicting. The Labrador house purportedly averaged about twenty people aboriginally (Taylor 1984:513), far fewer than Greenland's communal houses did. Hawkes (1916:ix, 513) cites floor dimensions of "10 to 12 feet across" (3.0–3.7 m) for a house he saw in 1914. That date came decades after the transformation to one- and two-family dwellings had begun, however, and three details from Kleivan's Appendix illustrate this change (Kleivan 1966). In 1844 there were sixty-four people in three houses (i.e., 21.3 per house), whereas in 1862 and 1863 we see "some houses containing as many as ten persons." One village's Moravian congregation in 1892 consisted of "17 persons constituting 5 families," which, if an accurate census, means 3.4 members per family. This average might suit one or two such families in Hawkes' houses (i.e., 2.0 and 3.9 m²/person, respectively) but such a structure would hardly pamper twenty people (Hawkes 1916). In fact, the maximum area (3.7 m)² divided by twenty occupants equals only 0.7 m²/person! It appears, therefore, that Hawkes' 3 to 3.7-meter range is too small for a classic, indigenous communal house.

It may be plausible, on the other hand, to guess with equal or better certainty about an old-time *igluqsuaq*'s occupancy. Let us start with the largest of Schledermann's archaeological houses, the floor area of which is conservatively some 90 m² (approximately 12 by 7.5 m, or 39.4 by 24.6 ft) (see Schledermann 1976b:fig. 3). Consider next that it contained five lamp platforms (albeit only four are so labeled), hence five families. Using the various household data and a floor area of 90 m², the following results obtain:

Given 17 people (5 families), mean floor area/person = 5.3 m²
Given 20 people (per house), mean floor area/person = 4.5 m²
Given 21.3 people (per house), mean floor area/person = 4.2 m²

Compared to Greenlandic communal houses, then, floor areas per person for Labrador Eskimos might have been much greater in earlier days. This assumes of course that partitioned stalls each held about four family members, as they did in Greenland.

Illuvigaq, igluvi·gu'q, or *iglugeak* (snow house): Generalized comments indicate sleeping chamber diameters of 3.7 to 4.3 m (12–14 ft) and domes high enough to allow a six-foot-tall man to walk upright within them (Hawkes 1916:59; Hutton 1912:36).

IGLULIK

Qarmaq (autumn house): Stones formed a short, low, turf-covered entrance tunnel merely 3 m (10 ft) long and 0.6 m (2 ft) high (Parry 1824:230). At a site with five *qarmaq*s the largest one had a "base" of 5.2 to 5.5 m (17 to 18 ft) and stood about 2.7 m (9 ft) high (Lyon 1824:235). Presumably these were interior measurements because this house type had partitions (implying at least two families) and because other Eskimos normally built smaller winter dwellings for single families. Lyon inspected one home crammed with sixteen adults as well as "several" (thus, at least four?) children (Lyon 1824:280). Based on the data presented here, interpolating a rough lower limit on personal space in these houses looks quite plausible: the mean floor area (5.3 m or 17.5 ft), computed for a circle (= 22.3 m^2), then divided—minimally—by twenty people, yields a value of 1.1 m^2/person. In all probability, most *qarmaq*s were more roomy.

Iglo (many-domed multifamily snow house): In the first village that Lyon and Parry saw on shore, sixty-four people inhabited "five clusters of huts" and comprised thirteen families (Lyon 1824:115). The main chambers had diameters ranging from 4.3 to 5.5 m (14 to 18 ft), for which I assume a mean of 4.9 m (16 ft), although Hall reported 3 m (10 ft) as the norm (Lyon 1824:116; Nourse 1879:73; Parry 1824:411). These figures indicate 12.8 persons per household and families of about 4.9 individuals, and the usual number of domes seems to have been three (Parry 1824:134–135, 411). At another site on sea ice, there were five "snow-huts," containing twenty-eight people, or 5.6 per house (Parry 1824:349). With 1.38 children (or 0.75 in cases of polygyny) per two adults (Mary-Rousseliere 1984:Table 1), both Lyon's "families" and Parry's "households" might often comprise two to three nuclear families.

The mean floor area per person for a dome 4.9 m across, based on family member (4.9?) and occupancy (12.8/3 = 4.3) averages per dome, yields a generous range of 3.8 to 4.4 m^2. Therefore these houses, assuming the data are plausible, must have been astoundingly roomy. If Parry's smaller seal-hunting community also represents a single sleeping dome per "snow-hut," the floor area per person would be 3.2 m^2. That figure may be too liberal if sea ice villages were less elaborate (and probably employed smaller domes) because they tended to be used for shorter-term residence. A shore-based site in the 1920s, imaginably typical of the period, had no multiple sleeping domes (Mathiassen 1928:fig. 4). This might be taken to intimate, more recently, a declining emphasis on communal living.

Ice-slab house (*qarmaq*): In the 1920s these were 4 m (13.1 ft) in diameter (Mathiassen 1928:139). Based on a circular plan, this comes to a floor area of 12.6 m^2. For a family of 4.9, the mean floor area per person would be 2.6 m^2 per person; for an average household of 5.6 individuals, 2.2 m^2.

Tupeq (ridge tent): Depending on family sizes, a tent might range from 3 to 4.3 m (10 to 14 ft) in diameter toward the tent's round posterior reaches (Lyon 1824:229). Parry describes a much more oblong floor shape, 5.2 m (17 ft) long by 2.1 to 2.7 m (7 to 9 ft) wide (Parry 1824:244). Two households might even conjoin separate tents at their entrances to double their sheltering capacity, in which case the entrance would be centered in one long side (Lyon 1824:229). On one beach two sets of tents, totaling seventeen, housed about 120 people in all (Lyon 1824:230), which translates into 7.1 persons per tent. The fairly small size of Iglulik nuclear families, mentioned above, suggests that Iglulik tents probably protected no less than two families apiece. Accepting a mean diameter from Lyon, a circular tent would permit 1.5 m^2 per person. Parry's "oval" tent, computed as if it were straight-sided and round-backed and averaged 2.4 m wide by 5.2 m long, would accommodate one person per 1.7 m^2. Thus, not only was this tent smaller than a snow house, but it also harbored possibly more individuals in a tinier space.

Snowblock windbreaks: About 0.9 to 1.2 m (3 to 4 ft) high, these sometimes protected hunters who waited at seals' breathing holes.

CARIBOU ESKIMO

Iglo (snow house): Birket-Smith's rather thorough census produces a figure of about 4.3 persons per household, and he cites the near-breadth measurement of a small sleeping dome as 3.7 m (1929:1:67–68, 84). Birket-Smith says two or more "families" occasionally cohabit one *iglo*, but let us assume the following: first, that there was one household per dome and second, that a typical dome must have had at least a 4-meter (13.1-ft) diameter (Birket-Smith 1929:1:76). The resulting mean floor area per person, then, would be minimally 2.9 m^2. Albeit having less room than what Igluliks probably experienced, the Caribou Eskimos' lack of artificial household heat also meant they had less space to warm up. Obviously, more people per household would mean smaller floor area averages.

Tupeq (conical tent): By indirect methods, one can approximate a *tupeq*'s mean floor area per person. To start, Birket-Smith shows a party of Caribou Eskimo women erecting a tent frame as men stand nearby (Birket-Smith 1929:1:fig. 15). Photogrammetrically, the tent poles' basal spread is about two and one-third times the height of those men. Now, Birket-Smith (1940:58) lists the average height of Caribou Eskimo males as 1.61 m (5'3"), which yields, in the photograph, a tent diameter of just about 3.75 m. Relying on this, the tent's floor area would be at least 11.0 m^2. Seven people are clearly visible in the photograph so they would have an area of 1.6 m^2 each. Borrowing the average household figure of 4.32 people, and given that *iglo*s generally hold the same number as *tupeq*s (Birket-Smith 1929:1:76), a floor area of 2.6 m^2 results. These conclusions are not ideal but they do provide a range of sorts; it might be better to favor the lower quantity.

COPPER ESKIMO

Snow house: Nine appears to have been the upper limit for one-dome residents but five or six was still a large number. Mean floor areas per person must be generalized once again because of minimal data. Stefánsson cites typical floor dimensions of 1.5 to 2.1 m (5 to 7 ft) for two to three individuals (Stefánsson 1914:62). A larger house about 3 m (10 ft) in diameter (Stefánsson 1914:230) approximates another example (Jenness 1922:68–69) for three people that was 2.7 by 3.4 m (9 x 11 ft). For that number of residents, these measurements suggest a range of 0.88 to 2.4 m² per person. A crowded household of nine, assuming the same floor areas, drops the range to 0.3 to 0.8 m² per person, unquestionably too confining for ordinary homelife. Somewhere in between is an average of three children per couple (Jenness 1922:163–164), which Stefánsson (1914:62) indicates is a high number. Therefore, to calculate for five family members and for a more conservative estimate of four in the larger-sized houses, each member would have had from about 1.5 to 1.8 m² of floor space.

Semi-apsidal-floor ridge tent: Oddly, tents were ordinarily quite variable in plan view. A purportedly large one could cover 3.4 by 4.6 m (11 x 15 ft) of ground (Jenness 1922:78). Stefánsson quotes a confoundingly smaller floor shape for a *double* tent, i.e., 1.8 by 4.3 m (6 x 14 ft) (Stefánsson 1914:66). These disparate values yield a floor area range of 5.8 to 14.2 m². Falling back on an average of four and five residents per household, the mean floor area per person equals 2.8 to 3.5 m² for Jenness' large singleton tent versus 1.2 to 1.4 m² for Stefánsson's small double.

Conical tent: A certifiably conical tent was 5.5 m (18 ft) high and 6.1 m (20 ft) across (Jenness 1922:80). Its floor area per person, therefore, would range from 5.8 to 9.7 m² for five or three people, respectively. Considering this tremendous spaciousness, it might be more astute to assume a lesser diameter as the norm, say 2.7 m (9 ft). This produces a range between 1.8 and 2.0 m² per person, probably more realistic.

Qaggiq (dance house): Peak heights of 2.7 to 3.0 m (9 to 10 ft) were not uncommon (Rasmussen 1932:129; Stefánsson 1914:62).

NORTHWEST ARCTIC AND BERING STRAIT GROUPS

MACKENZIE ESKIMO

Iglu or *iglo* (wooden multifamily house): For unspecified reasons, Smith (1984:349) cites one nuclear family per sleeping platform, a low affair slightly higher than floor level. However, Petitot unquestionably indicates that a family would occupy one *side* of each alcove's platform (Petitot 1876:15; 1981:40). This means an *iglu* normally housed six families (Stefánsson 1914:166).

An exemplary house scrutinized in 1906 closely resembled Petitot's illustration, differing only in its barely extended space at the entryway (Stefánsson 1914:fig. 87–88). It provides a rare set of useful dimensions for a three-sleeping-alcove residence (Stefánsson 1914:fig. 88). With approximately 26.5 m² of floor area, its maximum size was about 5.7 m long by 7.3 m wide (roughly 19 x 24 ft). There is no list of residents for this particular house but assuming five to six families per house and extreme estimates of three to five people per family, the normal limits of occupancy would be fifteen to thirty to a household. That comes out as 0.9 to 1.8 m² of floor area per person for Stefánsson's measurements. Since this 1906-dated house had only an abrupt entrance alcove, it might be that earlier *iglu*s enclosed more space. Finally, Rasmussen writes about a chief's house, "an elegant log cabin very like a villa," with a "living room" measuring 7 m long, 5.5 m wide, and 3.2 m high (Ostermann 1942:33).

Iglo-riyiark (snow house): Some of Rasmussen's posthumous notes detail the residents, by number and name, of several communities he visited in 1924 (Ostermann 1942:36–44). One "settlement out on the ice," which connotes snow houses, had six homes averaging exactly five inhabitants each (Ostermann 1942:9, 36–37). Obviously this mean household figure contradicts the image of full-blown occupancies for wooden *iglo*s, and rightly so, for snow houses seem to have been nuclear family dwellings (Smith 1984:351). Assuming a maximum dome diameter of 3 m (10 ft) or less, the floor area per person would have been under 1.5 m^2.

In a second seal hunting village there were ten homes for forty-three people. Residents here varied between two and seven to a house. A third ice-borne settlement (Ostermann 1942:40–42) saw eighty people spread among nineteen snow houses (cf. Ostermann 1942:16, which says twenty houses). Unlike the first community, not one child is specified at either of the last two. This renders specious their average household sizes (4.3 and 4.2 persons, respectively).

Tupiq (conical tent): At an upriver site, an observer saw some 500 people sharing forty-two "big tents" (Petitot 1970:136) Given those numbers, a tent averaged about 11.8 persons, or two to three nuclear families.

Qargi (ceremonial house): Considering its implied enormity, 15.2 to 18.3 m (50 to 60 ft) on a side, a good 3 to 3.4 m (10 to 11 ft) high in the middle, and at least 1.8 m (6 ft) high around its wall-skirting benches, fuel costs must have been astronomical even as winter approached.

TAĠIUĠMIUT

Iglu (wooden house): It was commonplace for two families to share an *iglu*, and Murdoch writes of one house with thirteen customary inhabitants (Murdoch 1892:75). As added evidence for a local population decline, houses at the settlement nearest Point Barrow averaged about 6.4 people in 1853 despite famine's death toll (Simpson 1855:920). By 1883 households had diminished to 4.3 persons apiece (Ray 1885:49). Simpson expresses house floor sizes as ranging from 2.4 to 3.0 m (8–10 ft) wide by 3.7 to 4.3 m (12 to 14 ft) long (Simpson 1855:931). Calculating this with the larger household number, floor areas averaged 2.7 by 4.0 m (9 x 13 ft) and translated into 1.7 m^2 per person. Archaeological data reveal smaller measurements, though (see Reinhardt and Dekin, 1990:Table 4-1). Four protohistoric Barrow houses averaged only 6.9 m^2, or just over 2 by 3 m (6 x 9 ft). Considering 6.4 people per house as a low post-famine estimate, this suggests a *maximal* mean floor area of 1.1 m^2 per person in near-aboriginal times. One excavated house was closer to Simpson's dimensions, measuring 2.2 by 3.8 m (7 ft 4 in x 12 ft 4 in). Its mean floor area per person would be 1.3 m^2 (Ford 1959:72). Adding Ford's house to the archaeological sample leaves the figure at about 1.1 m^2. This boosts the average floor area per person compared to other Eskimo primary winter houses.

Apuyyaq (snow house): One comment on snow house size estimates that single families lived in rooms about 1.8 by 3.7 m (6 x 12 ft), or 6.7 m^2

(Murdoch 1892:81). However, the question of family strength still remains. If famine-reduced dual-family households consisted of 6.4 people, then a reasonably liberal one-family size might stand at four people. Given these approximations, an *apuyyaq* allowed about 1.7 m² of floor area per person. This seems large compared to the wooden *iglu*'s average, but no better data is available.

Tupiq (conical tent): Tent floors were generally 3.7 m (12 ft) in diameter and intended for single families (Murdoch 1892:84, 85). Resorting to a liberal estimate of four-person families, each person would have 2.6 m² of floor area. This is a guess, though, and perhaps peculiarly more area than either an *iglu* or *apuyyaq* offered.

Qargi (ceremonial house): Two large examples around Point Barrow measured 4.3 and 4.9 m (14 and 16 ft) wide by 5.5 and 6.1 m (18 and 20 ft) long, the bigger of which was 2.1 m (7 ft) tall in its center—mentioned above as having held sixty people (Murdoch 1892:80; Simpson 1855:933). A separate temporary variant was photographed in 1884 (figs. 105–106). Its span seems to be at least 2 by 9 m (7 x 30 ft) and its pitched (possibly hip) roof is about 2 m (7 ft) high in the middle.

NUNAMIUT

Itchalik (dome tent): The frame roughly described a hemisphere or semiellipsoid around 1.5 to 1.8 m (5 to 6 ft) high at its center. Indigenous Nunamiut settlements seldom witnessed more than five or six homes at a time (Campbell 1962:50). Nuclear families or small extended units lived together in their own tents, although one or more teenagers might occupy others in summer. Four separate accounts cite tent floors ranging anywhere from 2.7 to 3.7 m (9 to 12 ft) wide and 3.0 to 4.6 m (10 to 15 ft) long. However, the most-used phrase indicates a 3.7-meter (12-foot) diameter as normal. In the early 1960s ninety-six Nunamiut lived as smaller family units in twenty-eight summer tents, although the whole population of the village of Anaktuvuk Pass remained constant (Gubser 1965:347). Computing these figures yields 3.4 people to a summer tent and a mean floor area per person of 3.0 m². Winter residence compressed ninety-six individuals into eighteen modern-period sod houses. Assuming this to approximate winter tent occupancy in earlier times, the results would be 5.3 people on the average, each with about 2.0 m² of floor area. Both extremes of floor area per person, 2 to 3 m², suggest very capacious quarters, since a domed (and double-arch) tent's sides rise almost vertically. (Single-arch, ridge, and conical tent shapes, on the other hand, all have acutely inclining sides.)

Ivrulik, or *ibrulik, iwrulik, iwjulik*, etc. (pole-and-turf house): The only turf house (from 1960) with an accompanying occupancy (seven individuals) measured 4.9 by 7.3 m (16 x 24 ft) inside (Gubser 1965:xii). Its much-larger- than-aboriginal floor area, 35.7 m², and greater than average number of residents yields 5.1 m² per individual. Several archaeological turf houses range from about 2.1 to 4.4 m wide (6.8 to 14.4 ft) and 4.1 to 5.3 m (13.5 to 17.4 ft) long and average 15.7 m² (Corbin 1976:fig. 7–9, 10A; Hall 1976:fig. 4–6). Resorting to Gubser's mean winter household size of 5.3 people, they each would have 2.9 m² of floor area (Gubser 1965:347). Whether reliable or not, this accords acceptably with the domed tent's mean values.

KUUVAŊMIUT

Ukiivik (wooden house): Two small winter villages in the 1880s averaged 7 and 7.5 people to a house (Stoney 1900:39). [Other prehistoric house-floor data are available but not computed here (Giddings 1952).]

SOUTHWEST ALASKA, BERING SEA, SIBERIAN, AND GULF OF ALASKA GROUPS

UNALIGMIUT

Ini (wooden house): Average data on actual households, unfortunately, may be better reflections of floor area than occupancy. Zagoskin "never saw a house that measured more than 3 *sazhens* [2.1 m] square" (Michael 1967:115). On the other hand, Dall (1870:13) records house floors as "usually about twelve or fifteen feet [3.7 to 4.6 m] square," or an areal spread of 13.4 to 20.9 m². Jacobsen describes one house interior that measured 3.7 by 4.3 m (12 x 14 ft), or 15.6 m², and contained 26 people, some of whom were guests. Another house of unspecified dimensions, with sleeping platforms on three sides, sheltered nineteen individuals normally, this number being expressed as "typical of an Eskimo dwelling" (Jacobsen 1977:125, 131). Therefore the only information at hand reveals a seemingly paltry mean floor area per person of 0.8 m².

Qasgiq (men's house): *Qasgiq*s were also bigger than houses, averaging 6 to 9 m (20 to 30 ft) (Ray 1966:50) across, although the "largest in the country" boasted a floor 7.5 by 9.1 m (25 x 30 ft) and a skylight looming 4.6 m (15 ft) high (Dall 1870:126).

ALUTIIQ

Ciqlluaq (multifamily wooden house): Giving us an indirect impression of one house's overall size, Lisiansky notes its adjoining sleeping chamber was 4.2 by 4.4 m (13 ft 10 in x 14 ft 7 in), or about 18.5 m² (Lisiansky 1814:213). Thus it was larger than most of the *house* interiors described in this book. Floor area estimates are outside guesses at best. A community of ten to fifteen houses could represent 200 to 300 people, hence up to twenty per household (Clark 1984:191; Hrdlicka 1975:19). Father Gedeon intimates slightly elongate main chamber floors as typical, measuring 8.5 m (28 ft) long and 5.7 m (18.7 ft) wide, that is, 48.5 m² without sleeping chambers (Black 1977:90). [Father Gedeon further asserts these rooms were only 1.4 m (4.7 ft) high, which sounds absurd unless this refers to the height of wall stringers or to the ceilings of the sleeping chambers (*qawarik*).]

In one archaeological house, the square main chamber floor approximates 30.25 m². Combined with the total area of its four side chambers, the full living space equals 56.9 m² (see Knecht and Jordan 1985:24, fig. 6).

Taking two leaps of faith, first, that this house is "average" and second, that it contained no more than twenty people, the *minimum* mean floor area per person would be a resounding 2.8 m². Assuming that these calculations are reasonably valid and that we should even count the side-room areas, all of this implies Alutiiqs had fewer—or maybe different—constraints, compared to the other Eskimo winter houses, regarding personal in-house surface areas.

Some intriguing inquiries spring to mind: Could Alutiiqs afford more heated space, possibly because wood was handy as fuel? Does this follow from Reinhardt's (1986) assessment of the wealth of their subsistence economy? Does their much warmer environment have ameliorating impacts on fuel and/or food economics? Hayden et al. discuss relationships between floor area, occupancy, and outside temperatures (1996).

References

When [an elder] dies, it is as if a

library has burned to the ground.

(Alex Haley 1976:vii)

Ackerman, Robert A.

1970   Archaeoethnology, Ethnoarchaeology, and the Problems of Past Cultural Patterning. In: Ethnohistory in Southwestern Alaska and the Southern Yukon: Method and Content, Margaret Lantis, ed., 11–47. *Studies in Anthropology* 7. University Press of Kentucky, Lexington.

Aldrich, Herbert L.

1889   *Arctic Alaska and Siberia, or, Eight Months with the Arctic Whalemen.* Rand, McNally and Co., Chicago.

Alsayyad, Nezar

1989   Dualities in the Study of Traditional Dwellings and Settlements. In: *Dwellings, Settlements and Tradition: Cross-Cultural Perspectives*, Jean-Paul Bourdier and Nezar Alsayyad, eds., 527–532. University Press of America, Lanham, MD.

Anderson, H. Dewey, and Walter Crosby Eells

1935   *Alaska Natives: A Survey of Their Sociological and Educational Status.* Stanford University Press, Stanford.

Anonymous

1825   *A Peep at the Eskimo; or, Scenes on the Ice. To which is annexed, A Polar Pastoral. With Forty Coloured Plates, from Original Designs. By A Lady.* 2d ed. H. R. Thomas, London (1st ed. 1825).

Balikci, Asen

1970   *The Netsilik Eskimo.* Natural History Press, Garden City, New York.

Beechey, Frederick William

1831   *Narrative of a Voyage to the Pacific and Beering's Strait to Co-operate with the Polar Expeditions: Performed in His Majesty's Ship Blossom . . . in the Years 1825, 26, 27, 28.* 2 vols. Henry Colburn and Richard Bentley, London.

Belcher, Edward

1855   *The Last of the Arctic Voyages . . .* 2 vols. Lovell Reeve, London.

Bessels, Emil

1884   The Northernmost Inhabitants of the Earth: An Ethnographic Sketch. *American Naturalist* 18:861–882.

Best, George

1867   *The Three Voyages of Martin Frobisher: In Search of a Route to Cathaia and India by the North-west, A.D. 1576–1578*, R. Collinson, ed. Hakluyt Society 38, from the original 1578 text of George Best. Hakluyt Society, London.

Bilby, Julian W.

1923   *Among Unknown Eskimo: An Account of Twelve Years of Intimate Relations with the Primitive Eskimo of Ice-Bound Baffin Land, with a Description of Their Ways of Living, Hunting Customs & Beliefs.* Seeley Service & Co. Limited, London.

Bird, Junius B.

1945   Archaeology of the Hopedale Area, Labrador. *Anthropological Papers of the American Museum of Natural History* 39:119–186.

Birket-Smith, Kaj

1924   Ethnography of the Egedesminde District, with Aspects of the General Culture of West Greenland. *Meddelelser om Grønland* 66, 1:1–484.

1928   The Greenlanders of the Present Day. *Greenland* 2:1–207. Oxford University Press, London.

1929   The Caribou Eskimos: Material and Social Life and Their Cultural Position, 1–2. *Report of the Fifth Thule Expedition 1921–1945*, Knud Rasmussen, ed. Gyldeddalske (sic) Boghandel, Nordisk Forlag, Copenhagen.

1936   *The Eskimos*, trans. by W. E. Calvert. Methuen, London.

1940   Anthropological Observations on the Central Eskimos. *Report of the Fifth Thule Expedition 1921–1924, 3, 2.* Gyldendalske Boghandel, Nordisk Forlag, Copenhagen.

1945   Ethnographical Collections from the Northwest Passage. *Report of the Fifth Thule Expedition 1921–1924, 6, 2.* Gyldendalske Boghandel, Nordisk Forlag, Copenhagen.

1953   *The Chugach Eskimo.* Nationalmuseets Skrifter, Ethnografiske Raekke 6. National Museum, Copenhagen.

Black, Lydia T. (translator and editor)

1977   The Konyag (The Inhabitants of the Island of Kodiak) by Iosaf [Bolotov] (1794–1799) and by Gideon (1804–1807). *Arctic Anthropology* 14:79–108.

Boas, Franz

1888   The Central Eskimo. In: *Sixth Annual Report of the Bureau of Ethnology for the Years 1884–1885*, 399–675. Government Printing Office, Washington, DC. (reprinted 1964, University of Nebraska Press, Lincoln).

1901   Eskimo of Baffin Land and Hudson Bay. *Bulletin of the American Museum of Natural History*, 15.

1904   The Folklore of the Eskimo. *Journal of American Folklore*, 8, 45:1–13.

Bockstoce, John R.

1980   Battle of the Bowheads. *Natural History* 89, 5:51–61.

1988   The Journal of Rochfort Maguire 1852–1854: Two Years at Point Barrow, Alaska, Aboard HMS Plover in the Search for Sir John Franklin, John Bockstoce, ed. 2 vols. *Hakluyt Society, Second Series* 60. The Hakluyt Society, London.

Bogojavlensky, Sergei

1969   *Imaangmiut Eskimo Careers: Skinboats in Bering Strait.* Ph.D. dissertation, Department of Social Relations, Harvard University.

Bogoras, Waldemar

1913   The Eskimo of Siberia [The Jesup North Pacific Expedition 8, 3], Franz Boas, ed. *Memoirs of the American Museum of Natural History* 12:417–456.

Borden, Courtney Louise

1928   *The Cruise of the Northern Light; Explorations and Hunting in the Alaskan and Siberian Arctic.* McMillan and Co., New York.

Bourdier, Jean-Paul, and Nezar Alsayyad, eds.

1989   *Dwellings, Settlements, and Tradition: Cross-Cultural Perspectives.* University Press of America, Lanham, MD.

Brower, Charles D.

1950   *Fifty Years Below Zero.* Gosset and Dunlap, New York.

Brown, Emily Ivanoff (Tickasook)

1956   *Inupiut (Eskimo) Homes.* Unalakleet, AK (privately printed).

Browne, Belmore

1946   Let's Build a Snowhouse. *Natural History* 55,10:460–465, 486.

Burch, Ernest S., Jr.

1971   The Non-Empirical World of the Arctic Alaskan Eskimos. *Southwestern Journal of Anthropology* 27, 2:148–165.

1983   Socio-Demographic Correlates of House Structures in Three Beringian Populations: An Exploratory Study. In: *Cultures of the Bering Sea Region: Papers from an International Symposium,* Henry N. Michael and James W. VanStone, eds., 112–139. International Research and Exchanges Board, New York.

1998   The Iñupiaq Eskimo Nations of Northwest Alaska. University of Alaska Press, Fairbanks.

Burch, Ernest S., Jr., and Werner Forman

1988   *The Eskimos.* University of Oklahoma Press, Norman, Ok.

Bushnell, David I., Jr.

1928   Drawings by John Weber of Natives of the Northwest Coast of America, 1778. *Smithsonian Miscellaneous Collections* 80, 10:112ff).

Call, S. J., Surgeon

1899   [Medical] Report of Overland Expedition. In: *Report of the Cruise of the U.S. Revenue Cutter* Bear *and the Overland Expedition for the Relief of the Whalers in the Arctic Ocean, From November 27, 1897, to September 13, 1898,* 114–127. Government Printing Office, Washington, DC.

Campbell, John M.

1962   Cultural Succession at Anaktuvuk Pass, Arctic Alaska. In: Prehistoric Cultural Relations between the Arctic and Temperate Zones of North America, John M. Campbell, ed., 39–54. *Arctic Institute of North America, Technical Paper* 11. Arctic Institute of North America, Montreal.

1998   *North Alaska Chronicle: Notes from the End of Time: the Simon Paneak Drawings.* Museum of New Mexico Press, Santa Fe.

Cantwell, John C.

1887   A Narrative Account of the Exploration of the Kowak River, Alaska. In: *Report of the Cruise of the Revenue Marine Steamer Corwin in the Arctic Ocean in the Year 1885,* by M. A. Healy, 21–52. Government Printing Office, Washington, DC.

1889a   A Narrative Account of the Exploration of the Kowak River, Alaska. In: *Report of the Cruise of the Revenue Marine Steamer Corwin in the Arctic Ocean in the Year 1884,* by M. A. Healy, 53–74. Government Printing Office, Washington, DC.

1889b   Exploration of the Kowak River, Alaska. Ethnological Notes. In: *Report of the Cruise of the Revenue Marine Steamer Corwin in the Arctic Ocean in the Year 1884*, by M. A. Healey, 75–99. Government Printing Office, Washington, DC.

Carius, Helen Slwooko
1979   *Sevukakmet: Ways of Life on St. Lawrence Island*. Alaska Pacific University Press, Anchorage, AK.

Choris, Louis [Ludovik]
1822   *Voyage Pittoresque Autour du Monde*. Firmin Didot, Paris.

Clark, Donald W.
1984   Pacific Eskimo: Historical Ethnography. In: *Handbook of North American Indians 5*, Arctic, David Damas, ed., 185–197. Smithsonian Institution Press, Washington, DC.

Collignon, Béatrice
2001   "Esprit des lieux at modèles culturels: La Mutation des Epaces domestiques en arctique inuit," *Annales de Géographie* 110, 62:383–404.

Collins, Henry B., Jr.
n.d.   "Two Kinds of Houses—Summer and Winter." Smithsonian Institution, National Anthropological Archives, Henry B. Collins papers, Box 46, File "Miscellany."

1935   Archeology of the Bering Sea Region. Smithsonian Annual Report for 1933, pp. 453–468. Washington: Government Printing Office.

1937   Archaeology of St. Lawrence Island. *Smithsonian Miscellaneous Collections 96*, 1. Smithsonian Institution, Washington, DC.

Cook, James, and J. King
1784   *A Voyage to the Pacific Ocean Undertaken, by the Command of His Majesty, for Making Discoveries in the Northern Hemisphere. Performed Under the Direction of Captains Cook, Clarke, and Gore, in His Majesty's Ships the Resolute and Discovery; in the Years 1776, 1777, 1778, 1779, and 1780.* 3 vols. G. Nicol and T. Cadell, London.

Corbin, James E.
1976   Early Historic Nunamiut House Types: An Ethnographic Description with Archaeological Identification, Comparison, and Validation. In: Contributions to Anthropology: The Interior Peoples of Northern Alaska, Edwin S. Hall, Jr., ed., 135–176. *National Museum of Man, Mercury Series, Archaeological Survey of Canada, Paper* 49. National Museums of Canada, Ottawa.

Coxe, William
1966   *Russian Discoveries between Asia and America*. University Microfilms, Inc., Ann Arbor, MI. (Originally published 1780, *Account of the Russian Discoveries between Asia and America*, 2d ed., T. Cadell, London.)

Crantz, David
1767   *The History of Greenland 1*. Brethren's Society for the Furtherance of the Gospel among the Heathen, London.

Cremeans, Lola M.
1931   Homes of the Eskimos on St. Lawrence Island. *Journal of Home Economics* 23, 2:129–131.

Crowell, Aron L.
1988   Dwellings, Settlements, and Domestic Life. In: *Crossroads of Continents: Cultures of Siberia and Alaska*, William W. Fitzhugh and Aron Crowell, eds., 194–208. Smithsonian Institution Press, Washington, DC.

Crowell, Aron L., and Daniel Mann
1998   *Archaeology and Coastal Dynamics of Kenai Fjords National Park, Alaska*. National Park Service, Anchorage, AK.

Crowell, Aron L., Amy F. Steffian, and Gordon L. Pullar, eds.
2001   *Looking Both Ways: Heritage and Identity of the Alutiiq People*. University of Alaska Press, Fairbanks.

Curtis, Edward S.

1907–   *The North American Indian: Being a Series of Volumes Picturing*
1930   *and Describing the Indians of the United States and Alaska* 20,
         Frederick W. Hodge, ed. (reprinted 1970, Johnson Reprint, New York).

Dall, William H.

1870   *Alaska and Its Resources.* Lee and Shepard, Boston.

Damas, David

1984a   "Copper Eskimo." In: *Handbook of North American Indians* 5, Arctic,
         David Damas, ed., 397–414. Smithsonian Institution Press, Washington,
         DC.

Damas, David, ed.

1984b   *Handbook of North American Indians* 5, Arctic. Smithsonian Institution
         Press, Washington, DC.

Davydov, G[avriil] I.

1977   Two Voyages to Russian America, 1802–1807, ed. by Richard A. Pierce,
         trans. by Colin Bearne. *Materials for the Study of Alaska History* 10. Lime-
         stone Press, Kingston, Ontario.

Dawson, Mary R.

1983   Arctic Environments. In: *Arctic Life: Challenge to Survive*, M. M. Jacobs
         and J. B. Richardson, eds., 19–34. Carnegie Institute, Pittsburgh.

Dawson, Peter C.

2001   Interpreting Variability in Thule Innit Architecture: A Case Study from the
         Canadian High Arctic. *American Antiquity* 66, 3:453–470.

De Laguna, Frederica

1956   *Chugach Prehistory.* University of Washington Press, Seattle.

Devine, Edward J.

1905   Across Wildest America: Newfoundland to Alaska, with the Impressions
         of Two Years' Sojourn on the Bering Coast Profusely Illustrated. *The Ca-
         nadian Messenger*, Montreal.

Dickie, Francis

1959   Synthetic Igloo. *Forest and Outdoors* 55, 5:117.

Diebitsch-Peary, Josephine

1894   *My Arctic Journal: A Year among Ice-Fields and Eskimos.* The Contempo-
         rary Publishing Company, New York.

Douglas, Mary

1971   Symbolic Orders in the Use of Domestic Space. In: *Man, Settlement and
         Urbanism*, Peter Ucko, Ruth Tringham, and G. W. Dimbleby, eds., 513–
         527. Schenkman Publishing Company, Cambridge, MA.

Duhaime, Gerard

1985   *De l'Igloo au H.L.M.: Les Inuits Sédentaires et l'Etat-providence.* Centre
         d'études nordique (Collection Nordica 48). Université Laval, Quebec.

Dyke, Arthur S., John England, Erik Reimnitz, and Hélène Jetté

1997   Changes in Driftwood Delivery to the Canadian Arctic Archipelago: The
         Hypothesis of Postglacial Oscillations of the Transpolar Drift. *Arctic* 50,
         1:1–16.

Eek, Ann Christine

1998   "The Roald Amudsen Photographs of the Netsilik People." In: *Imaging
         the Arctic*, J. C. H. King and Henrietta Lidchi, eds. British Museum: Lon-
         don.

Egede, Hans P.

1745   *A Description of Greenland, Shewing the Natural History, Situation, Bound-
         aries, and Face of the Country . . . .* C. Hitch, London (reprinted 1818, T.
         and J. Allman, London).

Ekblaw, W. Elmer

1927–   The Material Response of the Polar Eskimos to Their Far Arctic
1928   Environment. *Annals of the Association of American Geographers*
          17, 4:147–198; 18, 1:1–24.

Faegre, Torvald

1979   The Inuit Tent. In: *Tents: Architecture of the Nomads*, 125–131. Anchor-
          Doubleday, Garden City, NJ.

Fair, Susan W.

in press The Northern Umiaq: Boundary, Shelter, Identity. In: *Perspectives in Ver-
          nacular Architecture IX*, Alison K. Hoagland and Ken Breisch, eds., University
          of Tennessee Press, Nashville.

1997   Story, Storage and Symbol. In: *Perspectives in Vernacular Architecture,
          VII*, Annmarie Adams and Sally McMurry, eds., 167–182. University of
          Tennessee Press, Nashville.

Fair, Susan, W., James Creech, Gideon K. Barr, Sr., and Edgar Ningeulook

1996   The Hope and Promise of Ublasaun. In: *Ublasaun: First Light*, Jeanne Schaaf,
          ed., 62–93. National Park Service, Anchorage, AK.

Fienup-Riordan, Ann

1990   *Eskimo Essays: Yup'ik Lives and How We See Them.* Rutgers University
          Press, New Brunswick, NJ.

1995   *Freeze Frame: Alaska Eskimos in the Movies.* University of Washington,
          Seattle.

1996   *The Living Tradition of Yup'ik Masks.* University of Washington, Seattle.

2000   *Where the Echo Began and Other Oral Traditions from Southwestern Alaska
          recorded by Hans Himmelheber.* University of Alaska Press, Fairbanks.

Forbin, Victor

1926   Industrie et commerce chez les Esquimeaux. *Nature* 54, 2706:97–100.

Ford, James A.

1959   Eskimo Prehistory in the Vicinity of Point Barrow, Alaska. *Anthropologi-
          cal Papers of the American Museum of Natural History* 47, 1.

Franklin, John

1823   *Narrative of a Journey to the Shores of the Polar Sea, in the Years 1819,
          20, 21, and 22.* John Murray, London.

Frederiksen, V. C.

1912   Fund af Eskimohuse af Kap York-typen. *Meddelelser om Grønland* 28:391–
          397.

Gabus, Jean

1940   La construction des iglous chez les Padleirmuit. *Bulletin de la Societe
          neuchateloise de Geographie* 47:43–51.

1944   L'habitation. In: *Vie et Coutumes des Esquimaux Caribou*, 51–73. Librairie
          Payot, Lausanne.

1947   *Iglous: Vie des Esquimeaux-Caribou.* Editions Victor Attinger, Neuchatel.

1961   La maison des Esquimaux. Aspects de la Maison dans le Monde. *Memoirs
          du Centre International de la Maison dans le Monde*, Brussels.

Garber, Clark M.

1934   Some Mortuary Customs of Western Alaska Eskimos. *Scientific Monthly.*
          Sept.: 203–220.

Geist, Otto, and Froelich G. Rainey

1936   Archaeological Excavations at Kukulik, Saint Lawrence Island, Alaska:
          Preliminary Report. *University of Alaska MiscellaneousPapers* 2. Govern-
          ment Printing Office, Washington, DC.

Gerlach, S. Craig

1996   Historical Archaeology and the Early Twentieth Century Reindeer Herding Frontier on the Northern Seward Peninsula. In: *Ublasaun: First Light*, Jeanne Schaaf, ed., 94–109. National Park Service, Anchorage, AK.

Gibson, William, and John G. Comack

1940   Building a Snow House. *Beaver* 270, 4:40–41.

Giddings, James L.

1952   The Arctic Woodland Culture of the Kobuk River. *Museum Monographs, The University Museum*. University of Philadelphia.

1956   Forest Eskimos: An Ethnographic Sketch of Kobuk River People in the 1880s. *The University Museum Bulletin* 20, 2.

1957   Round Houses in the Western Arctic. *American Antiquity* 23, 2/1:121–135.

1961   Kobuk River People. *Studies of Northern People* 1. University of Alaska, College, AK.

Giffen, Naomi Musmaker

1930   *The Rôles of Men and Women in Eskimo Culture*. University of Chicago Press, Chicago.

Gilberg, Rolf

1984   Polar Eskimo. In: *Handbook of North American Indians 5*, Arctic, David Damas, ed., 577–594. Smithsonian Institution Press, Washington, DC.

Glassie, Henry

1975   Folk Housing in Middle Virginia. University of Tennessee Press, Knoxville.

Goddard, Pliny E.

1928   Native Dwellings of North America. *Natural History* 28:191–203.

Gordon, G. B.

1906   Notes on the Western Eskimo. *University of Pennsylvania, Transactions of the Department of Archaeology, Free Museum of Science and Art* 2, 1:69–101.

Graah, Wilhelm A.

1837   *Narrative of an Expedition to the East Coast of Greenland*. John W. Parker, London (reprinted 1932).

Graburn, Nelson H. H.

1969   *Eskimos without Igloos: Social and Economic Development in Sugluk*. Little, Brown and Company, Boston.

1972   A Preliminary Analysis of Symbolism in Eskimo Art and Culture. *Proceedings of the International Congress of Americanists* 2:165–170.

1976   Nulunaikutanga: Signs and Symbols in Canadian Inuit Art and Culture. *Polar-forschung* 46, 1:1–11.

Graburn, Nelson H. H., and Molly Lee

1990   The Arctic Culture Area. In: *Native North Americans: An Ethnohistorical Approach*, Daniel Boxburger, ed., 23–64. Kendall Hunt, Dubuque, IA.

Graburn, Nelson H. H., and B. Steven Strong

1973   *Circumpolar Peoples*. Goodyear, Pacific Palisades, CA.

Griggs, Robert F.

1917   The Valley of Ten Thousand Smokes: National Geographic Society Explorations in the Katmai District of Alaska. *National Geographic* 31:12–68.

1920   The Beginnings of Revegetation in Katmai Valley. In: Scientific Results of the Katmai Expeditions of the National Geographic Society, by Robert F. Griggs, J. W. Shipley, Jasper D. Sayre, Paul R. Hagelbarger, and James S. Hine, 318–342. *Ohio State University Bulletin 24, Contributions in Geographical Exploration* 1. Ohio State University.

1922 *The Valley of Ten Thousand Smokes*. National Geographic Society, Washington, DC.

Grinnell, George Bird
1910 The Natives of the Alaska Coast Region. In: *Harriman Alaska Series* 1: Narrative, Glaciers, Natives, John Burroughs, John Muir, and George Bird Grinnell, eds., 137–183. Smithsonian Institution, Washington, DC.

Gubser, Nicholas J.
1965 *The Nunamiut Eskimos*. Yale University Press, New Haven, CT.

Hall, Charles Francis
1864 *Arctic Researches and Life among the Eskimo: Being the Narrative of an Expedition in Search of Sir John Franklin, in the Years 1860, 1861, and 1862.* Harper & Brothers, New York.

Hall, Edwin S., Jr.
1976 A Preliminary Analysis of House Types at Tukuto Lake, Northern Alaska. In: Contributions to Anthropology: The Interior Peoples of Northern Alaska, 98–134. *National Museum of Man, Mercury Series, Archaeological Survey of Canada, Paper* 49. National Museums of Canada, Ottawa.

1990 *The Utqiagvik Excavations*. 3 vols. North Slope Borough Commission on Inupiat History, Language and Culture, Barrow, AK.

Handy, Richard I.
1973 The Igloo and the Natural Bridge as Ultimate Structures. *Arctic* 26, 4:276–81.

Hansen, Johannes, and G. Holm
1914 List of the Inhabitants of the East Coast of Greenland. In: The Ammassalik Eskimo 1, William Thalbitzer, ed. *Meddelelser om Grønland* 39:181–202.

Hantzsch, Bernard
1931–32 Contributions to the Knowledge of Extreme Northeastern Labrador. *Canadian Field Naturalist* 45, 3:49–54; 45, 4:85–89; 45, 5:115–118; 45, 6:143–145; 45, 7:169–173; 45, 8:194–8; 45, 9:222–4; 46, 1:7–11; 46, 2:34–35; 46, 3:64–66; 46, 4:84–88; 46, 5:112–115; 46, 6:143–144; 46, 7:153–161.

Hawkes, Ernest W.
1913a The Cliff-Dwellers of the Arctic. *Wide World Magazine* 30, 26:377–382.

1913b The "Inviting-In" Feast of the Alaskan Eskimo. *Canada Department of Mines, Geological Survey, Memoir 45, Anthropological Series 3.* Government Printing Bureau, Ottawa.

1914 The Cliff-Dwellers of King Island. *Wide World Magazine* 33, 6:81–91.

1916 The Labrador Eskimo. *Canada Department of Mines, Geological Survey, Memoir 91, Anthropological Series 14.* Government Printing Bureau, Ottawa (reprinted 1970, Johnson Reprint, New York and London).

Hayden, Brian D., Gregory A. Reinhardt, Dan Holmberg, and David Crellin
1996 Space Per Capita and the Optimal Size of Housepits. In: People Who Lived in Big Houses: Archaeological Perspectives on Large Domestic Structures. *Monographs in World Archaeology* 27, Gary Coupland and E. B. Banning, eds., 151–164. Prehistory Press, Madison, WI.

Hayes, Isaac I.
1885 *The Open Polar Sea: A Narrative of a Voyage of Discovery towards the North Pole, in the Schooner "United States."* George Routledge and Sons, London.

Healy, M. A.
1887 *Report of the Cruise of the Revenue Marine Steamer Corwin in the Arctic Ocean in the Year 1885.* Government Printing Office, Washington, DC.

1889 *Report of the Cruise of the Revenue Marine Steamer Corwin in the Arctic Ocean in the Year 1884.* Government Printing Office, Washington, DC.

Hieb, Louis A.
1990   The Metaphors of Hopi Architectural Experience in Cultural Perspective. In: *Pueblo Style and Regional Architecture*, Nicholas C. Markovich, Wolfgang F. E. Preiser, and Fred G. Sturm, eds., 122–132. Van Norstrand Reinhold, New York.

Himmelheber, Hans
1980   Ethnographische Notizen von den Nunivak-Eskimo. In: *Abhandlungen und Berichte des Staalichen Museums fur Volkerkunde, Dresden* 38:5–45.

1993   *Eskimo Artists*. University of Alaska Press, Fairbanks.

Hoffman, Walter James
1897   The Graphic Art of the Eskimos. *Annual Report of the Board of Regents of the Smithsonian Institution for 1895, Report of the U.S. National Museum*, 739–968. Government Printing Office, Washington, DC.

Holm, Gustav
1914   Ethnological Sketch of the Angmagsalik Eskimo. In: The Ammassalik Eskimo 1, William Thalbitzer, ed. *Meddelelser om Grønland* 39:1–147.

Holtved, Erik
1967   Contributions to Polar Eskimo Ethnography. *Meddelelser om Grønland* 182, 2.

Hooper, Calvin L.
1881   *Report of the Cruise of the U. S. Revenue Steamer* Corwin *in the Arctic Ocean, November 1, 1880*. U. S. Government Printing Office, Washington, DC.

Hooper, William H.
1853   *Ten Months among the Tents of the Tuski with Incidents of an Arctic Boat Expedition in Search of Sir John Franklin as Far as the Mackenzie River and Cape Bathurst . . . .* John Murray, London.

Hough, Walter
1898a   The Lamp of the Eskimo. In: *U.S. National Museum Report, 1896*, 1025–1057. Government Printing Office, Washington, DC.

1898b   The Origin and Range of the Eskimo Lamp. *American Anthropologist* 11:116–122.

Hrdlička, Aleš
1975   *The Anthropology of Kodiak Island*. AMS Press, New York. (Originally published 1944, Wistar Institute of Anatomy and Biology, Philadelphia).

Hughes, Charles
1984   Siberian Eskimo. In: *Handbook of North American Indians* 5, Arctic, David Damas, ed., 247–261. Smithsonian Institution Press, Washington, DC.

Hunter-Anderson, Rosalind L.
1977   A Theoretical Approach to the Study of House Form. In: *For Theory Building in Archaeology*, Lewis R. Binford, ed., 287–315. Academic Press, New York.

Hutton, S. K.
1912   *Among the Eskimos of Labrador*. J. B. Lippincott, Philadelphia, and Seeley Service Co., London.

Ingstad, Helge
1954   *Nunamiut: Among Alaska's Inland Eskimos*. W. W. Norton & Company, New York (British edition published 1954).

Jacobsen, Johan Adrian
1977   *Alaskan Voyage, 1881–1883: An Expedition to the Northwest Coast of America*, trans. by Erna Gunther. University of Chicago, Chicago.

Jenness, Diamond
1922   The Life of the Copper Eskimos. *Report of the Canadian Arctic Expedition, 1913–1918* 12. F. A. Ackland, Ottawa.

1924   Eskimo String Figures. *Report of the Canadian Arctic Expedition, 1913–1918* 13b. F. A. Ackland, Ottawa.

Jochelson, Waldemar

1906   Past and Present Subterranean Dwellings of the Tribes of North Eastern Asia and North Western America. In: *Congrès International des Américanistes*, 15me Session, 2:115–128. Quebec. (Reprinted 1968, Kraus Reprint, Nendeln/Liechtenstein.)

1933   *History, Ethnology and Anthropology of the Aleut.* Carnegie Institution of Washington Publication 432. Washington, DC.

Jolles, Carol

(in press)   Celebration of a Life: Remembering Linda Womkon Badten, Yupik Educator. In: Many Faces of Gender: Roles and Relationships through Time in Indigenous Northern Communities, Lisa Frink, Rita S. Shepard, and Gregory A. Reinhardt, eds. University Press of Colorado, Boulder.

Kaalund, Bodil

1983   *The Art of Greenland*, trans. by Kenneth Tindall. University of California Press, Berkeley.

Kane, Elisha Kent

1854   *The U.S. Grinnel Expedition in Search of Sir John Franklin: A Personal Narrative.* Harper & Brothers, New York.

1856   *Arctic Esplorations in the Years 1853, '54, '55.* 2 vols. Childs and Peterson, Philadelphia.

1881   *Als Eskimo unter den Eskimo.* A. Hartleben, Vienna.

King, Richard, M.D.

1836   *Narrative of a Journey to the Shores of the Arctic Ocean, in 1833, 1834, and 1835, under the Command of Capt. Back, R. N. R.* 2 vols. Bentley, London.

1847   "The Industrial Art of the Esquimaux." *Edinburgh New Philosophical Journal* 42:112-135.

Kennan, George

1870   *Tent Life in Siberia, and Adventures among the Koraks and Other Tribes in Kamtchatka and Northern Asia.* G. P. Putnam & Sons, New York.

Kleivan, Helge

1966   *The Eskimos of Northeast Laborador: A History of Eskimo-White Relations, 1771–1955.* Oslo.

Kleivan, Inge

1985   *Eskimos, Greenland and Canada.* E. J. Brill, Leiden.

Klutschak, Heinrich.

1987   *Overland to Starvation Cove: With the Inuit in Search of Franklin, 1878–1880.* Trans. and ed. by William Barr. University of Toronto Press, Toronto.

Knecht, Richard A.

1995   The Late Prehistory of the Alutiiq People: Culture Change on the Kodiak Archipelago from 1200–1750 A.D. Ph.D. Dissertation. Bryn Mawr College, Bryn Mawr, PA.

Knecht, Richard A., and Richard H. Jordan

1985   Nunakakhnak: An Historic Period Koniag Village in Karluk, Kodiak Island, Alaska. *Arctic Anthropology* 22, 2:17–35.

Kroeber, Alfred L.

n.d.   A New Type of Arch: The Peculiar Spiral Arch of the Eskimo Snow House. A. L. Kroeber Papers, Bancroft Library, University of California, Berkeley (unpublished manuscript).

1900   The Eskimo of Smith Sound. *Bulletin of the American Museum of Natural History* 12:265–327.

Kus, Susan, and Victor Raharijaona

2000 House to Palace, Village to State: Scaling Up Architecture and Ideology. *American Anthropologist* 102, 1:98–113.

Kuznecov, M. A.

1964 The Problem of the Origin of the Snow Igloo [title translated from the Russian]. *Letopis' Severa* 4:239–244.

Lantis, Margaret

1938 The Mythology of Kodiak Island, Alaska. *Journal of American Folklore* 51:123–172.

1947 Alaskan Eskimo Ceremonialism. American Ethnological Society, Monograph XI. J. J. Augustin, New York.

1984 The Aleut. *Handbook of North American Indians 5*, Arctic, David Damas, ed., 161–184. Smithsonian Institution Press, Washington, DC.

Lantis, Margaret

1946 The Social Culture of the Nunivak Eskimo. *Transactions of the American Philosophical Society* 35:153–323.

Larsen, Helge

1958 The Material Culture of the Nunamiut and Its Relation to Other Forms of Eskimo Culture in Northern Alaska. In: *Proceedings of the 32d International Congress of Americanists 1956*, 574–582. Munksgaard, Copenhagen.

Larsen, Helge, and Froelich Rainey

1948 Ipiutak and the Arctic Whale Hunting Culture. *Anthropological Papers of the American Museum of Natural History*, 42.

Leechman, Douglas

1945 Igloo and Tupik. *Beaver* 275, 4:36–39.

Levin, M. G., and L. P. Potapov, eds.

1964 *The Peoples of Siberia*, trans. by Scripta Technica. University of Chicago Press, Chicago.

Lisianski, Urey

1814 *A Voyage Around the World in the Years 1803, 4, 5, & 6*. John Booth and Longham, Hurst, Rees, Orme, & Brown.

Low, Albert P.

1906 *Report on the Dominion Government Expedition to Hudson Bay and the Arctic Islands on Board the* D.G.S. 'Neptune,' *1903–4*. Government Printing Bureau, Ottawa.

Lowenstein, Tom

1992 *The Things that Were Said of Them: Shaman Stories and Oral Histories of the Tikigaq People Told by Asatchaq*. University of California Press, Berkeley.

Lowie, Robert H.

1937 *The History of Ethnological Theory*. Holt, Rinehart and Winston, New York.

Lyon, George F.

1824 *The Private Journal of Capt. G. F. Lyon of* H.M.S. 'Hecla,' *During the Recent Voyage of Discovery under Captain Parry*. John Murray, London.

MacDonald, John

1998 *The Arctic Sky: Inuit Astronomy, Star Lore, and Legend*. Royal Ontario Museum, Toronto, and Nunavut Research Institute, Iqaluit, NWT, Canada.

Maressa, John

1986 *Maqiuq: The Eskimo Sweat Bath*. Klaus Renner, Munich.

Martin, George C.

1913 The Recent Eruption of Katmai Volcano in Alaska. *National Geographic* 24, 2:131–181.

Mary-Rousseliere, Guy
1984   Iglulik. *Handbook of North American Indians 5*, Arctic, David Damas, ed., 431–446. Smithsonian Institution Press, Washington, DC.

Mathiassen, Therkel
1927a   Archaeology of the Central Eskimos. *Report of the Fifth Thule Expedition, 1921–24*, 4, 1. Gyldendalske Boghandel, Nordisk Forlag, Copenhagen.

1927b   Archaeology of the Central Eskimos. *Report of the Fifth Thule Expedition, 1921–24*, 4, 2. Gyldendalske Boghandel, Nordisk Forlag, Copenhagen.

1928   Material Culture of the Iglulik Eskimos. *Report of the Fifth Thule Expedition, 1921–24*, 6, 1. Gyldendalske Boghandel, Nordisk Forlag, Copenhagen.

1936   The Eskimo Archaeology of the Julianehaab District. *Meddelelser om Grønland* 118, 1.

Mauss, Marcel, and Henri Beuchat
1979   *Seasonal Variation of the Eskimo: A Study in Social Morphology*, trans. by James J. Fox. Routledge and Kegan Paul, London. (Originally published 1904–1905, *Année Sociologique* 9).

McGhee, Robert N.
1974   Beluga Hunters: An Archaeological Reconstruction of the History and Culture of the Mackenzie Delta Kittegaryumiut. *Newfoundland Social and Economic Studies* 13. Institute of Social and Economic Research, Memorial University of Newfoundland.

1983   "Eskimo Prehistory." In: *Arctic Life: Challenge to Survive*, edited by Martina Magenau Jacobs and James B. Richardson III, pp. 73-112. Carnegie Museum of Natural History, Carnegie Institute, Pittsburgh.

McGuire, Randall H., and Michael B. Schiffer
1983   A Theory of Architectural Design. *Journal of Anthropological Archaeology* 2:227–303.

Merck, Carl Heinrich
1980   Siberia and Northwestern America, 1788–1792: The Journal of Carl Heinrich Merck, Naturalist with the Russian Scientific Expedition led by Captains Joseph Billings and Gavriil Sarychev, ed. by Richard A. Pierce, trans. by Fritz Jaensch. *Materials for the Study of Alaska History* 17. Limestone Press, Kingston, Ontario.

Merrill, George P.
1889   On hornblende andesites from the new volcano on Bogoslov Island in Bering Sea. In: *Report of the Cruise of the Revenue Marine Steamer Corwin in the Arctic Ocean in the Year 1884*, by Capt. M. A. Healy, 46–48. Government Printing Office, Washington, DC.

Michael, Henry N., ed.
1967   Lieutenant Zagoskin's Travels in Russian America, 1842–1844: The First Ethnographic and Geographic Investigations in the Yukon and Kuskokwim Valleys of Alaska. *Arctic Institute of North America, Anthropology of the North: Translations from Russian Sources* 7. University of Toronto Press.

Michea, Jean P.
1957   L'iglou. *Géographia* 75:53–60.

Miraglia, Rita A.
n.d.   The Chugach Smokehouse: A Case of Mistaken Identity. Paper presented at the 27th annual meeting, Alaska Anthropological Association, Anchorage, Alaska, March 24, 2000. On file, U.S. Bureau of Indian Affairs, ANCSA Office, Anchorage, AK.

Moore, Riley D.
1923   Social Life of the Eskimo of St. Lawrence Island. *American Anthropologist* 25, 3:339–375.

Morrison, David
    1991   The Diamond Jenness Collections from Bering Strait. *Archaeological Survey of Canada, Mercury Series Paper* 144. Canadian Museum of Man, Ottawa.

Muir, John
    1917   *The Cruise of the Corwin: Journal of the Arctic Expedition of 1881 in Search of De Long and the Jeanette*, William Frederic Bade, ed. Houghton Mifflin, Boston.

Murdoch, John
    n.d.   John Murdoch Journals, 1881–1883. Record Unit 7203, Smithsonian Institution Archives.

    1892   Ethnological Results of the Point Barrow Expedition. In: *Ninth Annual Report of the Bureau of Ethnology for the Years 1887–88*, 3–441. Government Printing Office, Washington, DC. (reprinted 1988, Smithsonian Institution Press, Washington, DC.).

Murdock, George Peter
    1967   *Ethnographic Atlas*. University of Pittsburg Press, Pittsburg.

Nabokov, Peter, and Robert Easton
    1989   Winter House, Iglu, and Tent. In: *Native American Architecture*, 188–208. Oxford University Press, New York.

Nansen, Fridtjof
    1894   *Eskimo Life*, trans. by William Archer. 2d ed. Longmans, Green, and Co., London.

Nelson, Edward W.
    1899   The Eskimo about Bering Strait. In: *Eighteenth Annual Report of the Bureau of American Ethnology for the Years 1896–97*, 3–518. Government Printing Office, Washington. (Reprinted 1983, Smithsonian Institution Press, Washington, DC.).

Nourse, J. E.
    1879   *Narrative of the Second Arctic Expedition Made by Charles F. Hall*. Government Printing Office, Washington, DC.

Oliver, Ethel Ross
    1989   Recording. Archives, Alaska and Polar Regions Department, Elmer E. Rasmuson Library, University of Alaska, Fairbanks, AK.

Oliver, Paul
    1977   *Shelter, Sign & Symbol*. Overlook Press, Woodstock, NY.

Ostermann, H., ed.
    1938   Knud Rasmussen's Posthumous Notes on the Life and Doings of the East Greenlanders in Olden Times. *Meddelelser om Grønland* 109, 1.

    1942   The Mackenzie Eskimos [After Knud Rasmussen's Posthumous Notes]. *Report of the Fifth Thule Expedition, 1921–24*, 10, 2. Gyldendalske Boghandel, Nordisk Forlag, Copenhagen.

Oswalt, Wendell H.
    1953   The Saucer-Shaped Eskimo Lamp. *Anthropological Papers of the University of Alaska* 1, 2:15–23.

    1967   *Alaskan Eskimos*. Chandler Publishing, San Francisco.

    1979   *Eskimos and Explorers*. Chandler & Sharp, Novato, CA.

Oswalt, Wendell H., and James W. VanStone
    1967   The Ethnoarcheology of Crow Village, Alaska. *Smithsonian Institution, Bureau of American Ethnology, Bulletin* 199. Government Printing Office, Washington, DC.

Packard, A. S.
    1877   The Eskimaux of Labrador. In: *The Indian Miscellany*, W. W. Beach, ed., 65–73. J. Munsell, Albany, NY.

1885 Notes on the Labrador Eskimo and Their Former Range Southward. *American Naturalist* 19, 5:471–560.

Parry, William E., Sir
1821 *Journal of a Voyage for the Discovery of a North-West Passage from the Atlantic to the Pacific: Performed in the Years 1819–1820.* John Murray, London.

1824 *Journal of a Second Voyage for the Discovery of a North-West Passage from the Atlantic to the Pacific; Performed in the Years 1821-22-23, in His Majesty's Ships Fury and Hecla.* . . . John Murray, London (reprinted 1969, Greenwood Press, New York).

Paulson, Ivor
1952 The "Seat of Honor" in Aboriginal Dwellings of the Circumpolar Zone, with Special Regard to the Indians of Northern North America. In: *Indian Tribes of Aboriginal America: Selected Papers of the 29th International Congress of Americanists*, Sol Tax, ed., 63–65. University of Chicago Press, Chicago.

Peary, Robert E.
1898 *Northward Over the "Great Ice."* 2 vols. Frederick A. Stokes Co., New York.

Petitot, Emile
1876 *Monographie des Esquimaux Tchiglit du Mackenzie et de L'Anderson*, Ernest Laroux, ed. Librairie de la Société Asiatique, Paris.

1887 *Les grands Esquimaux.* E. Plon, Paris.

1970 The Amérindians of the Canadian Northwest in the 19th Century, as Seen by Emile Petitot, 1, The Tchiglit Eskimos, Donat Savoie, ed. *Northern Science Research Group, Mackenzie Delta Research Report* 9, Department of Indian Affairs and Northern Development, Ottawa.

1981 Among the Chiglit Eskimos, trans. by E. Otto Hohn. *Boreal Institute for Northern Studies, Occasional Publication* 1. University of Alberta, Edmonton.

Petroff, Ivan
1884 *Report on the Population, Industries, and Resources of Alaska.* Department of the Interior, Census Office. Government Printing Office, Washington, DC.

Pierce, Richard A., ed.
1978 The Russian Orthodox Religious Mission in America, 1794–1837, trans. by Colin Bearne. *Materials for the Study of Alaska History* 11. Limestone Press, Kingston, Ontario.

Pinart, Alphonse
1873 Eskimaux et Koloches: Idées Réligieuses et Traditions des Kaniagmioutes. In: *Revue d'Anthropologie* 2:673–680.

Polglase, Christopher R.
1990 The Mound 44 Kitchen Excavations. In: *The Utqiagvik Excavations* 3, Excavation of a Prehistoric Catastrophe: A Preserved Household from the Utqiagvik Village, Barrow, Alaska, Edwin S. Hall, Jr., ed., 161–194. North Slope Borough Commission on Inupiat History, Language and Culture, Barrow, AK.

Porsild, Morten P.
1915 Studies on the Material Culture of the Eskimo of West Greenland. *Meddelelser om Grønland* 51, 5.

Portlock, Nathaniel
1789 *A Voyage Round the World; But More Particularly to the North-west Coast of America: Performed in 1785, 1786, 1787, and 1788, in the King George and Queen Charlotte, Captains Portlock and Dixon.* John Stockdale and

George Goulding, London. (Reprinted 1968, N. Israel, Amsterdam, and Da Capo Press, New York.)

Rainey, Froelich G.

1947 The Whale Hunters of Tigara. *Anthropological Papers of the American Museum of Natural History* 47, 2:231–283.

Rapoport, Amos

1969 *House Form and Culture*. Prentice-Hall, New York.

Rasmussen, Knud

1926 Rasmussens Thulefahhrt: 2 Jahre im schlitten durch unerforschtes Eskimoland. Frankfurter Societäts-Druckerei G.M.B.H. Abteilung Buchverlag, Frankfurt am Main.

1927 *Across Arctic America*. G. S. Putnam & Sons, New York.

1929 Intellectual Culture of the Iglulik Eskimos. *Report of the Fifth Expedition, 1921–24, 7, 1*. Gyldendalske Boghandel, Nordisk Forlag, Copenhagen.

1930 Observations on the Intellectual Culture of the Caribou Eskimos. *Report of the Fifth Thule Expedition, 1921–24, 7, 2*. Gyleddalske [sic] Boghandel, Nordisk Forlag, Copenhagen.

1931 The Netsilik Eskimos: Social Life and Spiritual Culture. *Report of the Fifth Thule Expedition, 1921–24, 8, 1–2*. Gyldendalske Boghandel, Nordisk Forlag, Copenhagen.

1932 Intellectual Culture of the Copper Eskimos. *Report of the Fifth Thule Expedition, 1921–24, 9*. Gyldendalske Boghandel, Nordisk Forlag, Copenhagen.

1952 The Alaskan Eskimos, as Described in the Poshumous Notes of Knud Rasmussen, Hother B. S. Ostermann and Eric Holtved, eds. *Report of the Fifth Thule Expedition, 1921–24, 10, 3*. Gyldendalske Boghandel, Nordisk Forlag, Copenhagen.

1975 *The People of the Polar North: A Record*, G. Herring, ed. Gale Research Co., Detroit (originally published 1908, Kegan Paul, Trench, Trubner & Co. Ltd., London).

Rausch, Robert

1951 Notes on the Nunamiut Eskimo and Mammals of the Anaktuvuk Pass Region, Brooks Range, Alaska. *Arctic* 4, 3:147–195.

Ray, Dorothy Jean

1960 The Eskimo Dwelling. *Alaska Sportsman* 26, 8:13–15.

1966 The Eskimo of St. Michael and Vicinity as Related by H. M. W. Edmonds. *Anthropological Papers of the University of Alaska* 13, 2.

1975 *The Eskimos of Bering Strait, 1650–1898*. University of Washington Press, Seattle.

1984 Bering Strait Eskimo. *Handbook of North American Indians 5*, Arctic, David Damas, ed., 285–302. Smithsonian Institution Press, Washington, DC.

Ray, P[atrick] H[enry]

1885 Ethnographic Sketch of the Natives of Point Barrow. In: *Report of the International Polar Expedition to Point Barrow, Alaska, in Response to the Resolution of the [U.S.] House of Representatives of December 11, 1884*, 35–87. Government Printing Office, Washington, DC.

Reinhardt, Gregory A.

1983 Excavations at Barrow, Alaska. *Archaeology at UCLA* 2, Ernestine S. Elster, ed., 10. Institute of Archaeology, University of California, Los Angeles.

1986 *The Dwelling as Artifact: Analysis of Ethnographic Eskimo Dwellings, with Archaeological Implications*. Ph.D. Dissertation. Department of

Anthropology, University of California, Los Angeles. University Microfilms, Ann Arbor, MI.

1991   Traditional Alutiiq Foodways Compared with Cultural Correlates in Two Other Alaskan Coastal Societies. Paper presented at the Alaskan Anthropological Association Annual Meetings, March 22–23, Anchorage, AK.

1997   Eskimo Art from Pingasugruk, Northern Alaska. Pictures of Record, Inc. Weston, CT.

n.d.   Unpublished field notes, Pingasugruk archaeological site (north Alaska coast) 1994-1996 field seasons.

Reinhardt, Gregory A., and Albert A. Dekin, Jr.

1990   House Structure and Interior Features. In: *The Utqiagvik Excavations* 3, Excavation of a Prehistoric Catastrophe: A Preserved Household from the Utqiagvik Village, Barrow, Alaska, Edwin S. Hall, Jr., ed., 38–112. North Slope Borough Commission on Inupiat History, Language and Culture, Barrow, AK.

Reinhardt, Gregory A., and Molly Lee

1997   *Encyclopedia of Vernacular Architecture of the World* 3, Paul Oliver, ed., 1795–1799, 1803–1804. Cambridge University Press, New York.

Renner, Louis L. (S. J.)

1979   *Pioneer Missionary to the Bering Strait Eskimos: Bellarmine Lafortune, S.J.*, with Dorothy Jean Ray. Binford & Mort, Portland.

Richardson, John

1852   *Arctic Searching Expedition: A journal of a Boat-Voyage through Rupert's Land and the Arctic Sea . . . .* Harper & Brothers, New York.

Riches, David

1990   The Force of Tradition in Eskimology. In: *Localizing Strategies: Regional Traditions of Ethnographic Writing*, Richard Fardon, ed., 71–89. Scottish Academic Press, Edinburgh.

Rink, Henry

1875   *Tales and Traditions of the Eskimo with a Sketch of their Habits, Religion, Language and Other Peculiarities*, Dr. Robert Brown, ed. William Blackwood and Sons, Edinburgh.

1877   *Danish Greenland: Its People and Its Products*, Dr Robert Brown, ed. Henry S. King & Co., London.

Ross, John

1835a   *Narrative of a Second Voyage in Search of a North-West Passage, and of a Residence in the Arctic Regions During the Years 1829, 1830, 1831, 1832, 1833.* A. W. Webster, London.

1835b   *Appendix to the Second Voyage in Search of a North-West Passage.* A. W. Webster, London.

Rowley, Graham

1938   Snowhouse Building. *Polar Record* 16:109–116.

Rudofsky, Bernard

1964   *Architecture without Architects* [exhibition catalog]. Museum of Modern Art, New York.

Saladin d'Anglure, Bernard

1975   Recherches sur le symbolisme inuit. *Recherches Amérindiennes au Quebec* 5, 3:62–69.

1984   Inuit of Quebec. In: *Handbook of North American Indians 5*, Arctic, by David Damas, ed., 476–507. Smithsonian Institution Press, Washington, DC.

Sarytschew, Gawrila

1806   *Account of a Voyage of Discovery to the North-East of Siberia, the Frozen Ocean, and the North-East Sea* 2. Richard Phillips, London.

Sauer, Martin
1802   *An Account of a Geographical and Astronomical Expedition to the Northern Parts of Russia, for Acertaining the Degrees of Latitude and Longitude of the Mouth of the River Kovima; of the Whole Coast of the Tshutski, to East Cape; and of the Islands in the Eastern Ocean, Stretching to the American Coast. Performed . . . by Commodore Joseph Billings, in the Years 1785, &c. to 1794.* T. Cadell, Juneau, AK.

Savelle, James M.
1984   Cultural and Natural Formation Processes of a Historic Inuit Snow Dwelling Site, Somerset Island, Canada. *American Antiquity* 49, 3:508–524.

Schaaf, Jeanne, ed.
1996   *Ublasaun: First Light.* National Park Service, Anchorage, AK.

Schledermann, P.
1976a   The Effect of Climatic/Ecological Changes on the Style of Thule Culture Winter Dwellings. *Arctic and Alpine Research* 8, 1:37–47.

1976b   Thule Culture Communal Houses in Labrador. *Arctic* 29, 1:27–37.

Schwatka, Frederick
1883   The Igloo of the Innuit. *Science* 2, 28:182–184; 2, 29:216–218; 2, 30:259–262; 2, 31:304–306; 2, 32:346–349.

1884a   The Implements of the Igloo. *Science* 4, 77:81–85.

1884b   The Netschilluk Innuits. *Science* 4, 98:543–545.

Schweitzer, Peter, and Molly Lee
1997   The Arctic Culture Area. In: *Native North Americans: An Ethno-historical Approach*, 2d ed., Molly Mignon and Daniel Boxburger, eds., 29–84. Kendall/Hunt, Dubuque, IA.

Sczawinski, Timothy M.
1981   The Little Diomede Kugeri. *Northern Engineer* 13, 4:19–25.

Senn, Nicholas
1907   *In the Heart of the Arctics.* W. B. Conkey, Chicago.

Senungetuk, Joseph E.
1971   *Give or Take a Century: An Eskimo Chronicle.* The Indian Historian Press, San Francisco.

Sheehan, Glenn W.
1985   Whaling as an Organizing Focus in Northwestern Alaskan Eskimo Society. In: *Prehistoric Hunter Gatherers: The Emergence of Cultural Complexity*, T. Douglas Price and James A. Brown, eds., 123–154. Academic Press, New York.

1990   Excavations at Mound 34. In: *The Utqiagvik Excavations* 2, Additional Reports of the 1982 Investigations by the Utqiagvik Archaeology Project, Barrow, Alaska, Edwin S. Hall, Jr., ed., 181–325. North Slope Borough Commission on Inupiat History, Language and Culture, Barrow, AK.

Simpson, John
1855   Observations on the Western Eskimo and the Country They Inhabit, from Notes Taken During Two Years at Point Barrow. In: *Further Papers Relative to the Recent Arctic Expeditions in Search of Sir John Franklin and the Crews of H. M. S. "Erebus" and "Terror,"* 917–942. [Great Britain Admiralty] George Edward Eyre and William Spottiswoode, London (reprinted 1875, in *Arctic Geography and Ethnology*, 233–275, John Murray, London).

Slaughter, Dale C.
1982   The Point Barrow Type House: An Analysis of Archaeological Examples from Siraaġruk and Other Sites in North Alaska. *Anthropological Papers of the University of Alaska* 20, 1–2:141–158.

Smith, Derek G.
1984 Mackenzie Delta Eskimo. In: *Handbook of North American Indians 5*, Arctic, David Damas, ed., 347–358. Smithsonian Institution Press, Washington, DC.

Smith, Timothy
1990 The Mound 8 Escavations. In: *The Utqiagvik Excavations* 1, Excavation of a Prehistoric Catastrophe: A Preserved Household from the Utqiagvik Village, Barrow, Alaska, Edwin S. Hall, Jr., ed., 84–111. North Slope Borough Commission on Inupiat History, Language and Culture, Barrow, AK.

Spencer, Robert F.
1959 The North Alaskan Eskimo: A Study in Ecology and Society. *Smithsonian Institution, Bureau of American Ethnology, Bulletin* 171. United States Government Printing Office, Washington, DC.

1984a North Alaska Eskimo: Introduction. In: *Handbook of North American Indians 5*, Arctic, David Damas, ed., 278–284. Smithsonian Institution Press, Washington, DC.

1984b North Alaska Coast Eskimo. In: *Handbook of North American Indians 5*, Arctic, David Damas, ed., 320–337. Smithsonian Institution Press, Washington, DC.

Staley, David P.
1985 Driftwood Tipi Structures on the Seward Peninsula Coast. Paper presented at the Alaskan Anthropological Association Annual Meetings, March 1–2, Anchorage, AK.

Steensby, Hans P.
1910 Contributions to the Ethnology and Anthropogeography of the Polar Eskimos. *Meddelelser om Grønland* 34, 7:253–405.

1917 An Anthropogeographical Study of the Origin of the Eskimo Culture. *Meddelelser om Grønland* 53:39–228.

Stefansson, Vilhjalmur
1913 *My Life with the Eskimo*. Macmillan, New York.

1914 The Stefansson-Anderson Arctic Expedition of the American Museum: Preliminary Ethnological Report. *Anthropological Papers of the American Museum of Natural History* 14, 1.

1921 *The Friendly Arctic: The Story of Five Years in Polar Regions*. Macmillan, New York.

1922 *Hunters of the Great North*. Harcourt, Brace, and Co., New York.

1944 *Arctic Manual*. MacMillan, New York.

Steltzer, Ulli
1981 *Building an Igloo*. Douglas and McIntyre, Vancouver.

Stoney, George M.
1900 *Naval Explorations in Alaska: An Account of Two Naval Expeditions to Northern Alaska, with Official Maps of the Country Explored*. United States Naval Institute, Annapolis, MD.

Strub, Harold
1996 *Bare Poles: Building Design for High Latitudes*. Carleton University Press, Ottawa.

Taylor, J. Garth
1974 *Netsilik Eskimo Material Culture: The Roald Amundsen Collection from King William Island*. Universitetsforlaget, Oslo, Bergen, Tromsø.

1984 Historical Ethnography of the Labrador Coast. In: *Handbook of North American Indians 5*, Arctic, David Damas, ed., 508–521. Smithsonian Institution Press, Washington, DC.

1990   The Labrador Inuit Kashim (Ceremonial House) Complex. *Arctic Anthropology* 27, 2:51–67.

Thalbitzer, William, ed.
1914   Ethnographical Collections from East Greenland (Angmagsalik and Nualik). In: The Ammassalik Eskimo, 1. *Meddelelser om Grønland* 39:319–755.

1924   Cultic Games and Festivals in Greenland. *Proceedings of the Twenty-First International Congress of Americanists* 2, 236–255. Gothenburg.

1941   The Ammassalik Eskimo, 2, 2d half-volume. *Meddelelser om Grønland* 40:565–740.

Thornton, Harrison Robertson
1931   *Among the Eskimos of Wales, Alaska, 1890–93*, Neda S. Thornton and William M. Thornton, Jr., eds. Johns Hopkins Press, Baltimore.

Townsend, Charles H.
1887   Notes on the Natural History and Ethnology of Northern Alaska. *Report of the Cruise of the Revenue Marine Steamer* Corwin *in the Arctic Ocean in the Year 1885*, by Capt. M. A. Healy, 81–102.

Turner, Lucien M.
1894   Ethnology of the Ungava District, Hudson Bay Territory. In: *Eleventh Annual Report of the Bureau of Ethnology for the Years 1889–90*, 159–350. Government Printing Office, Washington, DC.

Upton, Dell
1983   The Order of Things: Recent Studies in Vernacular Architecture. *American Quarterly* 35, 3:262–279.

U.S. Bureau of Indian Affairs, ANCSA Office
1995   Nunivak Overview: Report of Investigations for BLM AA-9238 et al., Kenneth L. Pratt, compiler, ed., and principal author. 6 vols. Copy on file, BIA ANCSA Office, Anchorage, AK.

VanStone, James
1962   *Point Hope: An Eskimo Village in Transition*. University of Washington Press, Seattle.

1970   Akulivikchuk: A Nineteenth Century Eskimo Village on the Nushagak River, Alaska. *Fieldiana: Anthropology* 60.

1977   A. F. Kashevarov's Coastal Explorations in Northwest Alaska, 1838. Fieldiana: Anthropology 69.

1984   Mainland Southwest Alaska Eskimo. In: *Handbook of North American Indians 5*, Arctic, David Damas, ed., 224–242. Smithsonian Institution Press, Washington, DC.

1989   Nunivak Island Eskimo *(Yuit)* Technology and Material Culture. *Fieldiana: Anthropology*, New Series 12.

Van Valin, William B.
1941   *Eskimoland Speaks*. Caxton Press, Caldwell, ID.

von Langsdorff, George H.
1968   Voyages and Travels in Various Parts of the World 2. *Bibliotecha Australiana* 41. N. Israel, Amsterdam, and Da Capo Press, New York (originally published 1813–1814, H. Colburn, London).

Waterman, T. T.
1924   Houses of the Alaskan Eskimo. *American Anthropologist* 26:289–291.

Weyer, Edward Moffat
1932   The Eskimos: Their Environment and Folkways. Yale University Press, New Haven, CT.

Whitney, Harry
1910   *Hunting with the Eskimos*. The Century Co., New York.

Wickersham, James

1902   The Eskimo Dance House. *American Antiquarian and Oriental Journal* 24:221–223.

Wiggins, Ira L.

1953   North of Anaktuvuk. *Pacific Discovery* 6:8–15.

Wulsin, Frederick R.

1949   Adaptations to Climate among Non-European Peoples. In: *Physiology of Heat Regulation and the Science of Clothing: Prepared at the Direction of the Division of Medical Sciences*, Louis Newburgh, ed., 3–24. Saunders, Philadelphia.

Names Index

A

Aldrich, Herbert L., 114
Alsayyad, Nezar, 1, 162
Amundsen, Roald, 45, 59
Anderson, H. Dewey, 128

B

Balikci, Asen, 61, 64
Beauchat, Henri, 5, 170
Beechey, Frederick William, 94, 107
Belcher, Edward, 54
Bessels, Emil, 31, 174
Best, George, 2
Beuchat, Henri, 44, 75
Bilby, Julian W., 57, 67, 68
Bird, Junius B., 36
Birket-Smith, Kaj, 3, 5, 11, 13, 14, 18,
    22, 24, 26, 27, 28, 30, 31, 32, 32n.2,
    33n.15, 38, 40, 41, 44, 48, 50, 51, 52,
    54, 55, 60, 62, 63, 65, 66, 67, 69, 71,
    94, 143, 144, 145, 150, 151, 153, 155,
    157n.12, 157n.21, 163, 177
Black, Lydia T., 139, 140, 144, 153, 154,
    157n.10
Boas, Franz, 1, 6n.3, 19, 33n.8, 33n.10,
    33n.19, 35, 39, 43, 44, 45, 46, 51, 52,
    53, 54, 57, 58, 63, 64, 67, 69, 70, 71,
    164, 168
Bockstoce, John R., 78, 114

Bogojavlensky, Sergei, 89, 106, 109
Bogoras, Waldemar, 131
Bourdier, Jean-Paul, 1
Brower, Charles D., 98
Browne, Belmore, 52
Burch, Ernest S., Jr., 3, 69, 71, 163

C

Call, S. J., 106
Campbell, John M., 82, 92, 96, 99, 100,
    180
Cantwell, John C., 84, 93, 98, 103, 104,
    106, 110, 111, 113
Carius, Helen Slwooko, 132, 133, 135,
    156
Choris, Louis [Ludovik], 148
Clark, Donald W., 139, 143, 150, 181
Collignon, Béatrice, 2
Collins, Henry B., Jr., 126, 133
Comack, John G., 71
Cook, James, 138, 139, 145, 146
Corbin, James E., 80, 82, 116n.11,
    117n.23, 180
Coxe, William, 150
Crantz, David, 10, 11, 12, 13, 14, 23, 24,
    27, 30, 33n.15, 172, 174
Crellin, David, 171, 182
Cremeans, Lola M., 135

Crowell, Aron L., 79, 140, 143, 150,
    156n.8
Curtis, Edward S., 84, 92, 93, 101, 104,
    126, 129, 152

D

Dall, William H., 120, 121, 123, 126,
    127, 129, 146, 153, 154, 156n.6, 181
Damas, David, 3, 6n.2, 35, 47, 63
Davydov, G[avriil] I., 141, 150, 152, 153,
    154, 155, 157n.10, 157n.22
Dawson, Mary R., 4, 52, 167
Dekin, Albert A. Jr., 79, 80, 116n.7, 179
de Laguna, Frederica, 143
Devine, Edward J., 107–108
Dickie, Francis, 51
Diebitsch-Peary, Josephine, 27
Douglas, Mary, 162
Duhaime, Gerard, 2
Dyke, Arthur S., 32n.1, 75

E

Easton, Robert, 2, 163
Eek, Ann Christine, 58
Eells, Walter Crosby, 128
Egede, Hans P., 13, 24, 33n.15
Ekblaw, W. Elmer, 4, 5, 10, 14, 15, 16,
    20, 21, 27, 30, 174

Elson, Thomas, 94
England, John, 75

F

Faegre, Torvald, 64, 99
Fair, Susan, W., 87, 152, 157n.18
Fienup-Riordan, Ann, 120, 122, 123, 124, 125, 129, 130, 131, 145, 152, 155, 156, 156n.6, 156n.7, 164
Forbin, Victor, 71
Ford, James A., 79, 116n.7, 179
Forman, Werner, 3, 163
Franklin, John, 43
Frederiksen, V. C., 11

G

Gabus, Jean, 60, 71
Garber, Clark M., 107
Geist, Otto, 131, 132, 152, 155, 156n.8
Gerlach, S. Craig, 87
Gibson, William, 71
Giddings, James L., 83, 84, 85, 92, 93, 94, 100, 101, 104, 106, 107, 109, 113, 117n.20, 117n.30, 181
Giffen, Naomi Musmaker, 21, 64
Gilberg, Rolf, 31
Glassie, Henry, 163
Glotoff, Stephen [Stepan Glotov], 150
Goddard, Pliny E., 5
Gordon, G. B., 114, 153
Graah, Wilhelm A., 24
Graburn, Nelson H. H., 2, 20, 47, 52, 54, 163
Griggs, Robert R., 138, 140, 142
Grinnell, George Bird, 136, 137
Gubser, Nicholas J., 80, 82, 92, 99, 100, 107, 109, 112, 113, 180, 181

H

Hall, Charles Francis, 49
Hall, Edwin S., Jr., 80, 117n.23, 180
Handy, Richard I., 47
Hansen, Johannes, 172
Hantzisch, Bernard, 16, 64
Hawkes, Ernest W., 36, 38, 41, 42, 50, 56, 57, 62, 63, 66, 67, 71, 89, 102, 106, 109, 115, 154, 155, 156n.6, 175
Hayden, Brian D., 162, 171, 182
Hayes, Isaac I., 18, 44
Healy, M. A., 81, 103, 104, 105, 106, 134, 149
Hieb, Louis A., 164
Himmelheber, Hans, 123, 129, 153, 155, 156n.6

Hoffman, Walter James, 166, 168
Holm, Gustav, 11, 13, 18, 19, 21, 22, 23, 25, 28, 30, 117n.27, 171, 172
Holmberg, Dan, 171, 182
Holtved, Erik, 15, 16, 18, 22, 24, 27, 28, 30, 32n.5, 33n.7, 174
Hooper, Calvin L., 78, 97
Hooper, William H., 95, 98
Hough, Walter, 20
Hrdlička, Aleš, 141, 153, 154, 181
Hughes, Charles, 135, 148
Hunter-Anderson, Rosalind L., 116n.7, 162, 163
Hutton, S. K., 36, 37, 42, 56, 175

I

Ingstad, Helge, 82, 83, 92, 96, 98, 99, 100, 104, 112

J

Jacobsen, Johan Adrian, 115, 121, 123, 153, 154, 157n.22, 181
Jenness, Diamond, 5, 32n.3, 41, 42, 43, 44, 48, 50, 51, 54, 55, 58, 60, 62, 63, 64, 65, 66, 67, 68, 70, 71, 116, 117n.27, 177, 178
Jetté, Hélène, 75
Jochelson, Waldemar, 3, 159
Jolles, Carol, 138
Jordan, Richard H., 3, 138, 139, 140, 141, 152, 181

K

Kaalund, Bodil, 30, 115
Kane, Elisha Kent, 1, 16, 17, 18, 22, 29, 30, 174
Kaplan, Lawrence, 6n.2, 98
Kashevarov, A. F., 91
Kennan, George, 135
King, J., 111, 138, 139, 145, 146
Kleivan, Helge, 14, 36, 38, 56, 175
Klutschak, Heinrich, 59
Knecht, Richard A., 3, 138, 139, 140, 152, 181
Kroeber, Alfred L., 18, 19, 24, 41, 47, 174, 175
Kuznecov, M. A., 38

L

Lantis, Margaret, 110, 141, 153, 154, 157n.16
Larsen, Helge, 82, 92, 96, 98, 99, 104, 109, 112, 113
Lee, Molly, 4, 6n.2, 23, 36, 43, 52, 58, 74, 79, 83, 98, 138, 163, 168

Leechman, Douglas, 65
Lisiansky, Urey, 139, 141, 153, 157n.23, 181
Low, Albert P., 65
Lowie, Robert H., 170
Lyon, George F., 1, 39, 50, 51, 56, 58, 63, 64, 66, 69, 176, 177

M

MacDonald, John, 70, 114
Magnus, Olaus, 1
Mann, Daniel, 143, 150
Maressa, John, 129, 152, 157n.19
Martin, George C., 138
Mary-Rousseliere, Guy, 176
Mathiassen, Therkel, 11, 20, 39, 40, 43, 44, 46, 47, 48, 50, 51, 53, 55, 58, 62, 63, 65, 66, 67, 69, 71, 176
Mauss, Marcel, 5, 44, 75, 170, 172
McGhee, Robert N., 4, 75, 76, 89, 104, 110
McGuire, Randall H., 167
Merck, Carl Heinrich, 139, 141, 152, 154
Merrill, George P., 77
Michae, Jean P., 71
Michael, Henry N., 121, 129, 147, 155, 181
Milne, Murray, 61, 144, 166
Miraglia, Rita A., 144
Moore, Riley D., 135, 156n.8
Morrison, David, 116
Muir, John, 88, 89, 95, 102, 106
Murdoch, John, 9, 20, 76, 78, 79, 80, 91, 94, 95, 96, 104, 106, 107, 109, 111, 112, 116n.7, 122, 131, 145, 154, 179, 180

N

Nabokov, Peter, 2, 163
Nansen, Fridtjof, 11, 14, 19, 27, 174
Nelson, Edward W., 51, 87, 88, 89, 94, 95, 98, 101, 102, 104, 106, 120, 121, 128, 129, 131, 132, 133, 135, 136, 138, 143, 146, 147, 148, 151, 152, 153, 154, 156n.3, 156n.8, 164
Nourse, J. E., 44, 69, 71, 176

O

Oliver, Ethel Ross, 82–83, 99, 100
Ostermann, H., 11, 30, 77, 91, 93, 111, 117n.16, 179
Oswalt, Wendell H., 1, 4, 9, 25, 35, 71, 73, 84, 85, 119, 121, 127, 140, 155, 156n.2

P

Packard, A. S., 36, 63, 67

Parry, William E., 1, 33n.19, 44, 50, 51, 52, 53, 54, 56, 58, 60, 61, 64, 65, 66, 67, 69, 176, 177

Paulson, Ivor, 16

Peary, Robert E., 1, 5, 15, 16, 18, 19, 32n.5, 33n.10, 33n.11, 174

Petitot, Emile, 74, 75, 76, 89, 90, 95, 96, 98, 107, 117n.19, 178, 179

Petroff, Ivan, 143, 145

Pierce, Richard A., ed., 141, 153, 154

Polglase, Chistopher R., 80

Porsild, Morten P., 30

Portlock, Nathaniel, 144, 151, 157n.17

R

Rainey, Froelich G., 80, 106, 112, 116, 131, 132, 152, 155, 156n.8

Rapoport, Amos, 2, 6n.1, 102, 170

Rasmussen, Knud, 18, 33n.14, 44, 51, 56, 58, 59, 67, 68, 69, 70, 77, 178

Rausch, Robert, 98, 99

Ray, Dorothy Jean, 3, 77, 94, 95, 98, 104, 106, 117n.25, 120, 121, 123, 129, 130, 131, 143, 144, 145, 147, 152, 153, 156n.3, 157n.24, 179, 181

Reimnitz, Erik, 75

Reinhardt, Gregory A., 2, 4, 23, 24, 28, 33n.14, 36, 43, 58, 66, 67, 74, 79, 80, 83, 96, 98, 116n.7, 121, 138, 139, 159, 163, 170, 171, 179, 182

Renner, Louis L., 102

Richardson, John, 89, 110, 114, 116n.5, 116n.13

Riches, David, 6

Rink, Henry, 10, 12, 14, 18, 21, 32n.2, 174

Ross, John, 20, 35, 39, 52, 54, 60, 61

Rowley, Graham, 71

Rudofsky, Bernard, 1

S

Saladin d'Anglure, Bernard, 56, 59, 71, 164

Sarytschew, Gawrila, 139

Sauer, Martin, 139, 141

Savelle, James M., 39

Schaaf, Jeanne, 168

Schiffer, Michael B., 167

Schledermann, P., 4, 11, 36, 175

Schwatka, Frederick, 20, 40, 42, 50, 51, 54

Schweitzer, Peter, 4, 6n.2, 168

Sczawinski, Timothy M., 88, 89, 106, 109

Senn, Nicholas, 17

Sheehan, Glenn W., 80, 111, 114, 115

Simpson, John, 78, 80, 85, 91, 95, 106, 111, 112, 114, 116n.9, 179, 180

Slaughter, Dale C., 78

Smith, Derek G., 71, 76, 78, 116n.3, 178, 179

Spencer, Robert F., 79, 98, 99, 116n.7, 116n.8, 116n.10, 117n.24

Staley, David P., 104, 107

Steensby, Hans P., 4, 5, 14, 15, 16, 18, 19, 21, 27, 30, 31, 33n.10, 106, 159, 174

Stefansson, Vilhjalmur, 20, 35, 38, 39, 40, 41, 43, 51, 55, 60, 63, 64, 65, 66, 68, 69, 75, 76, 77, 81, 89, 90, 91, 98, 100, 104, 106, 111, 112, 117n.14, 117n.16, 177, 178

Steltzer, Ulli, 41

Stoney, George M., 83, 92, 93, 104, 109, 112, 113, 117n.17, 117n.18, 181

Strong, Steven B., 47

Strub, Harold, 167, 170

T

Taylor, J. Garth, 36, 48, 56, 61, 67, 175

Thalbitzer, William, 11, 13, 14, 18, 20, 21, 23, 24, 25, 28, 30, 31, 33n.15, 33n.16, 159, 172

Thornton, Harrison Robertson, 33n.17, 94, 115

Townsend, Charles H., 84

Turner, Lucien M., 48, 55, 56, 63, 65, 71

U

Upton, Dell, 2

U.S. Bureau of Indian Affairs, ANCSA Office, 123, 153, 154

V

VanStone, James W., 79, 91, 123, 124, 126, 127, 129, 150, 152

Van Valin, William B., 92, 98, 102, 106, 107

W

Waterman, T. T., 163

Weyer, Edward Moffat, 163

Whitney, Harry, 29

Wickersham, James, 109, 115

Wulsin, Frederick R., 71

Z

Zagoskin, Lavrentiy, 147, 181

Subject Index

Page numbers in *italics* refer to illustrations and diagrams.
See the Names Index for authors and explorers.

A

Alaska and Siberia, 119–57, 181–82, *see also entries beginning with Alaska and Siberia*
    area of study, 118 (map), 119
    ceremonial structures, 127–31, 154, 156n.6, 181
    history and dwellings, 121, 131
    household life, 121–23, 125, 129–31, 135–38, 141, 152–53
    household sizes and dwellings, 181–82
    lesser structures, 152–53
    rituals and beliefs, 129, 154–56
    special-use structures, 127, 152–54
    summer houses, 145–51, 159–64
    types and classification of houses, 159–63, 165
    winter houses (men's and women's), 119–44, 159–62
Alaska and Siberia special-use structures, 152–54
    birth, menstrual, and mourning huts, 153
    ceremonial houses, 154
    lesser structures, 152–53
Alaska and Siberia summer houses, 145–51, 159–63
    alternative summer dwellings, 150–51
    gender separation, 145
    Kodiak Island grass huts (shalash), 148–50
    Norton Sound dome tents, 147
    Norton Sound wooden houses, 145–47
    Prince William Sound plank huts, 150
    Siberian Eskimo double-arch tents, 131, 148, *149*
    transitional dwellings, 144–45

umiak lean-tos, 150
Yukon River wooden houses, 126–28, *146*, 147–48
Alaska and Siberia winter houses (men's and women's), 119–44, 159–62
    alternative winter dwellings, 143–44
    Chugach smokehouses (transitional dwelling), 144–45
    gender separation, 129–30, 145, 165–66
    heating, 122–23, 125, 129, 131, 133, 135, 167
    Hooper Bay (Yukon River) wooden houses, 126–28
    household life, 121, 129, *131*
    Kodiak Island alternative dwellings, 143–44
    Kodiak Island year-round wooden houses (*ciqlluaq* or barabara), 138–43
        idealized house design, *138*
    Norton Sound snow tent (alternative dwelling), 143
    Norton Sound year-round men's wooden house (*qasgiq*; Unaligmiut), 120–23, *128*, *129*, 155–56
        idealized house design, *120*
    Nunivak Island year-round wooden houses (*qasgiq*; Nunivaarmiut), 123–26, 127, 155
        connected housing complexes, 123–25
        idealized house design, *124*
        isolated houses, 126
    Prince William Sound wooden houses, 143
    Siberian Chukchi new-style hide-roofed houses (*mangtaha.aq*), 131, *134*, 135–38, *137*
    Siberian Yupik old-style wooden houses (*nenglu*), 131–34
    Southwest Alaska men's houses (*qasgiq*; Unaligmiut), 127–31, 154, 155
    transitional dwellings, 144–45
    wooden houses (other Central Yup'ik), 126–28

Aleuts, 3, 139, 157n.16

Algonkian Indians, 59

Alutiiq (Chugach Eskimo and Koniag). *see also* Alaska and
  Siberia; Kodiak Island, Alaska; Prince William Sound, Alaska
    beliefs and rituals, 155
    birth and menstrual huts, 153, 157n.22
    ceremonial houses *(qasgiq)*, 154
    grass huts, 148–50
    mourning hut, 153
    research on, 3, 138–39
    steam baths, 152, 154
    umiak lean-tos, 129n.26, 150, 162
    wooden year-round houses *(ciqlluaq* or barabara), 138–43
      idealized house design, *138*

Ammassalik. *see* East Greenland (Ammassalik)

Angmagsalik, 28. *see also* East Greenland (Ammassalik)

antlers. *see* caribou

architecture, Eskimo, 1–9, 159–70. *see also* art and artifacts;
  gender
    art and artifacts, 166
    classification principles, 22, 159–65
    climate, 4–5, 162–63
    culture and, 1–3, 162–70
    distribution of dwellings
        summer dwelling types, 159–63
        winter and transitional dwelling types, 161–62
    energy requirements (energistics), 68, 167
    gender studies, 165
    household sizes and dwellings (dimensions; area per person),
      171–82
    research possibilities, 164–68
    settlement patterns, 5–6, 39–40, 55, 116n.11, 163, 167
    spatial analyses, 51, 164–65
    symbolic dimensions, 165–66
    taxonomy and survey, 2–4, 35
    terms, 1, 6n.1, 6n.2, 71n.1
    uniformity and variation, 4, 163, 168–70

arch tents. *see* double-arch tents; single-arch tents; tents

Arctic (Central), 35–71, 159–62, *see also entries beginning with
  Arctic (Central)*
    alternative dwellings, 48, 62–63
    area of study, 34 (map), 35, 71n.1
    birth, menstrual, and death huts, 66–67
    ceremonial houses, 67–69
    household life, 48, 50–52, 58, 60, 63–67
    household sizes and dwellings, 175–78
    lesser structures, 66–69
    rituals and beliefs, 69–70
    special-use structures, 66
    summer dwellings, 55–69
    transitional dwellings, 52–55
    types and classification of houses, 159–63, 165
    winter dwellings, 36–55

Arctic (Central) summer dwellings, 55–69, 159–63
    alternative summer dwellings, 62–63
    Baffin Island pole-ridged tent, 56, *57, 58*
    Baffin Island tandem tents, 63
    Caribou Eskimo long-pole conical tents *(tupeq)*, 60, 64, 177
      idealized tent design, *60*
    Caribou Eskimo shelters, 63, 66

conical tents, 59–61, 65

Copper Eskimo ceremonial houses *(qaggiq)*, 68–69, 178

Copper Eskimo lean-tos and shelters, 63, *64, 66*

Copper Eskimo long-pole conical tents, 55, 178

Copper Eskimo pole-ridge tents, 57–59, 63, 65, 178
    idealized tent design, *60*

erecting tents, steps for, 64–65

gender roles, 60, 63–66

household life, 58–60, 63–66

Iglulik ridge tents *(tupeq)*, 56–57, 63, 65, 176–77
    idealized thong-ridged tent, *58*

Iglulik shelters, 63, 177

Indian influences, 59, 71n.10

Labrador Eskimo long-pole conical tent, 62, 65, 71n.10

Labrador Eskimo shelters, 63

Labrador Eskimo thong- or pole-ridge tents, 55–56, 65
    idealized tent design, *56*

Netsilik ridge tents, 58, 64

Netsilik short-pole conical tents, 60–61, 64

Québec long-pole conical tents *(nuirtaq)*, 59

Québec ridge tents, 56

ridge tents, 55–59, 65

rituals and beliefs, 69–70

Sallirmiut double-arch tents, 61–62

tandem tents, 61, 63

tent poles, 55, 56, 63–65

tent raising, steps in, 60, 64–65

tent rings and weights, 55, 56, 63, 65

tent skins, 55, 56, *58*, 60, 63

tent types, 55, 59, 60–61, 163, 165

transporting, 64

windbreaks and shelters, 62–63

Arctic (Central) winter houses, 36–55, 159–62, 175–78
    alternative dwellings, 48
    Baffin Island ceremonial houses, 67–69
    Baffin Island snow houses, 18 19, 44, *45, 46*
    Caribou Eskimo ceremonial houses *(qaggiq)*, 67
    Caribou Eskimo snow houses *(iglo)*, 44, *49*, 51, 55, 177
      idealized snow house design, *43*
      idealized travelers' snow house design, *49*
    communities and settlements, 39–40, 50, 167
    Copper Eskimo ceremonial houses *(qaggiq)*, 68–69
    Copper Eskimo snow houses, 41, 44, 48, 51, 66, 177–78
      idealized house design, *43*
    distribution of, 159–62
    gender roles, 42, 48
    heating and insulation, 41–42, 44, 48, 50, 71n.11, 167
    history of, 36–38
    household life, 48–52
    ice autumn houses, 53–55
    Iglulik ceremonial houses *(qaggiq)*, 67–69
    Iglulik ice autumn houses *(qarmaq)*, 53–55, 176–77
    Iglulik snow houses *(iglo)*, 44, 48, 50, 66, 176
      idealized house design, *43*
    Iglulik transitional houses, 52
    Labrador ceremonial houses *(qaggiq)*, 67
    Labrador snow houses, 55, 175
    Labrador stone communal houses *(igluqsuaq* or *iglu)*, 36–
      38, 175
      idealized stone communal house design, *36*
    lamps, 48, 50
    Netsilik ice autumn houses *(qarmat/qarmaq)*, 53–55, 71n.4

Netsilik snow houses, 42, *45*, *50*
rituals and beliefs, 69–70
Sallirmiut stone houses, 47–48
site locations, 39–40, *49*
snow houses (common design), 38–47
    design variations, 42–47
    how to construct, *38–42*, 71n.5
    travelers' temporary, 48
snow vent-hole plugs, 43, 48, 71n.6
stone/bone/turf autumn houses, 52–53
transitional dwellings, 52–55
windows and skylights, 42, *45*, 48, *49*, *51*

Arctic (Northwest) and Bering Strait, 73–117, 178–81, *see also entries beginning with Arctic (Northwest)*
    area, 72 (map), 73
    ceremonial houses, 108–13
    history and dwellings, 80–82, 94, 98, 116n.11
    household sizes and dwellings, 116n.7, 129n.22, 178–81
    lesser structures, 104–6
    population, 73, 80, 82, 116n.1, 129n.22
    rituals and beliefs, 113–16
    special-use structures, 104–13
    summer dwellings, 94–104, 159–63
    types and classification of houses, 73, 80–82, 159–63, 165
    winter dwellings, 73–94, 177

Arctic (Northwest) and Bering Strait special-use structures, 104–13
    birth and death huts, 106–7
    burial structures, 107–8
    ceremonial men's houses, 108–13, 180
    lesser structures, 104–6
    rituals and beliefs, 113–16

Arctic (Northwest) and Bering Strait summer houses, 94–105, 159–63
    alternative summer dwellings, 104, *105*
    Bering Strait stilt houses *(inipiaq or tuviq)*, 101–2, *103*, *105*
    heating and insulation, 100, 102, 167
    household life, 94, 96, 98–100, 102
    Kuuvaŋmiut bark houses *(aurivik)*, 100–101
        idealized house design, *100*
    Kuuvaŋmiut conical tents, 98, 104
    Kuuvaŋmiut live spruce houses *(miluq)*, 94
    Kuuvaŋmiut willow-framed houses *(echellek)*, 93–94
    lighting, *95*, 102
    Mackenzie Eskimo short-pole conical tents *(tupiq)*, 94–96, 179
        idealized tent design, *94*
    Nunamiut short-pole conical tents *(nappaqtaq)*, 96, 104
    Nunamiut year-round domed tent *(echellek)*, 93–94
    Nunamiut year-round domed tent *(itchalik* and *qaluugvik)*, 98–100, 180
        idealized tent design, *98*
    short-pole conical tents, 94–98
        idealized tent design, *94*
    Taġiuġmiut ceremonial houses *(qargi)*, 111–12, 114–15, 180
    Taġiuġmiut conical tent *(tupiq)*, 96, 179
    Tagiugmiut dome tent, 98–99
    tent types, 93–94, 98, 159–63, 165
    transitional dwellings, 93–94

Arctic (Northwest) and Bering Strait winter houses, 73–94, 159–62
    alternative dwellings, 89–93
    area of study, 75

Bering Strait Islands stone pit-houses, 87–89, *103*
heating and insulation, 76, 80, 82–83, 116n.10, 167
household life, 76–77, 79–80, 84, *86*, 90, 91
Kuuvaŋmiut moss houses *(ivrulik)*, 92–93, 104
Kuuvaŋmiut pole-and-turf houses *(ukiivik)*, 83–85, 90, 181
    idealized house design, *83*
Kuuvaŋmiut transitional houses *(miluq* and *echellek)*, 93–94
Mackenzie Eskimo ceremonial houses *(qargi)*, 110–11, 179
Mackenzie Eskimo snow houses *(iglo-riyoark)*, 89–91, 179
Mackenzie Eskimo wooden houses *(iglu* or *iglo)*, 73–77, 178
    idealized house design, *74*
Malemiut wooden houses (Kotzebue Sound), 85
Nunamiut pole-and-turf houses, 80–83, 90, 116n.10, 180–81
    idealized house design, *82*
Nunamiut snow houses *(aniguyyaq* and *apuyyaq)*, 91–92, 143
pole-and-turf houses, 80–83, 178
Seward Peninsula wooden houses, 86, 87
Taġiuġmiut snow houses *(apuyyaq)*, 91–92, 179–80
Taġiuġmiut wooden houses *(iglu)*, 77–80, 179
    idealized house design, *79*
transitional dwellings, 93–94
types, 73, 91, 93–94, 129n.17, 159–62, 165
wood sources, 73, 75

art and artifacts, 166
    bone engraving (Bering Strait), *166*, *167*
    ceremonial houses, 115, *122*, *129*
    double faced wooden mallet (Little Diomede), 116, *166*
    drawing of tents (Ammassalik), *25*, *166*
    first published engraving of Western Eskimo dwelling, 145
    ivory comb (Sallirmiut), *62*, *166*
    masks, 30, 116, *125*, 156
    prevalence and meaning, 166
    tobacco pipe (Kuskokwim River), *166*
    ulu handle (Pingasugruk), 96, *97*, *166*
    whaling ceremonies, 116

B

Baffin Island Eskimos, Canada. *see also* Arctic (Central)
    ceremonial houses, 67–69
    early depiction of, 2
    pole-ridged tent, 56, *57*, *58*
    snow houses, 18–19, 44, *45*, *46*
    tent designs (Greenland), 24, 33n.10, 64
Baker Lake, Canada, 69–70
bark houses
    Chugach, 143–45
    Chugach lean-tos, 151
    Kuuvangmiut *(aurivik)*, 93, 100–101, 104
    Prince William Sound plank huts, 150
    Yukon River wooden, 147–48
baths. *see* sweat or steam baths
Belcher Island, Canada, 59
beliefs. *see* rituals and beliefs
Bering Sea. *see* Alaska and Siberia
Bering Strait. *see* Arctic (Northwest) and Bering Strait; Big and Little Diomede Islands (Bering Strait); King Island (Bering Strait)

Big and Little Diomede Islands (Bering Strait). *see also* Arctic (Northwest) and Bering Strait
    art and artifacts, 116
    ceremonial houses, 109
    double faced wooden mallet, 116, 166
    geographic area, 73
    rituals and beliefs, 114
    stilt houses *(inipiaq* or *tuviq)*, 101–2, *103*, *105*
    storage, 106
    winter stone pit-houses, 87–89
birth huts
    Central Arctic, 69, 129n.27
    Chugach, 157n.21
    common use, 66–67, 106–7, 129n.27
    Greenland, 30, 129n.27
    Northwest Arctic, 106–7
    Southwest Alaska, 153
    umiaks as, 30
Bladder Festival (Alutiiq), 155
blinds. *see* hunters and hunting structures
boats. *see* kayaks; umiaks
bones and skulls. *see* caribou; walrus; whales and whaling
buildings and materials. *see* bark houses; pole-and-turf houses; snow houses; stone houses; wood houses
burial structures and rituals. *see also* death rituals, beliefs, and structures
    art and, 166
    Central Yup'ik, 153–54
    chambers (Alutiiqs), 154
    cones (Northwest Eskimo), 107–8
    snow (Copper Eskimo), 67

C

caches, 30, 66, 100, 106
Canada. *see* Arctic (Central)
Cape Dorset, Canada, 52
Cape Nome, Alaska, 87, 120
Cape Prince of Wales, Alaska, *86*, 109, 115
caribou
    antlers as building materials, 47, 56, 160
    antlers as tent poles, 56, 160
    household life and, 20, 28, 33n.19, 40, 63, 84, 99, 100, 106, 121
    membrane skylights, 84
    nostril plugs, 33n.19
    rituals and beliefs, 70
    shelters and lean-tos, 62–63
    storage racks (antlers), 20, *50*
    tent skins
        Arctic (Central), 55, *59*, 60
        Arctic (Northwest) and Bering Strait, 94–98, 100, 110
        general use and preparation, *21*, 33n.12, 63–65, 160
Caribou Eskimos. *see also* Arctic (Central)
    ceremonial houses *(qaggiq)*, 67
    household sizes and dwellings, 177
    long-pole conical tents *(tupeq)*, 60, 64, 177
        idealized tent design, *60*

snow houses (Central Arctic design), 38–47
snow houses *(iglo)*, 44, *49*, 51, 54–55, 177
    idealized travelers' house design, *49*
spirit beliefs and site selection, 69
windbreaks and shelters, 62–63, 66
caves, 91
ceremonial structures
    Alaska and Siberia, 127–31, 154, 156n.6, 181
    Arctic (Central) *(qaggiq/qargi/qasgiq)*, 67–69, 178
    Arctic (Northwest) men's *(qargi)*, 108–15, 179, 180
    art and artifacts, *115*, *122*, *129*
    gender and, 28, 30, 67–69, 165
    Greenland men's *(qagsse)*, 28
    history and prevalence, 28, 67, 164
    terms for, 33n.13
    whales and whaling, 69, 110–11, 114–15
cheek plugs, *112*
childbirth. *see also* birth huts
    miniature tents (Northwest Arctic), 106
    miscarriage and hunting, 33n.14
    rituals and beliefs (Central Arctic), 69
    without assistance (Central Yup'ik), 153
Chugach Eskimo. *see* Alaska and Siberia; Alutiiq (Chugach Eskimo and Koniag)
Chukchi Peninsula, Siberia. *see also* Alaska and Siberia
    new-style hide-roofed houses, 131, *134*, 135–38
    old-style wooden houses *(nenglu)*, 131–34
clothing. *see* household life
conical tents. *see also* long-pole conical tents; short-pole conical tents; tents
    conical tents, 59–61, 65
Copper Eskimo. *see also* Arctic (Central)
    birth huts, 129n.27
    burial, death, and mourning structures, 67
    ceremonial houses *(qaggiq)*, 67–69, 178
    household sizes and dwellings, 177–78
    pole-ridge tents, 55, 57–59, 64, *65*, 66, 178
        idealized tent design, *60*
    snow houses, 44, 47, 48, 51, 66, 177–78
        idealized house design, *43*
        transitional, *55*
    snow houses (Central Arctic design), 38–47
    windbreaks, lean-tos, and shelters, 62–63, 66
crania as building material. *see* walrus; whales and whaling
Crow Village, Alaska, 127

D

death rituals, beliefs, and structures. *see also* burial structures and rituals
    abandonment and reoccupation of dwellings, 31, 113, 114, 123, 154–55
    corpse removal, 31, 107–8, 154–55
    death at home, 69, 107, 113, 154–55
    death huts, 33n.14, 66–67, 69, 107
    death prevention, 31
    memorial poles, *151*
Diomede Islands. *see* Big and Little Diomede Islands (Bering Strait)

dogs
    snow houses, *17, 30, 52, 66*
    tent skin transport, 64
dome tents. *see also* tents
    Norton Sound dome tents, 147
    Nunamiut year-round domed tent (*echellek*), 93–94
    Nunamiut year-round domed tent (*itchalik* and *qaluugvik*), 98–100, 180
        idealized tent design, *98*
    Taġiuġmiut dome tent, 98
double-arch tents. *see also* tents
    Sallirmiut double-arch tents, 61–62, 177
    Siberian Eskimo double-arch tents, 131, 148, *149*
    West Greenland double-arch tent (*erqulik* or *igdlerfiusaq*), 24, 26, 27, 28, 64
drying racks. *see also* storage
    Alaska and Siberia, *137*, 144–45
    Arctic (Central), *46*, 51
    Arctic (Northwest), 80, 91, *93*, 102, *103*, *105*, 115, *167*
    general use, 160
    Greenland, *12, 17, 31*
dwellings, Eskimo. *see* architecture, Eskimo

E

East Cape, Siberia, 133, *134, 138*
East Greenland (Ammassalik). *see also* Greenland
    area of study, 8 (map), 9
    art and artifacts, 30, 166
    beliefs and rituals, 30–32
    household sizes and dwellings, 171–72
    lesser structures, 30
    single-arch tent (*tupeq*), 22–28, 64, 172
        idealized tent design, *23*
    special-use structures, 28–30, *31*, 129n.27
    stone communal house (*itte*), 10–14, 171–72
        idealized house design, *11*
    stone transitional houses, 22
    temporary snow houses (*uttisaawt*), 18
Egedesminde District, Greenland, 24
Eskimo, as term, 6n.2. *see also* architecture, Eskimo

F

fishes and fishing
    fish-skin skylights, 123
    huts and weirs, 30, 66, 106
    salmon tent skins, 56
furnishings. *see* household life

G

games, string figure, 70, 114
gender
    roles and separation
        Alaska and Siberia (separation), 119–20, 129–30, 145
        Arctic (Central), 42, 48, 60, 63–66
        Arctic (Northwest) and Bering Strait, 95, 98–99
        Greenland, 19–21, 27–28
    studies, 165
grass huts (Alutiiq), 148–50

Greenland, 9–33, 159–63, 171–74, *see also entries beginning with Greenland*
    area of study, 8 (map), 9–10
    ceremonial men's houses (*qagsse*), 28
    climate, 4, 10
    history of dwellings, 9, 10–11, 14, 28
    household life, 19–21, 27–28
    household sizes and dwellings, 171–74
    Kalaallit, as term, 6n.2, 9
    rituals and beliefs, 30–32
    special-use structures, 28–30
    summer dwellings, 22–28, 159–63
    types and classification of houses, 161–63, 165
    winter dwellings, 9–21, 159–62, 171–75, 177
Greenland summer dwellings, 22–28, 159–62
    East Greenland single-arch tent (*tupeq*), 22–28, 64, 172
        idealized tent design, *23*
    gender roles, 27–28
    household life, 27–28
    Polar Eskimo arch tent (*tupeq qanisaling*), 27, 33n.10, 174
        idealized tent design, *27*
    transitional dwellings, 22
    West Greenland double-arch tent (*erqulik* or *igdlerfiusaq*), 24, 26, 27, 28, 64
    West Greenland single-arch tent (*tupinaq*), 10, 22–28, 64, 174
        idealized tent design, *23*
Greenland winter and transitional houses, 9–22, 159–62, 171–75
    alternative dwellings, 18–19
    ceremonial men's houses (*qagsse*), 28
    East Greenland stone communal house (*itte*), 10–14, 171–72
        idealized house design, *11*
    East Greenland temporary snow houses (*uttisaawt*), 18
    East Greenland transitional stone houses, 22
    gender roles, 13, 19–21
    household life, 19–21
    lamp (*qulliq*), 14, 19–21
    Polar Eskimo stone one- to two-family houses (*iglu, qarmaŋ* or *qaŋma*), 14–18, 174
        dimensions, 14, 32n.4, 174
        idealized house design, *14*
    Polar Eskimo temporary snow houses (*iglooyak* or *igluiya*), 18, *19*, 32n.5, 174–75
    Polar Eskimo transitional stone houses (*qarmaq*), 22
    reuse or abandonment, 9–10, 15, 18
    site selection, 9–10
    snow houses for temporary use, 18–19
    transitional dwellings, 22
    West Greenland stone communal houses (*igdlo/illu*), 10–14, 172–74
        idealized house design, *11*
    West Greenland transitional stone houses, 22
Gulf of Alaska. *see* Alaska and Siberia

H

heather (*Cassiope* sp.), 24, 51, 55, 68
heating and insulation. *see also* household life; lamps
    Alaska and Siberia, 122–23, 125, 129, 131, 133, 135
    Arctic (Central), 41–42, 44, 48, 50–51, 71n.11

Arctic (Northwest) and Bering Strait, 76–77, 80, 82–83, 100, 102, 110–11, 116n.10
body heat, 19, *50*, *122*, 167
energy requirements (energistics), 68, 167
fire-drill, *25*
Greenland, 14, 18, 19–21, 27–28
Hooper Bay, Alaska, 126, 152
Hotham Inlet, Alaska, *106*
household life. *see also* lamps; rituals and beliefs
Alaska and Siberia, 121–23, 125, 129–31, 135–38, 141–43, 152
Arctic (Central), 48–52, 56–57, 59, 63–67
Arctic (Northwest) and Bering Strait (summer houses), 94–95, 96, 98–100, 102
Arctic (Northwest) and Bering Strait (winter houses), 75–76, 79–80, 84, 90, 91
cooking, 71n.12
energy requirements (energistics), 68, 167
Greenland, 19–21, 27–28
mosquitoes and dwelling designs, 59, 101
sewing and lacing, 27–28, *60*, 70, 106
sleeping customs, 16
household sizes and dwellings (includes area per person), 171–82
Alaska and Siberia, 181–82
Arctic (Central), 175–78
Arctic (Northwest) and Bering Strait, 178–81
Greenland, 171–74
houses, Eskimo. *see* architecture, Eskimo
hunters and hunting structures
blinds, 30, 66, 152
rituals and beliefs, 32, 33n.14, 70, 155
snow houses, 89–91

I

ice-slab houses, 53–55
Icy Cape, Alaska, 110, *111*
igloo *(iglu)*, as term, 1. *see also* snow houses
Iglulik. *see also* Arctic (Central)
ceremonial houses, 67–69
death huts, 67
household sizes and dwellings, 176–77
ice autumn houses *(qarmat/qarmaq)*, 53–55, 176–77
ridge tents *(tupeq)*, 56–57, 63, 65, 176–77
idealized tent design, *58*
snow houses (Central Arctic design), 38–47
snow houses *(iglo)*, 44, 48, 50, 66, 176
idealized house design, *43*
tents, 71n.8
transitional houses, 52
windbreaks, 63, 66, 177
Ignituk, Alaska, *121*
Ikogmiut Eskimos, 152
Indian influences
Algonkian Indians, 59
Arctic (Central) summer dwellings, 59, 71n.10
canoes, *93*
Tlingit Indians, 143
insulation. *see* heating and insulation
Inuit as term, 6n.2. *see also* Arctic (Central)

inuksuk (stone cairns), 182
Inuvialuk/Iñupiaq Eskimos, 71n.2. *see also* Arctic (Northwest) and Bering Strait
Inviting-In Ceremony (Unaligmiut), 129
ivory. *see* art and artifacts; walrus

K

Kalaallit (Greenlandic Eskimos), 6n.2, 9. *see also* Greenland
Karluk Lagoon, Kodiak Island, 139
Katmai volcano and Kodiak Island, Alaska, *140*, *142*, 143
Kauwerak, Alaska, 120
kayaks
general use, 5, *95*, *105*
Greenland, *10*
storage of, *49*, *54*, 66, 102, 106, *127*, 152
King Island (Bering Strait). *see also* Arctic (Northwest) and Bering Strait
ceremonial houses *(qargi)*, 109
stilt houses *(inipiaq* or *tuviq)*, 101–2, *103*, *105*
winter stone pit-houses, 87–89
King William Island, Canada, 59
Kobuk River, Alaska. *see* Kuuvaŋmiut
Kodiak Island, Alaska. *see also* Alaska and Siberia
alternative dwellings, 143–44
birth and menstrual structures, 153, 157n.23
grass huts *(shalash)*, 148–50
Katmai volcano effects, *140*, *142*, 143
research issues, 143
umiak lean-tos, 150
year-round wooden houses *(ciqlluaq* or *barabara)*, 138–43, 181–82
idealized house design, *138*
Koniag Eskimo. *see* Kodiak Island, Alaska
Kotzebue Sound, Alaska
death and burial, 108
trade fairs, *97*, 98, 104, *105*
Kusquqvagmiut (Kuskokwim River), 150
Kuuvaŋmiut. *see also* Arctic (Northwest) and Bering Strait
bark houses *(aurivik)*, 100–101
idealized house design, *100*
birth and menstrual huts *(miluq)*, 106–7
ceremonial houses *(qargi)*, 109, 113
conical tents, 98, 104
household sizes and dwellings, 181
moss houses *(ivrulik)*, 92–93, 104
pole-and-turf houses *(ukiivik)*, 83–85, 90, 181
idealized house design, *83*
rituals and beliefs, 113–14
transitional houses *(miluq* and *echellek)*, 93–94
watercraft lean-tos, 150

L

Labrador Eskimos. *see also* Arctic (Central)
ceremonial houses *(qaggiq)*, 67
history of dwellings, 36–38
household sizes and dwellings, 175
lesser structures, 63, 66
long-pole conical tent, 62, 65, 71n.10

snow houses (Central Arctic design*)*, 38–47
snow houses *(illuvigaq)*, 175
stone communal winter houses, 36–38, 175
    idealized house design, *36*
thong- or pole-ridge tents, 55–56, *57, 58,* 65
    idealized tent design, *56*
lamps, 19–21
  ceremonial houses, *68*
  design and construction, 20, 32n.6, 84, 116n.8
  heat and, 71n.7, 167
  operation, 19–21, 90
  replacements (nontraditional), 14, 156n.7
  snow and ice houses, 48, 50, 54
  symbol and meaning, 20
lean-tos, *62,* 94, 104, *105,* 129n.26, 148–50, 162
lighting. *see* lamps; skylights; windows
Little Diomede Island. *see* Big and Little Diomede Islands (Bering Strait)
long houses, 11. *see also* Greenland winter and transitional houses
long-pole conical tents
  Caribou Eskimo long-pole conical tents *(tupeq),* 60, 64, 177
    idealized tent design, *60*
  Copper Eskimo long-pole conical tents, 55, 178
  Labrador Eskimo long-pole conical tent, 62, 65, 71n.10
  Québec long-pole conical tents *(nuirtaq),* 59

M

Mackenzie Eskimos. *see also* Arctic (Northwest) and Bering Strait
  ceremonial houses *(qargi),* 110–11, 114–15, 179
  household sizes and dwellings, 178–79
  rituals and beliefs, 113, 129n.27
  shelters and windbreaks, 71n.2, 104–6
  short-pole conical tents *(tupiq),* 94–96, 179
    idealized tent design, *94*
  snow houses *(iglo-riyiark),* 89–91, 179
  wood multifamily houses *(iglu* or *iglo),* 73–77, 178–79
    idealized house design, *74*
  wood supplies, 73
Mackenzie River and Delta, Canada, 73, 75
Malemiut wooden houses, *85*
maps
  Alaska and Siberia, 118
  Arctic (Northwest) and Bering Strait, 72
  area of study, 3
  Central Arctic, 34
  Greenland, 8
  summer dwelling types, 163
  winter and transitional dwelling types, 162
masks, 30, 116, *125,* 156
menstrual huts and taboos, 66–67, 106–7, 153, 157n.22
metaphors and dwellings, 155–56, 164, 165–66
miniatures and models
  as art, 166
  ceremonial houses (Southwest Alaska), *122, 129*
  snow houses (Central Arctic), 52, 66
  tents (Northwest Arctic), 106
  winter dwellings (Greenland), 28

mosquitoes and dwelling designs, 59, 101
mourning beliefs and structures, 66–67, 69–70, 153

N

narwhal
  building material in Greenland, 4
  sinew thread in Greenland, 27
  tusks as tent poles, 33n.11, 56, 63
Nelson Island, Alaska, 120, 155–56
Netsilik Eskimos. *see also* Arctic (Central)
  ice autumn houses *(qarmat/qarmaq),* 53–55, 71n.4
  ridge tents, 58, 63–64
  rituals and beliefs, 69
  short-pole conical tents, 60–61, 63–64
  snow houses, *42, 45,* 51
  snow houses (Central Arctic design), 38–47
  windbreaks, 66
North Alaska. *see* Arctic (Northwest) and Bering Strait
Northumberland Island, Greenland, 15
Norton Sound, Alaska. *see also* Alaska and Siberia; Saint Michael, Alaska
  birth and menstrual huts, 153
  burial structures *(nuiqsaq),* 107–8
  dome tents, 147
  first published depiction of Western Eskimo dwelling, 145
  gender separation, 145
  Saint Michael dwellings, 126, *128, 129,* 156n.6
  snow tent *(aniguyuk),* 143–44
  wooden houses, 145–47
  year-round men's wooden houses *(qasgiq),* 120–23, *128, 129,* 155–56, 181
    idealized house design, *120*
nostril plugs, 33n.19
Nunagiak, Alaska, *99*
Nunamiut. *see also* Arctic (Northwest) and Bering Strait
  ceremonial houses *(qargi),* 109, 112–13
  folk tales and dwellings, 114
  household sizes and dwellings, 180–81
  old-style winter houses *(ivrulik),* 82
    idealized house design, *82*
  pole-and-turf houses, 80–83, 90, 116n.10, 180–81
    idealized house design, *82*
  short-pole conical tents *(nappaqtaq),* 96, 104
  snow houses *(aniguyyaq* and *apuyyaq),* 91–92, 143–44
  special-use huts, 107
  year-round domed tent *(echellek),* 93–94
  year-round domed tent *(itchalik),* 98–100, 180
    idealized tent design, *98*
Nunivaarmiut. *see also* Alaska and Siberia
  birth and menstrual huts, 153
  year-round wooden houses, 123–26
    connected housing complexes, 123–25
    idealized house design, *124*
    isolated houses, 126
Nunivak Island, Alaska. *see also* Alaska and Siberia
  burial practices, 154, 155
  ceremonial houses, 156n.6
  lesser structures, 152–53
  wooden year-round houses *(qasgiq; Nunivaarmiut),* 123–26, 127, 155

connected housing complexes, 123–25
idealized house design, *124*
isolated houses, 126
Nushagak River, Alaska, 127

O

oral tradition, 32, 67, 70, 114, 157n.18, 164, 165–66

P

Pingasugruk, Alaska, 79, 96, 97, 116n.7, 166
Plover Bay, Siberia, *134, 136, 137, 149*
Point Barrow, Alaska. *see also* Arctic (Northwest) and Bering Strait
    ceremonial houses, 111–12, 114–15
    dome tents, *81,* 96, 98
    rituals and beliefs, 114–15
    transitional houses, *169*
    winter houses, 73, 77–80
Point Belcher, Alaska, 99
Point Hope, Alaska, 116. *see also* Arctic (Northwest) and Bering Strait
    burial structures, *106*
    ceremonial houses, 112
    conical tents, 95
    death rituals, *106*
    winter houses, 73, 77–80, *81, 169*
Polar Eskimos (Northwest Greenland). *see also* Greenland
    arch tent (*tupeq qanisaling*), 27, 33n.10, 174
        idealized tent design, *27*
    area, 8 (map), 9
    death beliefs and dwellings, 30, 33n.14
    household sizes and dwellings, 174–75
    snow houses for temporary use (*iglooyak* or *igluiya*), 18–19, 174–75
    special-use structures, 28–30
    stone one- to two-family houses (*iglu, qarmaŋ* or *qaŋma*), 14–18, 174
        idealized house design, *14*
    storage spaces, 30
    wood, 32n.4, 33n.11
pole-and-turf houses, 80–85, 159–62
    distribution maps, *162, 163*
    Kuuvanmiut pole-and-turf houses (*ukiivik*), 83–85, 90, 180–81
        idealized house design, *83*
    Nunamiut pole-and-turf houses, 80–83, 90, 116n.10, 180–81
        idealized house design, *82*
poles, tent. *see* tents
population, Eskimo
    Alaska and Siberia, 119
    Arctic (Central), 35
    Arctic (Northwest) and Bering Strait, 73, 82, 116n.1, 129n.22
    Greenland, 9
    precontact, 4
Prince Albert Peninsula, Canada, 54, *64*
Prince William Sound, Alaska. *see also* Alaska and Siberia
    lean-tos and plank huts, 150–51

wooden houses, 143, 181–82
Punuk Island, Alaska, *133*

Q

Québec, Canada
    long-pole conical tents (*nuirtaq*), 59
    ridge tents, 56

R

racks. *see* drying racks; storage
ravens, 30
Razboinski, Alaska, *146,* 147–48
research possibilities, 164–68
ridge tents, 55–59. *see also* tents
    Baffin Island pole-ridged tent, 56, *57, 58*
    Copper Eskimo pole-ridge tents, 58–59, *60, 64, 65,* 178
        idealized tent design, *60*
    Iglulik ridge tents (*tupeq*), 56, 63–64, *65,* 176–77
        idealized thong-ridged tent, *58*
    Labrador Eskimo thong- or pole-ridge tents, 55–56, *65*
        idealized tent design, *56*
    Netsilik ridge tents, 58, *64*
    Québec ridge tents, 56
    ridge tents, 55–59, *65*
rituals and beliefs. *see also* birth huts; burial structures and rituals; death rituals, beliefs, and structures; menstrual huts and taboos areas
        Alaska and Siberia, 154–56
        Arctic (Central), 69–70
        Arctic (Northwest) and Bering Strait, 113–16
        Greenland, 30–32
    Bladder Festival (Nunivak Island), 155
    constellations, 114
    good luck, 30, 69, 70
    masks, 30, 116, *125,* 156
    sorcery protection, 31
    tent-to-house ceremony, 30, 115

S

Saint Lawrence Island, Alaska. *see also* Alaska and Siberia
    beliefs and rituals, 154–56
    ceremonial houses, absence of, 129
    double-arch tents, 148, *149*
    lamps, 32n.6
    Siberian Yupik new-style hide-roofed houses (*maŋtaŋa.aq*), *134,* 135–38
    Siberian Yupik old-style wooden houses, 131–34
    storage areas, 152
    summer houses, 131, 151
    Yup'ik/Yupik languages, 6n.2, 156n.1
Saint Michael, Alaska. *see also* Alaska and Siberia; Norton Sound, Alaska
    burial structures, *153*
    storage areas, 152
    wooden houses (others in area), 126–28
    year-round wooden houses, 120–23, *128,* 129, 156n.6
        idealized house design, *120*
Sallirmiut. *see also* Arctic (Central)

beliefs and rituals, 67
double-arch tents, 61–62, 161
fish caches, 66
ivory comb, 62, 166
stone winter houses, 47–48

salmon. *see also* fishes and fishing
caches and weirs, 66
tent skins, 56

scaffolds. *see* storage

scrimshaw. *see* art and artifacts

seal skins
tent skin preparation, 24, 27–28, 33n.9
tent skins, *10*, 33n.12, 56, 58, 95

settlement patterns, 5–6, 39–40, 55, 116n.11, 163–64, 167

Seward Peninsula wooden houses, 86, 87

sewing and lacing, 27–28, 60, 66, 70, 106

Shageluk, Alaska, *130*

Shaktolik, Alaska, 154

shaman (angakoq), *31*

shelters. *see* windbreaks and shelters

short-pole conical tents
Mackenzie Eskimo short-pole conical tents *(tupiq),* 94–96, 179
idealized tent design, *94*
Nunamiut short-pole conical tents *(nappaqtaq),* 96, 104
short-pole conical tents, 94–98
idealized tent design, *94*

Siberia. *see* Alaska and Siberia

Siberian Eskimo. *see also* Alaska and Siberia
double-arch tents, 131, 148, *149*
new-style hide-roofed houses, 131, *134,* 135–38
old-style wooden houses *(nenglu),* 131–34
Yup'ik/Yupik languages, 6n.2, 156n.1

Siberian Yupik. *see also* Alaska and Siberia
Siberian Yupik new-style hide-roofed houses *(maŋtaŋa.aq),* *134,* 135–38
Siberian Yupik old-style wooden houses, 131–34

single-arch tents. *see also* tents
East and West Greenland single-arch tent *(tupeq),* 22–28, 64, 172
idealized tent design, *23*
Polar Eskimo arch tent *(tupeq qanisaling),* 27, 33n.10, 174
idealized tent design, *27*

site location. *see also* death rituals, beliefs, and structures
Arctic (Central) snow houses, 39–40, 42, 49
Arctic (Central) tents, *49,* 55
factors influencing, 55, 167
Greenland, 4, 9–11
Northwest Alaska coast, 94, 98, 101–2, 114
reuse or abandonment, 9–10
rituals and beliefs, 69–70
snow houses, 9–11, 39–40, 42, *49*
Thule influence, 4

skins. *see* caribou; fishes and fishing; walrus; whales and whaling

skulls. *see* walrus; whales and whaling

skylights
arched, 91
ceremonial houses, 156n.6

gut properties, 15–16
movable (Malemiut), 85
pyramidal (North Alaska), *81*
rituals and beliefs, 129, 155
types (membrane, ice, fish-skin), 75, 76, 84, 88, 123, *130*

smokehouses (Chugach), 144–45

snow houses, 38–47, 159–62. *see also* Alaska and Siberia; Arctic (Central); Arctic (Northwest) and Bering Strait; Greenland
construction, steps in, *38–42,* 71n.5
cultural symbol, 1–2, 51–52
distribution maps, 162, 163
household life, 48–52
household sizes and dwellings, 171–82
idealized house designs
Caribou Eskimo snow houses *(iglo),* *43*
Caribou Eskimos travelers' snow houses *(iglo),* *49*
Copper Eskimo and Iglulik snow houses, *43*
igloo *(iglu),* as term, 1
knives (snow), *29,* 40
origin and prevalence, 35, 38–39
types and classification, 159–62, 165
windows (ice), 42, 48, 51, 76

sod. *see* pole-and-turf houses

sorcery, 30, *31*

Southhampton Island, Canada. *see* Sallirmiut

Southwest Alaska. *see* Alaska and Siberia

special-use structures. *see also* birth huts; burial structures; caches; death rituals, beliefs, and structures; storage; windbreaks
Alaska and Siberia, 152–54
Arctic (Central), 66–69
Arctic (Northwest) and Bering Strait, 104–13
definition, 28
Greenland, 28–30
types and significance, 28, 165

spiritual beliefs. *see* rituals and beliefs

steam baths. *see* sweat or steam baths

stilt houses (Bering Strait), 101–2, *103, 105*

stone houses, 159–63. *see also* Greenland; Labrador Eskimos
Arctic (Central) transitional stone/bone/turf autumn houses *(qarmat/qarmaq),* 52–53
Bering Strait stone pit-houses, 87–89, *103*
cairns *(inuksuk),* 166
distribution maps, 162, 163
Greenland transitional stone houses, 22
household sizes and dwellings, 171–82
idealized house designs
East Greenland (Ammassilik) stone communal houses *(itte),* *11*
Labrador Eskimo stone communal winter houses, *36*
Polar Eskimo one- to two-family stone houses *(iglu, qarmaŋ* or *qaŋma),* *14*
West Greenland Eskimos stone communal houses *(igdlo/illu),* *11*
Sallirmiut stone winter houses, 47–48
storage using raised stone, 30, 66
traps and trapping with stone piles, 33n.15, 33n.16
types and similarities, 159–62, 165

storage. *see also* drying racks
of kayaks, *49, 54,* 66, 102, 106, *127, 152*

regional
    Alaska and Siberia, 152–53
    Arctic (Northwest), 77, 88, 91, 106
    Central Arctic, 66
    Greenland, 13, 16, 30
    scaffolds (whale bones), 77, 81, 88, 106, 152

summer houses, 159–63. see also architecture, Eskimo; tents; wood houses; year-round houses
    Alaska and Siberia, 145–51, 162–63
    Arctic (Central), 55–69, 161
    Arctic (Northwest) and Bering Strait, 94–104, 161–63
    Greenland, 22–28, 161
    types and similarities, 5, 159–63

sweat or steam baths
    distribution, 157n.19
    uses of, 129, 131, 139, 152, 154, 155

T

Taġiuġmiut. see also Arctic (Northwest) and Bering Strait
    birth huts (sudliwin), 107
    ceremonial houses (qargi), 111–12, 114–15, 164
    conical tent (tupiq), 96, 180
    dome tent, 96, 98–99
    household sizes and dwellings, 179–80
    rituals and beliefs, 113–14
    snow houses (apuyyaq), 91–92, 179–80
    storage, 91, 106
    wooden houses (iglu), 77–80, 179
        idealized house design, 79

tents, 159–63. see also Arctic (Central); Arctic (Northwest) and Bering Strait; Greenland; Labrador Eskimos
    classification of, 22, 55, 159–63, 165
    common use, 22, 28
    distribution maps, 163
    drawing of tents (Ammassalik), 25, 166
    household life, 65–66
        Arctic (Central), 63–66
        Arctic (Northwest) and Bering Strait, 98–100
        Greenland, 27–28
    household sizes and dwellings, 171–82
    how to erect, 60, 64–65
    idealized tent designs
        arch tent (Polar Eskimo), 27
        domed tent (Nunamiut), 98
        long-pole conical tents (Caribou and Copper Eskimos), 60
        short-pole conical tents (Northwest Arctic), 94
        single-arch tent (East and West Greenland), 23
        thong- or pole-ridge tents (Labrador), 56
        thong-ridged tents (Iglulik), 58
    rituals and beliefs, 30, 115
    similarities of, 159–63
    skin preparation, 24, 27–28, 33n.9
    skin sewing and lacing, 27–28, 60
    skin types (caribou, walrus, salmon), 24–27, 33n.12, 56, 58, 59, 63–64, 148
    special-use structures, 67, 106
    summer settlement patterns, 5, 167
    tandem tents (Central Arctic), 63
    transportation, 24, 64
    types, 22, 55, 59, 60–61, 93–94, 98, 159–63, 165
    weights, 55, 63, 65

Thule influence on dwellings, 4, 39, 52, 57
Tlingit Indians, 143
tobacco pipe, 112
trade fairs (Alaska), 97, 98, 104, 105
traps and trapping, 30, 33n.15, 33n.16, 152. see also fishes and fishing
turf houses. see pole-and-turf houses

U

Ublasaun, Alaska, 87
ulu (woman's crescent knife)
    Pingasugruk, 96, 97, 166
    uses, 20, 27–28
umiaks
    birth hut, 30
    lean-tos, 105, 129n.26, 150, 151, 162, 165
    transporting tent skins, 24, 64
Unalaska, Aleutian Islands, 139
Unaligmiut. see also Alaska and Siberia
    ceremonial men's houses (qasgiq), 127–31, 156, 181
    household sizes and dwellings, 181
    snow tent, 143
    special-use structures, 152–53
    wooden year-round houses (ini), 120–23, 181
        idealized house design, 120
Uppernavik, Greenland, 29

V

Victoria Island, Canada, 62

W

walrus
    Bering Strait scaffolds and storehouses, 106
    Bering Strait stilt houses (inipiaq or tuviq), 87, 101–2, 103, 105
    bones and skin
        clothing, 149
        door curtains, 28, 63, 80
        floor board nails, 132
        kitchen utensils, 20
        skulls as building material, 49, 115
        storage racks (jaws), 77, 106
    ceremonial masks, 125
    Saint Lawrence Island alternative summer dwelling, 151
    Siberian Eskimo double-arch tents, 131, 148, 149
    Siberian Yupik new-style hide-roofed houses, 131, 134, 135–38
watercraft. see kayaks; umiaks
weirs. see fishes and fishing
West Alaska. see Alaska and Siberia
West Arctic. see Alaska and Siberia; Arctic (Northwest) and Bering Strait
West Greenland Eskimos. see also Greenland
    area, 8 (map), 9
    death beliefs and houses, 31
    double-arch tent (erqulik or igdlerfiusaq), 26, 27, 28, 64
    household sizes and dwellings, 172–74
    single-arch tent (tupinaq), 10, 22–28, 64, 174
        idealized tent design, 23

snowblock shelters, *29, 30*
stone communal houses *(igdlo/illu)*, 10–14
    idealized house design, *11*
stone transitional houses, 22
whales and whaling
    art and artifacts, 96, 116
    bones and skulls
        Alaska and Siberia, 124, 126, 131–34, *137*, 151, 152
        Arctic (Central), 36, 47, 52
        Arctic (Northwest) and Bering Strait, 77, 79, 80, *81,*
          106, 111
        Greenland, 22
        skulls, 79, 110, 114–15
    burial structures, *106*, 107
    ceremonial structures, 69, 110, 114–15
    household uses, 51, 135
    membrane for skylight, 88
    rafters, ribs as, 11, *52, 53*
    rituals and beliefs, 114–15
    storage scaffolds
        Alaska and Siberia, 152
        Arctic (Northwest) and Bering Strait, 77, *81,* 88, 106
    tent skins and poles, 56, 61, 63–64, 148
windbreaks and shelters, 28, *29, 30,* 55, 62–63, 66, 104
windows. *see also* skylights
    gut properties, 15–16
    ice, 42, 48, 51, 76
winter houses, 159–62. *see also* architecture, Eskimo; pole-and-turf houses; snow houses; stone houses; wood houses;
    year-round houses
        Alaska and Siberia, 119–44
        Arctic (Central), 36–55
        Arctic (Northwest) and Bering Strait, 73–94
        Greenland, 9–21
        types and similarities, 5, 159–62, 165
wood houses, 159–62. *see also* Alaska and Siberia; Mackenzie Eskimos
    distribution maps, 162, 163
    general use, 4, 32n.1, 32n.4, 33n.11, 73, 170

household sizes and dwellings, 171–82
idealized house designs
    Kodiak Island year-round wooden houses *(ciqlluaq* or barabara), *138*
    Mackenzie Eskimos wooden multifamily houses *(iglu* or *iglo), 74*
    Norton Sound, Alaska year-round wooden houses, *120*
    Nunivak Island year-round wooden houses *(qasgiq;* Nunivaarmiut), *124*
    Taġiuġmiut wooden houses *(iglu), 79*
reuse, 114, 123
rituals and beliefs, 114
similarities of, 159–62
stilt houses (Bering Strait), 101–2, *103, 105*
types and classification, 159–62, 165

Y

year-round houses
    Alutiiq wooden houses *(ciqlluaq* or barabara), 138–43, 181–82
    Norton Sound men's wooden houses *(qasgiq),* 120–23, *128, 129,* 155–56
    Nunamiut domed tent *(echellek* and *qaluugvik),* 93–94
    Nunamiut domed tent *(itchalik* and *qaluugvik),* 98–100, 180
    Nunivaarmiut wooden houses, 123–26
    Nunivak Island wooden houses *(qasgiq;* Nunivaarmiut), 123–26, 127, 155
    Saint Michael wooden houses, *128*
Yukon River, Alaska
    cache or storage shed, *151,* 152
    wooden houses, 126–28, *146,* 147–48
Yup'ik/Yupik languages, 6n.2, 156n.1